The Declining World Order

Other titles in the Global Horizons series, edited by Richard Falk, Lester Ruiz, and R.B.J. Walker

International Relations and the Problem of Difference
Naeem Inayatullah and David L. Blaney

Methods and Nations: Cultural Governance and the Indigenous Subject
Michael J. Shapiro

Bait and Switch: Human Rights and U.S. Foreign Policy
Julie A. Mertus

The Declining World Order
America's Imperial Geopolitics

Richard A. Falk

ROUTLEDGE
NEW YORK AND LONDON

A volume in the series Global Horizons, edited by Richard Falk, Lester Ruiz, and R.B.J. Walker.

Published in 2003 by
Routledge
29 West 35th Street
New York, NY 10001
www.routledge-ny.com

Published in Great Britain by
Routledge
11 New Fetter Lane
London EC4P 4EE
www.routledge.co.uk

Copyright © 2003 by Taylor and Francis Books, Inc.

Routledge is an imprint of the Taylor and Francis Group.

Printed in the United Stated of America on acid-free paper.

10 9 8 7 6 5 4 3 2

Library of Congress Cataloging-in-Publication Data

Falk, Richard A.
    The declining world order : America's imperial geopolitics /
Richard A. Falk.
        p. cm. — (Global horizons)
Includes bibliographical references and index.
    ISBN 0-415-94692-1 (alk. paper) — ISBN 0-415-94693-X (pbk. : alk. paper)
    1. International relations. 2. Globalization. 3. Imperialism. 4. War on Terrorism, 2001-.
5. United States—Foreign relations—2001-. I. Title. II. Series.
    JZ1308 .F35 2004
    327.1—dc22
                        2003022750

Dedication

For Karolin and Dimitri in celebration, with love

Introduction

This book is essentially an inquiry into why the end of the Cold War, along with the end of colonialism and apartheid, did not bring moderation and a sense of hope to our understanding of present trends and future prospects bearing on the organization of the political life of the planet. It is argued that there are no simple or authoritative explanations, although particular attention is paid to the failures of American leadership during a period of unprecedented historic opportunity. The United States, following the collapse of the Soviet Union, was indisputably the dominant political actor on the world stage, but its leaders and citizenry seemed generally uninspired by the occasion and acted with a pronounced complacency with respect to issues associated with unresolved conflicts, human suffering, and the growing need for equitable forms of global governance in an increasingly complex and fragile world. September 11 was a traumatic wakeup call, but a wakeup to what? The argument presented here is that the American response to the al Qaeda attacks has accentuated its earlier failures of global leadership, plunging the world into a struggle between two extremist visions of how to achieve world peace and global justice.

The role of the United States, however central to the unfolding cosmodrama of world order, is not the only interpretative standpoint adopted. It is also important to take note of the turn toward trade, investment, and finance in the 1990s, giving world order an economistic orientation that gave rise to the terminology of "globalization," elaborated in various ways to take account of its several dimensions. This book assesses the relevance of globalization by distinguishing between corporate, civic, imperial, apocalyptic, and regional globalizations as a way of bringing clarity to the interplay of tendencies associated with contending approaches to the unacknowledged central challenge of achieving global governance, and the most prominent tensions associated with the auspices and ideological outlook shaping the response to this challenge. In particular, the 1990s began as if global governance would be mainly entrusted to the forces and ideas associated with what is here called corporate globalization. Important in this regard was the degree to which the outlook associated with corporate globalization fell under the influence of a particular variant of capitalism associated with maximum autonomy for market forces and a corresponding skepticism about the role of government beyond that of facilitator. This orientation, identified as "neoliberalism" or "the Washington consensus," was championed by the private sector, achieving ideological hegemony in such arenas as the annual World Economic Forum held each year in the Alpine town of Davos.

Various expressions of discontent were associated with this preoccupation with world economic growth. Increasingly, civil society related the miseries of the poor in the world to the impact of corporate globalization, and disparate elements organized oppositional events of protest and resistance. This dynamic was both local and transnational, searching for ways to be effective, civil society actors, building on the earlier efforts of environmentalists and human rights activists, making use of arenas associated with high profile conferences organized by the United Nations on global policy issues and then, when these became unavailable in the 1990s, presenting their grievances mainly through mass protests at symbolic meetings of the corporate globalizers, especially those of the International Monetary Fund, World Bank, and World Trade Organization. Such a presence was initially identified as "an anti-globalization movement," but is here labeled as "civic globalization," an alternative globalization with its own vision of the future.

Since September 11 the globalization narrative has taken on new twists, reconfiguring the worldview of divergent globalizers in several directions. The most salient of these involves the confrontation between the United States and al Qaeda, a reassertion of security concerns as the core problematique of world politics. September 11, combined with the fortuitous circumstance of the presidency of George W. Bush, enabled the radical right to seize the policy initiative in Washington during this critical period of responding to the al Qaeda confrontation. This neocon influence, reinforced by the religious right, emphasized the role of the United States as the militarily dominant state in providing the world (and itself) with a durable form of global governance. I identify this world order fix as "imperial globalization." Its credibility in part rests on the formidable asymmetric and innovative capabilities of the al Qaeda network to inflict severe harm and to strike fear into the hearts of Western secular societies. Such political violence is directed primarily, although not exclusively, at civilian targets, giving rise to a new perception of terrorism as a war making instrument — here called here "megaterrorism" to distinguish it from earlier variants. The visionary worldview of Osama bin Laden, as endorsed by a variety of Islamic extremists, is identified in this book as "apocalyptic globalization" to emphasize its radical program for restructuring political life on the basis of religious orthodoxy, which also can be interpreted as an approach to global governance. It is far from clear that either of these globalizations will persist, at least in the forms manifest since 2001. The American electorate may disavow imperial globalization, reacting to its costs, burdens, and unpopularity, while Islamic radicals may refashion their tactics and aims in a less visionary and more sustainable form.

When conceiving globalization, it is also relevant to take account of regionalizing tendencies, especially the gradual emergence of Europe as an inchoate "regional state." Depending on developments elsewhere, including a possible reliance on regional governance as a response to the other forms of globalization, it is possible that in the decade or so ahead, there could arise regional actors that provide an approach to global governance that is intermediate between the global democratic aspirations of civic globalization and the global security goals of imperial globalization.

Globalization is not the only useful approach to thinking about this conjuncture of historical forces. This book also seeks to explore the interface between modernity and postmodernity to call attention to the fundamental destabilization of the established categories of analysis applicable to world order and global governance. The modernist framing of world order is associated with the rise of the state and the organization of the state system, as it evolved from the Peace of Westphalia, a seminal event that overlooks to some extent the degree to which ideas of territorial sovereignty and the realities of state formation preceded 1648. The Westphalian era exhibited both the evolution of the state through various stages and its geographic spread from Europe to the entire world. The formal organization of world society accorded primary relevance to the state as political actor, exemplified by the membership and voting rules of the United Nations. This experience of modernity also shaped international law as the rules and practices governing the relations among states and of warfare as violent conflict among states. There were always other important influences and actors, but it seemed accurate to conceive of world order as a framework for global governance based on the relations among states, with leading states playing a managerial role associated with their geopolitical status.

What has given postmodernity its relevance in the last decade or so in the setting of international relations theory and practice is the extent to which the state and the state system need to share the stage of global history with a variety of nonstate actors. As such, it is no longer clarifying to act as if we still inhabit a Westphalian world organized around territorial units whose governing authorities claim sovereign rights. Not that the state or the state system has been rendered obsolete. Instead, the framing of world order is a more tenuous and contested reality, particularly influenced by the behavior of various kinds of transnational networks, ranging from criminal to religious, by global corporations, banks, hedge funds, financial traders, by regional actors, by the leaders of the first "global state" (based on a combustible mixture of territorial authority and nonterritorial claims), and by a constellation of civil society actors pursuing an assortment of global policy agendas. The persuasiveness of this postmodern hypothesis is heavily affected by technological innovation, past, present, and future. The revolutionary effects of information technologies with respect to global integration and administration, as well as in relation to the nature of warfare and the character of power, lends plausibility to the redefinition of the defining reality of world order by reference to postmodernity.

Language and perception are both at issue here. In part, the perspective taken in the chapters that follow presupposes a constructivist outlook, but with a normative as well as an analytic aspect. By this is meant the conceptualizing of world order and global governance is inevitably an interpretative act that deserves respect to the extent that it seems to illuminate and clarify the puzzles presented by experience and perception. It is obvious that an interpreter does not "see" the state, the state system, globalization, or postmodernity. These are constructs of the informed mind, appeals to participants in the production and dissemination of knowledge, but subject to a process of assessment and refinement by the exchange of perceptions. They are also aspirational constructs, seeking to prefigure a preferred future, as well as to describe, explain, predict, and, as such, qualify as "normative (that is, value-laden) constructs." The social science predilections of the academy encourage hiding, if not repudiating, these normative dimensions, by an alleged fidelity to scientific method and an ethos of objectivity. But interpretative undertakings necessarily include subjective elements associated with an assortment of factors, including place, time, social location, educational and cultural background, and political bias. In my worldview, normative constructivism does not pretend to achieve objectivity or deny the relevance of preferences and hopes in the construction of reality. At the same time, it claims to be honest within its disclosed framework, acknowledging evidence adverse to its preferences.

There is a further issue of language present. It relates to the coloring of perception by media manipulation and mainstream politicians. This coloring has assumed acute proportions in the domain of political violence, especially after September 11. The inflammatory use of the word "terrorism" to associate certain forms of political violence with moral depravity and extreme criminality has had the double effect of repudiating one set of political projects while sanitizing those of adversaries, regardless of the scope and effects of their reliance on violence. Let us assume the common ethical ground of repudiating violence directed against civilians as totally unacceptable regardless of extenuating circumstances. Surely, such a standpoint repudiates nonstate tactics that rely on political violence, but what needs stressing is that state tactics with similar or greater consequences should also be repudiated, and perhaps more insistently as they generally derive from legitimated authority structures (that is, governments) that have set the rules governing political violence in human affairs. For this reason, I try my best to avoid using the terminology of "terrorism" in a one-sided fashion.

Can we be hopeful about the future? The title chosen suggests a dangerous downward pull exerted by the American empire-building project. This negativity is complemented by other tendencies associated with corporate and apocalyptic globalization, but it is offset to varying degrees by the energies associated with civic and regional globalization. The wrecking of world order, if that is what it is, also has some dialectical effects, encouraging receptivity to bolder thinking about the goals of the struggle against these darker forces — including a reevaluation of the spiritual message of the great world religions and the possibility of constructing human security on a foundation of nonviolent politics.

Acknowledgment

Work on a book of this sort has depended on an invisible network of collaboration, which in this case has been truly global in scope. It has also been premised on two central orienting principles: perceiving the political circumstances of the world from as many angles of observation as possible and keeping my authorial eye on horizons of hope without losing contact with present realities, and especially with notable situations of acute suffering and abusive economic, political, and social arrangements. In these senses, I would consider this book to be a contribution to "normative international relations," framing analysis with ethical, legal, and spiritual goals consciously and explicitly in view.

I should mention what may seem obvious. Although this manuscript was substantially completed before the September 11 attacks it was recast to take account of the momentous changes wrought by that event, and even more so by the American response. The future global role of the United States is both more contested than ever before in its history, and possibly subject to significant change. The Iraqi resistance to American occupation and the uncertainties associated with the outcome of the 2004 presidential elections make it difficult to anticipate adjustments that will be made in American grand strategy in the years ahead, as well as in the efforts by other political actors to play supportive or oppositional roles. The two most plausible futures for world order involve either a scenario of global domination by the United States or a collaborative world order that reinstates the primacy of "globalization" as it was being shaped at the end of the 1990s, including by the emergent forces of global civil society.

The last stages of this book were completed in Santa Barbara and Istanbul, both settings providing a happy combination of serenity and stimulation. I have been fortunate to be associated with the Global and International Studies Program of the University of California at Santa Barbara. I have found collegial warmth and intellectual stimulation in this atmosphere, and mention particularly Rich Applebaum, Giles Gunn, and

Mark Juergensmeyer in the program, as well as Juan Campo, Lisa Hajjar, Burleigh Wilkins, and Howard Winant in closely related endeavors. My time in Santa Barbara has also brought me closer to the Nuclear Age Peace Foundation and its dedicated president, David Krieger. The opportunity to work closely with David has also influenced the approach taken on a number of issues addressed here. And finally, being here has enabled me to renew my close working friendship with David Ray Griffin, whose recent interests increasingly converge with my own and whose explorations into the ways of American empire are breaking new ground.

While in Istanbul I had the opportunity to work in that most beautiful city, and to find the change of outlook of great value. I have learned from my friend Ahmet Davutoglu, who has so creatively built many bridges from present to past, from past to future, from politics to religion, from religion to politics, from intellectual studies to public service, and from public service to intellectual studies. Over the years the wisdom and insight of Murat Belge has also been invaluable in my efforts to understand the fascinating Turkish kaleidoscope.

I wish also to acknowledge the importance for my understanding of the world arising from taking part in the Independent International Commission on Kosovo. It provided an excellent opportunity to grasp first-hand the complexities associated with "humanitarian intervention." I was fortunate to have excellent colleagues in this endeavor, and worked especially closely with Richard Goldstone (chair), Carl Tham (co-chair), Mary Kaldor, Martha Minow, and Jacques Rupnik. The work of producing a report under time pressure was also greatly facilitated by the fiercely independent and talented Liam Mahoney and the graciously skillful executive director, Pia Övelius.

Throughout this period, as earlier, my friendship and collaboration with Chandra Muzaffar and JUST, the organization that he founded and headed, has helped me see the world through eyes that have an unimpeded vision of Western hegemony, as well as the limits of the Enlightenment legacy.

My approach to the role of the sovereign state in this evolving global setting was benefited by a project entitled "Global Governance in the 21st Century: Alternative Perspectives on World Order" that was established by the Swedish Government in 1995 under the auspices of its Expert Group on Development Issues (EGDI). The EGDI undertaking was expertly led by Bertil Odén and Björn Hettne, generating stimulating interplay among the participants.

I would finally mention my close collaboration with Andrew Strauss, especially as it relates to global democracy. Andy has made me see the importance of working to establish a global peoples parliament as soon as possible. In this respect, this effort complements the broader and more conceptual approaches taken to these issues by other close friends and collaborators Daniele Archibugi, David Held, Saul Mendlovitz, and Rob

Walker. During the course of writing this book, I (and the world) lost a dear, valued, and brave friend and brilliant scholar, Edward Said.

In a more personal vein, I want to thank my children, Noah, Dimitri, and Zeynep for their love and for reinforcing a sense of responsibility to the future. And most of all, as for the last decade, I am grateful beyond words for the companionship in all dimensions of experience of my wonderful wife, Hilal.

Richard Falk
Santa Barbara, California

Contents

Part One
Structures, Actors, and Agency

Chapter 1
The Future of the State and State System

This chapter considers the historically ambiguous circumstances of world order as contextualized by macrohistorical developments early in the twenty-first century, especially the overall impacts of the complex market-led phenomenon generally described as "globalization" and the more traumatic September 11 megaterrorist attacks on the United States that have given rise to a resurgence of security-oriented geopolitics. What these two seemingly disparate developments have in common is their subversive impact on a structure of world order long constituted overwhelmingly by the interplay of sovereign states. These complementary challenges each in their own way definitively undermine the regulative capabilities of states, thereby revealing the extraordinary potency of nonterritorial, networked forms of information-based organization. These fundamental shifts in the locus and nature of power are giving rise to profound doubts about the continuing viability of resource-based power and territorially delimited authority structures that have dominated international diplomacy and foreign policy for the last several centuries. This reconfiguration of power and structure is accentuated by the resurgence of global religion, the emergence of transnational social forces, the rise of transnational crime, the expansion of legal and illegal migration patterns, the impact of globally integrated TV, and the militarization of the planet under the aegis of a single political actor.

Revisiting Westphalia
Westphalian Benchmarks
To comprehend the significance of a post-Westphalian image of global politics, it is helpful to begin by clarifying the Westphalian reality to the

extent possible. In brief, the Westphalian rubric is ambiguous in its usage as it serves both as shorthand to designate a state-centric, sovereignty-oriented, territorially bounded framing of international authority and to identify a hierarchically structured world order shaped and managed by dominant or hegemonic political actors, the identity of which change with the ebb and flow of history. In effect, the term "Westphalia" contains an inevitable degree of incoherence by combining the territorial/juridical logic of equality with the geopolitical/hegemonic logic of inequality.

But the problems of conceptualization extend further. "Westphalia" is simultaneously used to identify an *event,* an *idea,* a *process,* and *a normative score sheet.*

As event, Westphalia refers provincially to the European peace settlement negotiated at the end of the Thirty Years War (1618–1648), which has also served as a convenient, although somewhat arbitrary, point of origin to establish the distinctively modern structural frame for world order that has endured, despite major modifications from to time to time, until the recent past. This structural persistence has been sufficient to give continuity to international relations, especially if the evolutionary experience is explicated by an historical approach.

As idea, Westphalia refers to the state-centric character of world order premised on full participatory membership accorded exclusively to territorially based political actors that qualify as sovereign states. As process, Westphalia refers to the changing character of the state, statecraft, and state system that have evolved during more than three hundred and fifty years since the 1648 treaties were negotiated. It takes into account the crucial stages of evolution associated with the rise and fall of Eurocentricism, as well as the related dynamic of colonialism and decolonization, the advent of weaponry of mass destruction, the establishment of international institutions, the rise of global market forces, the emergence of global civil society at the end of the last century, and the application of a series of revolutionary technologies to the organization of life on levels of societal action. As normative score sheet, Westphalia refers to the strengths and weaknesses, as conditioned by the long cycles of historical circumstances, of such a sovereignty-based system, shielding oppressive states from accountability and exposing weak and economically disadvantaged states to intervention and severe forms of material deprivation. Each of these dimensions could be elaborated upon in great detail, but their essential relationship to what is the focus of this study, the contemporary interface and overlap between Westphalian and post-Westphalian tendencies, does not depend on such a detailed exploration.[1] Nor does it depend on a judgment about historical reality as either reflecting cycles of repetition or some sort of linear path leading from past to future. A war/peace view of history encourages the adoption of a cyclical outlook, whereas a technological/scientific view encourages a linear perspective.

This long established statist/hegemonic structure of world order had been preceded in thought and practice by a medieval conception that emphasized with greater consistency the interaction between Christian universalism, establishing a normative community of belief among Christians, and territorial localism, associated with various heterogeneous forms of political control arising from feudal land tenure, employment relations, and geographically constrained communications and administrative capacities. These premodern foundations of world order, besides being implicitly and operationally Eurocentric, generated a sharp contrast in identity between the civilized "we" and the barbaric "them," which became formalized and ideologized much later in the colonial era. The initial breakdown of this pre-Westphalian framework was partly a consequence of cleavages within Christianity, especially the Protestant break with Rome, and partly a consequence of the military and economic benefits of more centralized political actors with greater capabilities to mobilize human and fiscal resources and establish order within large, yet manageable, territorial units.[2]

This Westphalian system originated in Europe, as set forth in the 1648 treaties, but enlarged by stages to encompass the world, combining at each stage its core statism (the logic of equality) with hegemonic actualities (the logic of inequality) particularly prominent in the extensive peripheries of the world system. The decades after World War II represented the organizational climax of the Westphalian conception of world order, that is, the extension of the states system to Asia and Africa via the dynamics of decolonization, the continued control over global economic policy by states, a preoccupation by governments with security in relation to war and peace, and a geopolitical focus on "bipolarity" that reflected the centrality of the antagonist and potentially apocalyptic encounter between two superpowers and their respective blocs of subordinate allies.

This Westphalian world was juridically structured through the agency of such foundational norms of international law as the equality of states, sovereign immunity, and the doctrine of nonintervention. This juridical conception of international society *as statist* has also controlled membership and participation in most of the significant international institutions, including the United Nations and the European Union. This impression of statist organization is misleading, as the most important international institutions have found ways to take inequalities of political and economic power into account. For elaboration, see Chapter 4. Only fully sovereign states are treated as possessing the qualifications for full membership and participation, although caucuses of groups of states and movements toward regional representation, especially for EU countries, have complicated the realities of global diplomacy. Matters of human rights, civil discord, and the choice of governing ideology are treated by the United Nations Charter as exclusively matters of "domestic jurisdiction" in deference to the Westphalian frame of reference. Such deference can also be explained as a recognition of the limited capabilities of the UN as the institutional expression of the organized international community. When these limits are not respected, as has been arguably the case with respect to humanitarian diplomacy in the 1990s, the UN is rendered ineffective, and its activities generate embittered criticism, which decreases its overall stature.[3] Such results also reflect the political will of principal members that can either endow or withhold the capabilities required for effective undertakings.

The Westphalian model also effortlessly accommodated the realities of radical inequality among states in size, wealth, power, and international role. This inequality generated its own distinctive form of "global governance," relying on the performance of special managerial roles by leading state actors known as "the Great Powers," and discussed by international relations theorists beneath the rubric of "hegemonic geopolitics."[4] Such a model was historically conditioned by the evolutionary dynamics of a Eurocentric world that included a variety of imperial forms of multistate governance, and was gradually challenged in the twentieth century by the rise of the United States and Russia.[4a] These states emerged as the first "superpowers" in the era of the Cold War, dominating tight alliances designed to deter expansion by their rivals while avoiding the onset of World War III, and possessing weaponry of mass destruction that could be delivered to any part of the planet in devastating quantities.

Since 1945, even the strongest states have been inherently vulnerable to catastrophic destruction as a result of the development of nuclear weaponry and increasingly accurate and diverse means for its delivery in minutes from great distances. As of 2004, every state is vulnerable to attacks with weaponry of mass destruction (including possibly from nonstate actors), and there exist many actors that possess such a capability to some degree. With the end of the Cold War, further restructuring has led Westphalian realists to view the hegemonic position of the United States as establishing "a unipolar moment" in the history of the state system, which is currently sustained by a combination of economic, technological, diplomatic, cultural, and military instruments of influence. Paradoxically, this unipolar power structure is also challenged in formidable ways by countermovements and patterns of resistance that are without historical precedent, extending from networks of extremists to highly visible actions by civil society actors. Such phenomena as the zero-casualty NATO War in 1999 over Kosovo and the American quest for nuclear ballistic defense and space-based weaponry manifest the practice and mentality of unipolarity, and the seemingly futile quest for hegemonic or imperial invulnerability. It also reflects a dramatic geopolitical shift from a traditional Westphalian search for balance, deterrence, countervailing power, and at most, military superiority, to a more controlling effort to establish and maintain dominance in the face of a revolutionary preoccupation with the menace of nonstate political actors.[5] With the cunning of history at the very moment when territorial invulnerability in relation to states is achieved, the capacity of nonstate actors to expose deep structures of vulnerability emerges, especially in relation to the most powerful of states. Put vividly, the United States and its citizenry are far more vulnerable to these forms of antagonism than is Norway and its citizenry.

It is important to note two further Westphalian features of world order. Against the background of Machiavelli, Hobbes, and Clausewitz, the prevailing view of international society has been one in which the role of law and morality has been kept marginal in relation to statecraft. To the extent that stability and order produce "peace," it arises from the capable and prudent management of relative power, and not from norms of law and morality. This marginality has been interpreted in the contemporary period by such thinkers as Hans Morgenthau, George F. Kennan, and Henry Kissinger on the basis of a skeptical view of human nature that is conditioned by ambition, fear, and selfishness, leading to a political orientation that regards security as virtually synonymous with "power," and an outlook toward conflict associated with differing forms and degrees of "realism."

Such thinkers as E. H. Carr, Raymond Aron, Hedley Bull, and Robert Cox have modified the outlook of pure realism.[6] These influential thinkers, although sharing a preoccupation with the security and power of states, have many differences in emphasis and outlook. For instance, Aron and Bull conceive of international virtue modestly as consisting of "prudence" in statecraft, as well as inferring from statism the existence of an "anarchical society," a minimal form of societal reality that depended upon a generalized recognition of the benefits of elementary forms of international cooperation arising from good faith compliance with international treaties, from customary respect for diplomatic immunities, and from a general willingness to abide by norms of nonintervention.

Carr and Cox are far more inclined to consider seriously alternative forms of future world order, based either on the relevance of "dreams" or on leverage that might be exerted over time by transnational social forces. The character of international society reflects the historical circumstances, including struggles between opposed worldviews, and evolves as these circumstances alter. Such an international society possesses limits of sociability that lead to disillusionment if exceeded. More specifically, realist patterns of thought conceive it to be futile and disillusioning to prohibit recourse to force international life or to attempt to punish leaders of sovereign states for their transgressions against international law.[7]

The Westphalian ethos has also generated variants of structural realism that relate behavioral features of international relations ahistorically to the way in which power is distributed among leading states. Such trust in the explanatory power of rational analysis is partly an effort to give the study of international relations a scientific basis. Realist critics imbued with classical approaches resting on the historical and conceptual interpretation of world politics regard this effort to achieve scientific rigor as essentially misconceived because the subject matter of international life is too variable and complex. As such, it is not susceptible to the levels of abstraction that would be needed to accumulate comparable "cases," carry out experiments, and deduce laws of social and political behavior, or to engage in deductive generalization on the basis of class structures and the ownership of the means of production. This whole enterprise of scientific explanation and historical determinism amounts in the end to little more than one more instance of a confusion of science with "scientism," whether articulated as social science or Marxism.[8]

To summarize, the Westphalian framework continues to contain dual reference points that encompass the equality of states under international law and the hierarchy of states in the actual operation of international relations. It is only by combining these contradictory ordering logics that the complex character of Westphalia is comprehended. The shared outlook of these two ideas relates to their focus on power either as the territorial sovereignty of the state or the geopolitical control of relations among states by way of hegemonic mechanisms (for instance, either Great Power diplomacy or superpower arrangements).

To the extent that "failed states" exist within recognized territorial boundaries and to the degree that no state or states exercise leadership roles, the quality of Westphalian order tends to diminish. This quality can also be diminished by the emergence of militarist and dissatisfied states and by the suppression of human rights at home and aggression abroad. The Westphalian approach to world order tends toward the fulfillment of its *normative* potential when governance at the state level is internally moderate, democratic, and observant of human rights (including economic, social, and cultural rights), and when leading states are externally dedicated to the promotion of global public goods as well as to the preservation of their specific strategic interests.

As a matter of historical experience, this normative potential has never been achieved, or even clearly and fully advocated, although the extent of failure has varied over time.[9] Genocidal politics and major international and civil wars are indicators of extreme failure, as assessed by common Westphalian standards of performance.

The degree to which legal obligations deserve respect in international political life remains a matter of controversy. According to the Hobbesian variant of Westphalian realism, law can function *within* the state because an agency of enforcement exists, but *outside* the state there is no enforcing mechanism. It is a war zone that can be kept nonviolent only by means of deterrence and containment. Bull, in particular, challenged this view, suggesting that a distinctive form of sociability among states is an imperative of international life, but that the maintenance of security depends on leading states retaining discretion to use force in times and places of their choosing, but within an ethos of prudence so as to maintain balance and stability among sovereign states.[10]

Throughout the Westphalian period there existed countertraditions that emphasized morality and law to a far greater extent and envisioned the gradual emergence of a normatively accountable global polity by stages. Such perspectives are often grounded in and inspired by Kant's seminal essay, *Perpetual Peace* (1795), which served as the starting point for such persisting perspectives as international liberalism and the related espousal of "democratic peace" — that is, the view that democratically organized states do not wage war against one another.[11] Between World War I and the end of the Cold War, the United States was the main champion of this countertradition, often called "idealism" in contrast with "realism" and associated with the formative ideas and outlook of Woodrow Wilson, but drawing on deeper and abiding ideas of American exceptionalism ("a Lockean nation in a Hobbesian world").[12] Whether this Wilsonianism persisted in the United States during the Cold War era, except rhetorically, is a matter of ongoing debate, but its weight was (and is) felt in liberal patterns of support for the United Nations, foreign economic assistance, humanitarian diplomacy, and human rights.[13]

These strands of liberal/idealist thought often derive from and are associated with *inclusive* forms of religious belief.[14] Inclusive orientations, whether religious or secular humanist, emphasize human solidarity as desirable and possible, thereby challenging either directly or indirectly Westphalian complacency about radical inequality and war as intrinsic to international reality, as well as the existential limits of community. The liberal/idealist outlook is more hopeful about human nature, species identity, and world order prospects than are realists. Secular versions of such idealism rest their underlying optimism upon the emancipatory impacts of human reason over time and, especially, on the degree to which technological innovation improves material well-being, lessens the relevance of material scarcities and unevenness in wealth and resources, and contributes to better communication and understanding among the peoples of the world. Of course, these simplistic distinctions miss some crucial aspects of hybridity of thought — realists who exhibit optimism about the persistence of a Westphalian world despite global warming, demographic pressures, ecological decay, and the spread of weaponry of mass destruction; and liberal/idealists who are convinced that such persistence will trigger a catastrophic breakdown of order, together with a major regression in human circumstances. The latter tend to believe that rational human action can prevent catastrophic future developments, whereas most realists mainly rely on little other than their capacity to inflict destruction on adversaries, and are skeptical about internationalism of all kinds (other than defensive alliances), especially institution-building, Of course, there are many varieties of realism distributed throughout a spectrum of views on such matters, some of which incorporate liberal convictions about human rights, democracy, and international institutions, and some of which are hostile to such goals.

Despite such normative countertraditions, the postulates of realism have principally shaped the behavior of states during the modern era with the possible exception of the behavior of the liberal democracies, especially the United States in the period between the end of World War I and the onset of World War II. Whether realism persists to the same degree in the aftermath of September 11 will be treated in Part Three. It would be a mistake to regard the establishment of the League of Nations or, later, the United Nations and the European Union as indications that the Westphalian statist/geopolitical framework was being superseded by either design or practice.[15] Such institutional innovations, although ambiguous with regard to overall purpose, mainly function as instruments for the attainment of statist objectives. The realist predominance is also manifested by the continuing tolerance of genocide, massive poverty, and acute civil discord in those realms of international society where a geopolitics of indifference prevails, contrasted with the emergence of patterns of robust intervention in circumstances where important strategic interests of the intervenors are at stake. It is a question of some significance for the assessment of post-Westphalian prospects to gauge the extent to which realism is intrinsic to a statist framework of world order, or is more of an expression of values prevailing in the political culture or of the ethics associated with the market. There is also a matter of whether realism is capable of conceiving of national and strategic interests as long term, which would enable a realist to be deeply concerned about the impacts of a generation or a century of environmental deterioration, either by way of global warming, ocean pollution, or otherwise.

One way to concretize such an inquiry is with respect to the viability of an approach to security at the level of the state that proposes reliance on "human security," a terminology recently introduced into the language of diplomacy to express a less militarist and statist conception of security, a conception more attentive to the concerns and insecurities of persons and peoples. Would a statist system genuinely operating on the basis of and organized in relation to human security continue to be usefully labeled as "Westphalian"? Or, would not the adoption of human security by leading governments have a transformative impact on world politics, validating a post-Westphalian designation?

To the extent that such questions relate to political discourse, they suggest that the Westphalian state-centric and geopolitically managed world presupposes a pluralist orientation toward the definition of human well-being, development, and destiny. Such pluralism would be consistent with extensive cooperation among political communities to address global-scale challenges to ecological sustainability. It would not, however, be arguably consistent with the elimination of warfare and other self-help features of a decentralized world order constituted by sovereign territorial states.

The relation of state and nation is also a crucial aspect of the Westphalian ethos. The invention of militant nationalism in the eighteenth century served to consolidate state power, enhancing its mobilizing capacity, as well as accentuating the contrasts between "inside" and "outside," "citizen" and "alien," and even "civilized" and "barbaric." The idea of "nation-state" served partly as a mobilizing fiction and project to ensure loyalty to the state, and partly as a legalistic designation of "nationality" as conferred by the state without regard to specific ethnic identity. Such "nationalism" weakened bonds with outsiders, but served over time to construct meaningful political communities, as well as to erode many hierarchies and patterns of discrimination based on class, race, and ethnic identity within territorial boundaries.

And yet, as of the early twenty-first century, an array of antistate and ethnic nationalisms pose a crucial challenge to political stability in many states. This challenge is directed not at statism as such, but at the failure of existing states to be "nation-states" in psychopolitical respects (that is, to succeed as "natural political communities") and toward overcoming the plight of "captive nations" and embittered micronationalisms trapped within the boundaries of existing states. The modern system of states was premised on secular assumptions of multiethnicity and juridical nationhood, and so any major trend in the direction of invalidating such states would tend toward the nullification of mature Westphalian forms of world order. For this reason, the practice and theorizing on the right of self-determination since the end of colonialism and the Cold War has placed in jeopardy the persistence of the modernist ethos a Westphalian world, which favored in principle states premised on ethnic diversity and religious pluralism.[16]

To the extent that three to eight thousand distinct ethnicities exist as "nations," the legitimation of the claims of even a fraction of these unrepresented peoples to political independence, or even autonomy (sometimes identified as "internal self-determination"), would alter world order in fundamental respects. In effect, the legitimacy of states that are ethnically diverse and, in this sense, multinational to the extent that minorities conceive of themselves as "nations" is an indispensable feature of the Westphalian world.

It is obvious that the state system is at the core of the Westphalian experience, but it is confusing, being both a guiding and incoherent myth that does not now and never did correspond with patterns of behavior in international politics that were shaped by war, social forces, civilizational and religious energies, and inequalities of power/wealth. What is more, the character of the state is fundamentally ambiguous on this central matter of the nation-state, and the operating modes of statecraft certainly evolve over time, especially reflecting the impact of changes in technology, values, geopolitical goals, guiding ideology, and revealing "exceptions" (for instance, religious and ethnic states). As such, it is misleading to essentialize the Westphalian reality as if it were not embedded in a changing historical matrix of incompatible ideas, technologies, ideologies, structures, and practices.

What endures to give world order its Westphalian shape over the centuries is the primacy of the territorial state as political actor on a global level, the centrality of international warfare, the autonomy of the sovereign state to govern affairs within recognized international boundaries, the generalized tolerance of "human wrongs" committed within the scope of sovereign authority, the special leadership role in geopolitics claimed by and assigned to leading state(s), the weakness of the rule of law, and the absence of strong institutions of regional and global governance.[17] The veto power conferred on the five Permanent Members of the United Nations Security Council is a major continuning formal and symbolic recognition of state inequality as part and parcel of the Westphalian reality as of the early twenty-first century. As such, it is an explicit acknowledgement that the sovereign equality of states is a diplomatic concept, but not one that is politically descriptive of the workings of world order.

The decision to abandon or alter the Westphalian label for world order is a matter of not only assessing empirical trends, but also advancing prescriptive goals. Embracing a post-Westphalian perspective involves an endorsement of certain forms of transformative agency currently active in the world, as well as a process of relabeling due to subversive trends that have been unleashed in recent decades. There are several types of actors pushing consciousness and perceptions beyond Westphalian categories: there are global corporations and banks that conceive of the world as a marketplace for production, consumption, and investment; there are the civil society transnational actors that conceive of the world as a human community in which the human needs and basic rights of all persons are upheld; there are transnational networks of political extremists animated by post-Westphalian visions of community (for instance, the Islamic *umma*); and there is a global state that projects power and claims to exercise authority with limited deference to sovereign boundaries. These transformative agents seek alignment with governments and popular movements, and each exerts a measure of influence.

Corporate and financial globalizers have enjoyed widespread support in promoting their objectives within government circles of the leading states. Civic globalizers have had to be more innovative, cobbling together ad hoc coalitions with shifting clusters of states seeking to ensure the production of global public goods in relation to such international goals as arms control, human rights, and environmental protection. The al Qaeda network has found varying and indeterminate amounts of support among those governments and constituencies discontented with Western penetration of the non-Western world and disillusioned with the capacity of governing elites to promote indigenous well being. And finally, the American project of global dominance has gained support from those who view a unipolar structure, even if it assumes an imperial character, as globally beneficial as compared to alternatives of widespread chaos or generalized gridlock.

A post-Wesphalian world is mainly *not yet*, although the dynamics of behavioral and discursive subversion are quickly eroding Westphalian foundations. Reliance on the descriptive terminology of "globalization" in some way expresses the insufficiency of early discussions of international relations that kept their entire focus on the state system. Also, the interest in civilizational perspectives, whether to depict new conflict formations or to encourage dialogic relations is another recognition that our interpretative categories need to be revised to capture the most significant aspects of contemporary reality.[17a] In some genuine sense, "the Westphalian world" no longer exists, and never existed,[18] but neither has a post-Westphalian world been brought into being.[19] Westphalian frames for international reality no longer generate confidence, but globalization as another framing is too vague and uncrystallyzed to be a serious candidate for replacement, while contentions of a nascent American global empire remain polemical.

A final feature of the Westphalian outlook was the horizoning of reality in relation to the state, whether on maps or in the political and cultural imagination, although there were notable exceptions who earlier conceived of collective human experience in civilizational terms.[20] Such horizoning could be reconciled with feeble forms of regionalism and globalism, but without much relevance for the lifeworld of human existence or political behavior, which was quite obviously dominated by states. For this reason, conjectures of the imagination that depicted such horizons as constitutive were generally derided as "cultural" or "utopian," more suitable for the realms of literature and religion. Utopia has, of course, the revealing and humbling etymology of meaning "no where." It is this shift in horizoning that may be the most decisive indication that we are currently experiencing a post-Westphalian dawn. It is no longer possible to ignore *politically* the following nonstatist horizons: those of "humanity," "globality," and "regionality."[21] Such shifts in language and political discourse signal deeper behavioral and perceptual adjustments, and parallel the radical behavioral implications of the global religious resurgence, the rise of civilizational thinking, and the onset of a borderless war pitting a concealed network against a global state.

The post-Westphalian framing of political reality must accordingly be mindful of this set of tendencies, identified most prominently in relation to an impending "clash of civilizations." Here, the Westphalian war system is given a renewed relevance by being resituated in civilizational rather than statist structures of conflict.[22] The religious resurgence adds weight and passion to this outlook, although migration patterns of intermingled civilizations make spatial mapping of intercivilizational relations impossible, and to the extent attempted, extremely misleading. The emphasis on a "dialogue of civilizations" is mainly a normative effort to appreciate the relevance and fundamental attractiveness of civilizational interpretations of the historical situation, but at the same time seeking to avoid reproducing the Westphalian war system in the emergent current intercivilizational context. It also seeks to avoid confusing geographical categories of delimited regions with civilizational contours that overlap one another to significant degrees.

The Post-Westphalian Perspective

The Prescriptive Imperative

Modernity has given rise to two sorts of escapist projections: a nostalgic return to small local communities premised on high degrees of integration, perhaps epitomized by premodern images of self-determination and social cohesion affirmed by many representatives of indigenous or traditional peoples; and an evolution toward encompassing functional communities that were premised on low degrees of integration, but looked toward the emergence of a planetary polity in some form that sustained peace and stability.

During the whole course of the Westphalian reality there were those on the sidelines of political life who dreamed of a unified world order that maintained peace and security, and spread a set of preferred values, almost always their own familiar form of governance generalized for the entire world.[23] Already in the fourteenth century, Dante gave expression to such a self-serving hope in his *De Monarchia*, conceiving of Rome as the foundation for achieving a much desired global political unity, a visionary solution to the problems of political fragmentation that was set forth long before the formation of the European state system. Subsequently, there were a stream of peace plans and visions of a stateless world that were viewed as part of a utopian tradition of reflection and aspiration, but that also tended to express in concealed forms grandiose expansions of the power structures associated with the various authors. Ever since Dante, such projects for world unification tended to emanate from the existing center of global dominance and institutionalize that reality in a morally attractive form that was presented as beneficial to the whole of humanity. Such visionary thinking seems generally to represent a good-faith effort to promote human well being, but it is often greeted with suspicion because such thinking invariably emanates from existing power centers, and it is assessed skeptically because such individuals are writing on their own without any political base that might make a transition from here to there more believable.

At least since the end of the nineteenth century, on the occasion of the Hague Peace Conferences of 1899 and 1907, there was a constituency for the thesis that war was at once integral to the Westphalian world of interacting sovereign states and increasingly intolerable as a recurrent international practice associated with conflict resolution. After World War I, the World Federalists put forward proposals for world government that attracted considerable support among influential citizens in Europe and North America. After World War II these proposals were revived, especially as a result of the shock effects associated with the development and use of the atomic bomb and the prospect of future wars being fought with catastrophic weaponry. There existed a temporary mood among world leaders of "utopia, or else." This outlook remained prominent in the months following Hiroshima and Nagasaki.

For the next decade or so, this kind of thinking was given some attention, possibly most influentially in the plan for a strengthened United Nations that would be converted into a type of limited world government published in a sequence of three editions by Grenville Clark and Louis B. Sohn under the title *World Peace through World Law*.[24] However, the Cold War managed to stifle such thinking about alternative world orders based on the centralization of authority over this new form of weaponry. The absence of any use of nuclear weaponry during the Cold War and the refusal of nuclear weapons states to part with these capabilities, even in the absence of strategic rivalry, has effectively removed disarmament proposals from serious consideration, even among anti-Westphalians. The Soviet Union was also widely interpreted as a failed utopian project that suggested the bloody dangers and fundamental misconceptions about human nature that pertained to all efforts to transform the utopian genre from an occasionally inspiring literary pursuit to guidance for lifeworld politics.

In a more academic, less Western format, the World Order Models Project (WOMP), working with a transnational group of scholars since 1967, produced a series of volumes under the title "preferred worlds for the 1990s," published between 1975 and 1980.[25] These volumes were designed to formulate "relevant utopias" that could achieve dramatic improvements in the human condition, but accompanied by a strategy that could credibly interpret "the political space" between what exists and what is preferred. Such projections were certainly less anchored in Westphalian assumptions than was mainstream thinking about global reform, especially with respect to the relevance of human solidarity and ethical considerations to the formation of global policy. Unlike the pessimism of realists, the WOMP conjectures, while generally accepting the persistence of the state as dominant actor, were far more optimistic about reformist potentialities, including substantial demilitarization and denuclearization, building up the United Nations and regional institutions, promoting Third World development, and overall establishing a more egalitarian, democratic, law-abiding, and sustainable world order.

A later extension of this line of prescriptive thinking looked hopefully at the emergence of transnational social movements as creating the political basis for a global civil society that could, over time, and in collaboration with progressive states, produce a structure of humane global governance. In a sense, this post-Westphalian outlook regarded the ecological stability of the planet and its increasing interdependence as establishing a functional foundation for moving beyond the operational codes of behavior in an anarchical society of unequal sovereign states. Such transnational activism was also viewed as a positive expression of resistance to the reach and impact of global corporations and banks.

It is also true that economistic versions of this kind of post-Westphalian world began to surface toward the end of the twentieth century. The image of a borderless world dominated by markets, global corporations, and banks attracted a certain following as a practical approach to world order that did not rely on bureaucratic centralization, which was widely viewed as giving rise to global tyranny. More recently, these images were reinforced by the rise of cyberconsciousness with its affinities for "self-organizing systems" and libertarian critiques of government. In these economistic/cybervisions of the future, the Westphalian system is displaced from within and below, rather than superseded by a layer of supranational institutions. The advent of megaterrorism has dampened enthusiasm for these nonstate solutions to the dilemmas of world order in the face of global interdependence.

A final important prescriptive conception is associated with the degree to which "human wrongs" (as explicated by Ken Booth) continue to be given "a safe haven" by the Westphalian charter of sovereignty. The failure of the world to react to the Nazi policies of persecution, or more recently to genocide occurring in Cambodia or Rwanda and severe abuses of human rights in many countries, has inspired critics to advocate the creation of international capabilities and the acceptance of global responsibilities for overriding deference to territorial supremacy. Proposals to establish genocide-prevention forces under UN authority is one direction of assault upon hard core Westphalian ideas of sovereignty.[26] Support for humanitarian intervention is another approach to the protection of vulnerable populations in the face of severe oppression, although a contested one, especially in the aftermath of the Kosovo and Iraq wars. The experience of the ad hoc tribunals in The Hague to prosecute those indicted for crimes in relation to the breakup of the former Yugoslavia, Rwanda, and the Ivory Coast, as well as the Pinochet litigation, are still other forms of response, indicating the existence of procedures for imposing international standards of accountability on leaders of sovereign states that commit crimes against their own peoples.[27]

As already mentioned, two other presciptive trends implicitly posit a post-Westphalian world: the transition from "national security" to "human security" as the basis for governmental engagement in world politics; and the insistence that, to be legitimate, states must be "nation-states" in an ethnically homogeneous or at least an existentially coherent community, rather than in a juridical sense. Note that the advocates of "democratic peace" do not challenge the essential character of the Westphalian framework, including its structure of radical inequality among states or the artificial cohesion of most larger states. Such a project of reformed statism seeks to reformulate the qualifications for international legitimacy of the state so as to reconcile the protection of basic political and civil rights at the level of the individual with the exercise of territorial sovereignty. This reconciliation is believed to enhance prospects for a generally stable, cooperative, and, above all, peaceful and moderate interaction among existing states.

From a prescriptive outlook, such views are post-Westphalian in partial and questionable respects: the obsolescence of international warfare and the development of modest mechanisms for external accountability to encourage compliance with international human rights standards. These reforms would qualify as basic and beneficial modifications of the Westphalian reality, *if systemically implemented*, but would seem insufficiently "transformational" so as to merit unfurling the "post-Westphalian" banner. Perhaps, instead, the label of "neo-Westphalian" would seem to offer an appropriate degree of acknowledgement that the framework had changed in important respects, but that its essential statist character remains the defining reality. As "constructivism" has emphasized, naming is an interpretative act with significant policy effects. The naming of world order, particularly its renaming, generates both expectations and controversy. It highlights disagreements about the direction of global trends, and it signals the wish to affirm or avoid the restructuring of authority patterns that give shape and direction to world order. In these respects, "reality" arises from the dynamics of social construction, of which the deployment of language is a crucial instrument.

As will be discussed in subsequent sections, the emergence of certain forms of regionalism and global democracy will be treated in this study as transformational, and thus cannot be conceptually accommodated within the Westphalian framework. Such an insistence does not imply "the end of the state," although it does mean that world order can no longer be usefully depicted by a more or less exclusive focus on the role and interactions of states. At the same time, the state and statecraft are sufficiently robust, ingrained, and resilient to remain essential features of any nonutopian form of post-Westphalian world order that can be set forth. All in all, if these democratizing and regionalizing developments come to pass, a new organizing concept will be needed, and until it can be agreed upon, the new reality is at least prefigured by employing the post-Westphalian label. The added advantage of this inconclusive labeling is also to avoid either accepting or rejecting the terminology of "globalization," which has become increasingly problematic as a defining framework after the September 11, 2001, attacks and the American response to them.

Some Empirical Observations

Relying on the terminology of "globalization" represents an attempt to highlight a major shift in global trends that have become especially pronounced during the 1990s following the end of the Cold War. It also disclosed an effort to find terminology that is less statist, and yet not overly suggestive of moral progress or drastic innovation. Globalization can be understood either modestly as identifying a dominant trend toward integration in an economistic era of late Westphalian geopolitics, or more fundamentally as signaling the birth of a planetary structure that is dominated by market forces. The slippery and ambiguous nature of the term "globalization" is partly a result of this uncertainty about whether, at this stage, to specify these emergent structures of world order that seem to be shaping current history in new directions. At issue, also, is the role and future of the territorial state, and that of the state system. Of concern is whether it is more accurate and helpful to conceive of globalization as merely the latest phase of the Westphalian Era or itself the constitutive process of radical restructuring associated with the claim that some variant of post-Westphalian reality is upon us. Of course, the debate was an interpretative one that reached its height in the 1990s and was never resolved.

The minimum content of globalization involved the compression of time and space on a planetary scale. Other aspects include the intensification of cross-border interactivity, the transnational penetration of territorial space, the effects of information technology (IT) on global business operations, the dissemination of a consensual view of political legitimacy based on market liberalism and elective constitutionalism, and the pervasive impingement of global market forces on governmental processes. Such a presentation of globalization emphasizes its linear character as a sequel to a more state-centric, war-oriented phase of international history. The state in the course of globalization was being reinstrumentalized by market forces to promote to a far greater extent than previously the priorities of business and finance as these relate to trade, investment, and consumption around the world. Not all states were reinstrumentalized to the same degree or with the same ideological attitude toward globalization, which contributed to an overall impression of the uneven relationship between globalization and policymaking by states.

This prevailing account of globalization missed some critical aspects of the new global reality, especially the challenge mounted by transnational social forces to alleged adverse impacts of globalization: rapidly increasing inequality at the level of society, of the state, of the region; the tendency toward the social disempowerment of the state; and the decline in support for public goods at all levels of social interaction. Expressions of a vibrant global movement that currently lacks clear goals and a consensus as to tactics are: the Seattle demonstrations against the World Trade Organization (WTO) at the end of 1999; the Genoa protest riots sparked by the Group of Eight (G-8) Annual Economic Summit held there in mid-2001; and other grassroots displays of antiglobalization that occurred with growing militancy at sites where globalization elites convene. Antiglobalization forces do possess a shared and deepening resolve to resist the social, economic, and cultural deformations attributed to corporate globalization, but their clear agenda priorities have been changing in response to American global militarism.

It seems more useful to consider this resistance to globalization as increasingly manifesting a commitment to "another globalization" rather than being merely a negative response in the spirit of antiglobalization. The more positive orientation of transnational activists was animated by strong commitments to the enhancement of human well-being by way of building global democracy. The intention was to give globalization a people-oriented rather than a market-driven character. At the same time, there was also a nationalistic component of this antiglobalization movement that tends toward protectionism and is centered upon a struggle to preserve a territorial conception of world order based on the primacy of the nation-state and its citizenry; parts of organized labor and noncompetitive sectors of national economies are hostile to globalization, mainly for materialist reasons and in the spirit of statist populism.

Such perspectives of economic nationalism were not particularly interested in the global democracy and human rights project that motivated many of the transnational social forces. There is a subsidiary component of the critical globalization movement that has a dark green hue, harboring strong suspicions about the effects of integrative technology, including IT. These green critics seek to encourage deindustrialization and favor an austere, minimalist economic approach that rejects global economic growth as a societal goal, opting for small-scale, environmentally benign technologies associated with sustainable and intimate political communities.[28]

I have elsewhere referred to patterns of corporate globalization as "globalization-from-above," and civic globalization as "globalization-from-below."[29] This dichotomizing terminology, although descriptive of the basic tension, is far from satisfactory, as it overlooks and homogenizes the distinct strands of belief that are bound together in these encompassing orientations. It also neglects the sort of patterns associated with collaboration between transnational social forces and governments that are themselves seeking to sustain their identity as socially responsible political actors with primary allegiance to the well-being of their citizenry.

Familiar examples of such collaboration include the overall political process that in the late 1990s produced the Anti-Personnel Landmines Treaty and the Rome Treaty establishing an International Criminal Court. These collaborative patterns, although exploratory and situational, do disclose the possibility of a new internationalism that is neither statist, nor populist, yet combines the capacities of states with the energies of people, and breaks down the state/society dividing line, which organizationally suggests an interesting form of political hybridity.

Putting this cosmodrama of globalization into the context of an inquiry into post-Westphalian prospects suggests that globalization is a decidedly unfinished narrative that could go forward in different directions, especially as again backgrounded by an awareness of America's global dominance project. This rather cautious line of interpretation suggests that the most fundamental impact of globalization will depend significantly on the outcome of the ongoing struggle for "the soul of the state."[30] At issue is whether the state continues to be predominantly instrumentalized by and responsive to market forces or manages to be socially reempowered through the agency of transnational activism as reinforced by social democratic elites and by an accommodation with what is called "humane regionalism" in a later section.

In the case that globalization-from-above wins out by instrumentalizing the state, completing the process of social disempowerment and political demobilization, then it would be appropriate to consider globalization as having produced one possible post-Westphalian scenario; but for reasons only alluded to, such an outcome should be treated as a dysutopia. If the state is socially reempowered, there would exist a renewed regulatory relationship of governance structures and processes to the market and a shift away from rigid adherence to the policy postulates of neoliberalism. If this eventuality fails to come to pass, then the locus of power would remain configured in such a manner as to reaffirm the persistence and legitimacy (although in somewhat contested and diluted condition) of the Westphalian framework, perhaps reinforced by novel forms of violent international conflict.

Of course, there are many intermediate positions relating to the role of the state and of the imperial scenario that could result in a variety of compromise outcomes. Different states might respond in quite disparate ways to the mobilization of and pressures exerted by reformist orientations with respect to the role of the state in relation to globalization and the dual dangers of global empire and megaterrorism. The responses range from accommodation to rejection, and both possibilities could occur under circumstances of varying balances of internal power. Differences in political culture and the presence or absence of effective leadership on one side or the other could also push the process of encounter in one direction or another.

The rise of transnationalism, the growth of human rights and associated ideas of criminal accountability of political leaders, and the role of international institutions might, if these tendencies persist, justify adoption of an ambivalent label such as "a neo-Westphalian" scenario — even without taking globalization into consideration.[31] A neo-Westphalian world order would continue to be understood primarily through the prism of statist geopolitics, although accompanied by a conceptual acknowledgement that normative concerns are integral (relevance of international law and morality) and that transnationalism (localism, regionalism, and cosmopolitanism) is significantly more relevant than in the Westphalian era.

The search for forms of global governance and the protection of vulnerable and disadvantaged peoples are also neo-Westphalian concerns. As already suggested, there is a subjective or constructivist element present.

The terminology chosen reflects the will and perceptions of the observer as well as the objective circumstances that arguably call for a relabeling of reality. The counterintuitive irony present in this analysis of globalization is that the more hopeful interpretation of its evolution now relies on the social and normative reinvigoration of the state, but not on its militarist revival.[32] More pessimistic lines of thinking anticipate the decisive weakening of the state or its remilitarization as assessed from either a humanistic perspective of global public goods or from a more Westphalian perspective of the well-being of the territorial citizenry. It should be understood that this qualified endorsement of a renewal of "the strong state" as the basis of regulating global market operations should not be confused with support for the military and coercive dimensions of state power. As the current approach of the United States Government suggests, high-intensity militarization is quite consistent with an ardent embrace of neoliberal ideology with regard to state/society relations. This deadly combination of militarism and globalization has been pursued all along by the United States, most explicitly in the aftermath of September 11, and is epitomized by the militarization of space and the establishment of regional military commands that encompass the globe.

What seems evident is that "globalization" conveniently encodes the confluence of empirical trends that dominated the political imagination of the years following the collapse of the Soviet Union. Whether these trends would have been better interpreted as establishing a new structure of interaction or involve merely a modification of the old structure now seems irrelevant, and was always an essentially unresolvable debate. As the next section argues, from a normative perspective of human values and from an empirical perspective of likely prospects, some of the more familiar projections of post-Westphalian outcomes are best treated as dead ends. Their advocacy is regressive in relation to the ripening goal of envisioning and realizing humane global governance as a practical and indispensable political project.

The most profound challenge to the political and moral imagination at the present time is to depict a post-Westphalian scenario that is sufficiently rooted in emergent trends to engender widespread hope and mobilize social forces on behalf of such a commitment. Of course, as should be evident, not all post-Westphalian forms of world order are being pursued by those seeking peace, sustainability, human rights, and global community — the main elements of what is here identified as "humane global governance." A post-Westphalian world organized around short-term market forces with ever-widening gaps, deepening pockets of poverty, numerous "black holes" consisting of collapsed governance structures, and control mechanisms dominated by increasingly sophisticated technology at the disposal of elites serving the interests of business/finance.

Other post-Westphalian dystopias that need to be taken seriously involve intensifying trends toward religious and ethnic exclusivism as the claimed basis for fulfilling a right of self-determination and an array of chauvinistic backlashes that seek to hijack government to carry out an anti-immigrant agenda. Of unquestionable significance, as well, is the rise of megaterrorism, allowing nonstate actors to become geopolitical players without having a discernible territorial base of legitimate operations. This challenge to the established world order strengthens the hand of those that insist on an integrated structure of global security, the practical effect of which is to provide a rationale for the reorganization of world order in the form of a post-Westphalian global empire administered by the United States, itself converted into a new hybrid political creature, at once the leading and most sovereignty-oriented territorial state and the nonterritorial overlord of the world. As of 2004, it is uncertain whether this encounter is an epiphenomenal disruption of the globalization scenario, which could pass from the scene with the withering away of al Qaeda and the removal from power in the United States of the reactionary cabal that has shaped foreign policy for the Bush administration since September 11.

Four Post-Westphalian Dead Ends

It is important to exclude certain commonly discussed post-Westphalian scenarios as essentially unattainable or undesirable, or both. Such scenarios distract attention from what is happening and, more significantly, from the genuine *normative potential* implicit in the present phase of global politics. A systematic exploration of normative potential is partly a prescriptive, partly an empirical assessment of the prospect for realizing a specific series of world order goals or values within a matter of years, or at least decades. These goals include an equitable and globally oriented approach to economic development, poverty reduction, human rights, peaceful settlement of disputes, ecological sustainability, global democracy, international rule of law, world health, and universal literacy and education. The World Order Models Project launched such an inquiry as a prelude to hoped-for political action, implicitly subscribing to the slogan, "thought without action equals zero."[33]

WOMP also endorsed even more confidently the corollary "action without thought is less than zero." Although these post-Westphalian scenarios are presented as "dead ends" either because of their lack of feasibility or their denial of widely shared world order values, it should be appreciated that each contains a measure of plausibility with respect to global trends and aspirations. Each also provides some insight into the troublesome originality of the present historical moment, but each also turns a blind eye to difficulties of realization as well as to pitfalls implicit in their image of a preferred future.

The Global Marketplace

One theme in post-Westphalian literature is associated with the global ascendancy of market-driven forms of politcal and ideational structure giving rise to the first genuinely global civilization. Such conceptions envision the radical subordination of territorial states, the anachronism of specific civilizational and religious identities, and the disappearance of such modalities of statecraft as diplomacy and warfare. At best, states would survive as subordinate facilitators of market relations and existing civilizations would become secondary sources of identity, providing some administrative backup and cutltural specificity for an otherwise homogenized "global civilization" premised on Western consumerist priorities and the alleged benefits of a stream of technological innovations.[34]

Such a conception of the future overlooks the dialectical character of globalization, which strengthens rather than overcomes civilizational, religious, and ethnic identities. It also underestimates the resilience of the state and the role of force and violent conflict in a world of persisting inequality of material standards. The only way that such a megacivilization could become a political project would be in relation to the hegemonic ambitions of an existing center of power to exert global dominance, and then it would almost certainly be inherently oppressive and provoke widespread, intense resistance. The darkest reading of the American global strategy is to presuppose an unconditional imperial vision of the future, but many would insist that such a reading probably exaggerates U.S. ambitions and underestimates the frictions and adverse consequences that would result from such a pursuit of global dominance. Already, the awakening of civilizational identity throughout the non-Western world, and even the forward momentum of European regionalism, can be seen partially as a defensive hedge against attempts at the Americanization of the world. This dynamic of imperial projection and anti-imperial resistance has been intensified due to the outbreak of the struggle between the United States and al Qaeda, with critics contending that the struggle is used to hide the imperial project, and the advocates insisting that worldwide security can only be attained by a global security regime maintained under U.S. control.

World Government

There has been a naïve view in the West that a peaceful and just world depends on the establishment of a centralized core of political institutions operating in accordance with a constitutional framework. Such a projection has been a frequent utopian refrain in the face of debilitating warfare for the last century or so, and even earlier, and was given a strong impetus by the carnage of the two world wars of the twentieth century and by the advent of nuclear weaponry. Long-range thinkers and reformers often posited world government as the only serious alternative to apocalyptic catastrophe. More idealistically, world government was envisaged as the natural sequel to the era of sovereign states, a culmination of an evolutionary march of reason toward the institutionalization of political and societal unity on an ever grander scale.[35]

As with other conceptions of unification, the idea of world government engenders skepticism and disbelief. The implicit transfer of peacekeeping authority, especially with respect to "security," seems so remote considering the continuing vitality of nationalist sentiments and statist structures as to be dismissed as hyperutopian. The inequality of material standards and emergent resource scarcities also make the acceptance of a common democratic framework appear threatening in opposite respects to both the rich and the poor. The former fear a leveling down in the name of global equity, while the latter fear the impact of coercive authority for the sake of freezing the status quo under the rubric of law and order designed to inhibit social activism and quell likely unrest. World government seems to lack any current mobilizing appeal, both because it seems unattainable and because its establishment is generally seen to be either as the triumph of global tyranny or as leading to menacing forms of large-scale "civil warfare." Nationalism and civilizational identities remain too robust to risk their absorption in the name of forming a global constitutional polity, and besides, the Westphalian structure ensures protection for diversity and experimentation.

Global Village

The influential media guru Marshall McLuhan insisted decades ago that the impact of TV would create such a sense of shared awareness and interconnectivity as to justify the label "global village." These undoubted insights into the effects of media and technological innovation have been extended in recent years to account for the impact of the Internet, information technology, and a generalized conviction that citizenship is being superseded by netizenship and cyberpolitics in some business and commercial settings.[36] Such perspectives tend to embrace a libertarian ethos that reinforces market distrust of regulation and public sector solutions for human suffering and societal deficiencies. As such, it reinforces the neoliberal downward pressure on the allocation of resources relating to the production of public goods, with the notable and revealing exception of defense. This cyberconsciousness is disposed toward a faith-based reliance on self-organizing systems and the flow of technological innovations to sustain societal and ecological balances, and generate a hopeful posture toward the future.

The deficiencies of this post-Westphalian scenario are associated with a kind of synecdoche that slyly substitutes a part for the whole. Undoubtedly, the advent of IT is significant, even crucial, but there is little prospect that it will overwhelm the structures and attitudes of modernity in the foreseeable future, rather than be mainly accommodated by them. Also, IT generates a dialectical response rather than merely a linear one, which leads to a variety of defensive strategies designed to maintain identity and autonomy in the face of admitted global village tendencies that are regarded by most of the non-Western world as hegemonic in intention and effect. Thus, regionalism, traditionalism, self-determination, and collective rights, as well as international terrorism and transnational criminalization, are among the reactions that make the emergence of global village consciousness and arrangements a confusingly contradictory experience.

There is in this scenario the possibility of a mutually reinforcing collaboration with the social forces associated with "globalization-from-above," but even so the resistance of an activated civil society, "globalization-from-below," seems capable of preventing the global village metaphor from becoming the defining reality of world order.[37] Such an outcome is even more likely to the extent that intensities of the encounter between networks of extremist resistance are locked in violent conflict with the global state and its allies.

Global Empire

The renewed focus on security brought on by the September 11 attacks combined with the seeming inability to address effectively the megaterrorist threats posed within a Westphalian frame have provided a rationale for an American-led effort to provide security for and impose order on the entire world. Such a grandiose global security project is supposedly indispensable given the globally networked and concealed character of al Qaeda, as well as the urgency of guarding against its extremist willingness to inflict harm on civilian society to the maximum extent possible. The undertaking rests on American military dominance, relying especially on the weaponization of space to provide missile defense and, more significantly, to achieve by surveillance an offensive capability to strike a decisive blow anywhere on the planet. This level of dominance is projected in such a way as to make it futile for *any* country to seek to challenge the U.S. role. Such a result would involve the establishment of a global empire, although not formalized as such, but also, as with al Qaeda, a global empire based on a concealed network whose effectiveness is dependent on the control and manipulation of information more than on the technology of destruction.

The idea of a global empire administered from Washington is also a dead end. It rests on a premise of permanent militarization and the submission of other constellations of power and influence. The perception of such imperial ambitions has throughout international history generated a reactive formation among states — alliances to defeat, or at least contain, the quest for global empire. There is every reason to suppose that the remainder of the world will not accept, without mounting some sort of resistance, this American bid to establish such a global empire. The result would be a high-risk rivalry, wasteful of resources, endangering catastrophic warfare among state actors, and shifting priorities of policymakers away from human rights, environmental sustainability, and equitable development. This determined pursuit of global empire has unleashed an illegal aggressive war against Iraq that could not be persuasively explained as a reasonable response to the al Qaeda threat. This is a post-Westphalian scenario that is both an example of dysutopia and a course of history that restores to political consciousness the achievements of the Westphalian solution of world order that is based on political pluralism and a high level of respect for sovereign rights.

The Post-Westphalia Prospect in the Early Twenty-First Century

Noting the Historical Moment of Lost Opportunity
As the Cold War ended, the Soviet Union disintegrated, the world economy flourished, constitutional democracy was robust — there existed a historical moment of unprecedented opportunity to salvage the Westphalian legacy. Salvaging would have involved a mixture of initiatives designed to promote humane global governance: especially demilitarization, the buildup of UN peacekeeping capabilities, and "a Marshall Plan" for Africa and the Caribbean. Seizing the occasion depended on American leadership, which was timid and ambivalent, retreating from any claim to promote what had earlier been called "liberal internationalism." Unlike the endings of the two world wars of the twentieth century, the end of the Cold War did not give rise to grassroots demands for global reform, nor were the leaders on the scene dedicated to achieving a peaceful settlement that addressed the major problems of world order. Instead, the prevailing mood was complacent and foolishly optimistic about the future, triumphalist in response to the outcome of the East/West struggle, economistic in its sense of what needed to be done to secure human well-being, and essentially unresponsive to the legitimate grievances of peoples in the South.

There was some recognition of the opportunities and challenges of the 1990s. George Bush in 1990–1991 temporarily aroused interest and built support during the lead up to the Gulf War by constantly referring to the possibility of establishing "a new world order," by which he meant a functioning collective security process under UN auspices. Humanitarian diplomacy was also taken seriously in this period, both in relation to the protection of the Kurdish minority in Iraq, the response to the humanitarian catastrophe in Somalia, and the effort to avoid "ethnic cleansing" in Bosnia. But for reasons too complicated to discuss here, disillusionment ensued, and the more promising implications of such initiatives never materialized. Among the more hopeful initiatives was the effort by Lloyd Axworthy, while foreign minister of Canada, to champion a shift from "national security" to "human security" as the basis for the role of the sovereign state, a conceptualization earlier given currency in an annual volume of the Human Development Report. Instead, the United States led a return to Westphalian geopolitics in its narrower state-centric ethos, a backlash against the United Nations, and a primary reliance on the world economy organized ideologically along neoliberal lines (with hypocritical self-serving exceptions to protect some private sectors from competitive pressures) to address problems of human suffering (including poverty and the AIDS epidemic) and ecological sustainability.

The opportunity to initiate comprehensive negotiations to abolish nuclear weapons was not even seriously considered during this period, nor were proposals to establish a UN volunteer peacekeeping force that could respond to humanitarian catastrophes rapidly and without passing through the realist, geopolitical, and nationalist filters of leading states. Such states were reluctant to bear the financial or human costs of a diplomacy that could not be validated by traditional criteria associated with national security and strategic overseas interests (for example, to put the matter most starkly, oil is worth dying for, but the prevention of genocide and crimes against humanity is not, especially in a Third World setting). As a result, the main deficiencies of Westphalia were preserved: the war system of global security and the vulnerability of the peoples of the world to various forms of oppressive governance exercised within territorial boundaries.

Nevertheless, the case for drastic global reform was being made in various arenas, and if not attainable within the Westphalian framework then possibly its realization could be achieved through the agency of transnational social forces and the emergence of post-Westphalian structures of governance. What was this case? What were these social forces? Essentially, the plausibility of post-Westphalian perspectives involved the rise to high visibility of a multidimensional normative agenda: implementation of human rights, accountability for past crimes of state, abridgements of sovereignty, the rise of humanitarian peacekeeping.

Beyond the agenda, steps were taken to achieve institutionalization: an increasing willingness of national judicial bodies to apply international legal standards as relevant; greater reliance on mulitlateral approaches to global security, especially under the auspices of the United Nations; and the impressive growth of regional governance, especially in Europe, with mandates to promote human rights, to sustain a social contract between citizens and market forces, and to facilitate trade and investment. Such goals by their nature could not be realized without compromising the internal autonomy of sovereign states, and this would not happen without the agency of political actors other than the state. In effect, drastic global reform, if it is to occur, will eventuate in a post-Westphalian scenario of transformed state structures and strengthened transnational, regional, and global formal and informal institutional procedures.[38]

The most currently promising of these developments is the campaign to promote global democracy and the various movements to build comprehensive regional frameworks for democracy, human rights, and political identity. If cumulatively effective, the impact will be to view the outcome as post-Westphalian: states become subject to external and internal standards of accountability, the rule of law is extended to the foreign policy of governments, and official policies are subject to the discipline of democratic practices; and regional institutions become vital actors that adhere to frameworks that ensure constitutionalism and collective well-being within regional boundaries, but also participate in efforts to increase the quantity and quality of global public goods. World order is thus no longer state-centric, although the role of states remains crucial, even if reconfigured in light of legal and ethical norms. The dusk of Westphalia can be best understood in relation to the setting sun of sovereignty and the rising sun of regional and global policy horizoning, rather than by supposing that the state itself will disappear by stages, or is in the process of being marginalized.

The Campaign for Global Democracy

Until recently, "pro-democracy" advocacy was understood exclusively in relation to ensuring that state/society relations provided electoral mechanisms to obtain the consent of the governed by way of periodic, free elections and sufficient constitutionalism to protect citizens from governmental abuse. Democracy and democratic theory were essentially *internal* frameworks for domestic governance. The operation of international institutions and global arenas of decision were from this perspective not treated as particularly relevant to the existence and establishment of democracy on a global scale. The annual assessments of "freedom" made by Freedom House presupposed that the state was the only significant unit of democratization, and that human rights were only of the civil and political variety. The Kantian tradition of speculating about the global effects of the adoption of democracy at the level of the state is a purely Westphalian approach that does not regard regional and global arenas of authority as constitutionally and structurally necessary or desirable.

Global democracy is being theorized in a much more extensive and inclusive manner. It regards democratic values as pertaining to all domains of life, although adjusted to reflect the particular setting. On the one side of everyday existence, democratic accountability, procedures of participation, and transparency extend their reach to the domains of gender and workplace relations, but also to the undertakings of governments themselves. No one is either above or below the law, which poses a mission impossible if directed at contemporary realities, given the radical inequalities that exist in relation to all dimensions of concern within the current system of world order, however labeled. On the other side, democratic participation, accountability, and transparency are to be extended to such international (regional and global) institutional settings as the United Nations, the International Monetary Fund (IMF), World Bank (WB), the WTO, and the European Union. Such extensions of democracy blur the inside/outside red line of sovereignty associated with international boundaries as well as the public/private sector blue line of domestic governance, and as such challenge the equality/inequality structure that has so far prevented equals (whether states, persons, groups) from being treated equally in the implementation of international standards.

From Seattle to Pinochet, there is a multidimensional ferment that seeks democratic procedures of accountability, participation, and the rule of law in *all* arenas of decision that affect human well-being. In effect, the campaign for global democracy is closely associated with establishing a regime of representative governance associated with human security, but assigning the role of ultimate guardian of rights and responsibilities to the peoples of the world by way of procedures and regimes subject to popular control. The overall character of global democracy is a work in progress. We will not even be able to discern its contours for some decades to come, but it is an emergent reality and it has become the unifying thread in the spectrum of undertakings associated with globalization-from-below. Some illustrative initiatives can be briefly mentioned to convey the spirit of this campaign.[39]

But first, some cautionary words. Globalization-from-below can be understood in at least two distinct ways: as the normative strivings associated with the various elements of the transnational movement resisting globalization-from-above, or as the general populist orientations of the political culture that is operative within the world at this point in history, and is segmented in terms of state, religion, ethnicity, and class. As the antiglobalization demonstrations have confirmed, among the participants are violently disposed anarchists (the so-called "black blocs") and anti-technologists (often identified as "Luddites" or "Neo-Luddites"). Such orientations cannot contribute positively to the realization of humane global governance, even if they join the ranks of those most militantly opposed to the regressive implications of globalization-from-above. If one thinks more broadly about political culture in general, then there are grounds for growing concern, as both consumerism and militarism seem to enjoy strong majoritarian support in the richest and most influential countries. It is quite possible that if globalization-from-below is identified with democratic preferences of society as a whole, then there exists little or no tension between governing elites and the citizenry, and that globalization-from-above is entitled to claim formal legitimation according to standard criteria of the consent of the people. Besides given the militancy of opposition, such an acceptance by majoritarian consent is not enough to ensure legitimacy, even if this opposition is acknowledged to be a minority. Yet such support does not address fundamental issues of viability, which require world order to be sustainable and minimally equitable if it is to be regarded as legitimate.

In this chapter, globalization-from-below is used in the narrower, normative sense of dissenting from the neoliberal ideology and practices associated with corporate globalization, but is not necessarily opposed to the application of technology to productive processes so as to achieve economic growth and a variety of social gains in such areas as health and education. The antiglobalization movement that is challenging the legitimacy of globalization-from-above in its current form puts its main stress on failures to distribute the gains of economic growth among the peoples of the world on an equitable basis and in greater accordance with human needs. The movement also is directed at the failure to provide democratic oversight with respect to the operation of global market forces, as well as its tendency to downgrade support for global public goods such as environmental protection and the operations of international institutions. The following projects promoted by the antiglobalization movement are illustrative of a commitment to humane global governance, but are selective in the sense of both rejecting violence as a means and accepting the contributions of technological innovations to make a better world.

International Criminal Court. The Rome Treaty of 1998 called for the establishment of an international criminal court (ICC) once sixty countries deposited instruments of ratification with the United Nations which was achieved by 2002. This was an impressive achievement considering the nature of the commitment and the opposition of the United States. Both the process and the outcome are essential building blocks for a global democratic framework premised on the rule of law, extending principles of accountability even to those persons who exercise preeminent political and military authority on behalf of sovereign states. The process by which this treaty became a part of international law was decisively facilitated by a coalition of civil society actors that pushed governments and collaborated with those governments seeking to reach a similar goal. In other words, the very act of establishment embodied "a new internationalism" that can be viewed as a Westphalian hybrid, combining transnational civil society activism with traditional state actors to reach a very non-Westphalian result.

This outcome represents a great victory for the ethos of accountability, making those who abuse governmental power face the possibility of being held criminally accountable for their misdeeds as measured by accepted *international* standards relating to human rights, crimes against humanity, and international humanitarian law. The detention of Pinochet; the indictment of Milosevic by the International Criminal Tribunal for the former Yugoslavia; the recent discussion of the indictability of Henry Kissinger, Ariel Sharon, and Saddam Hussein under the Belgian claim of universal jurisdiction; and the recent litigation in the United States associated with World War II slave labor and comfort women are suggestive of a broader trend toward accountability for crimes by states and their representatives.[40]

Of course, the accountability breakthrough, also discussed in relation to a backlash against "the culture of impunity," should not be exaggerated. The Rome Treaty contains many important concessions to Westphalian conceptions, including deference to the primacy of national criminal authority and a major role for the UN Security Council in authorizing or prohibiting prosecution, which gives several of the leading geopolitical actors an extensive veto. Such states are likely to remain outside the ICC legal regime for the foreseeable future. But the existence of a permanent international criminal court is a reminder to the representatives of state power that their officials are not above international law, even in the manner with which they treat their own citizens. The refusal to implement its authority in a consistent manner will also provide civil society, especially in liberal democracies, with a powerful instrument by which to challenge the legitimacy of a national government and of specific official conduct. Also, complementary mechanisms of accountability are likely to be emboldened; domestic courts especially will be more encouraged than ever to conceive of themselves as agents of the international legal order with respect to crimes of state.

Post-Pinochet discussion of these issues is already indicative of a trend toward international accountability, although there are also skeptical responses to these developments, as well as backlash efforts to turn back the clock of accountability.[41] Mention is made of the unevenness of implementation that is certain to damage the credibility of efforts to impose accountability on leaders for their official acts, and of the degree to which the pursuit of leaders holding office can disrupt diplomacy that is generally carried on without challenging the immunity of those representing states regardless of the extent to which their behavior departs from international legal norms of the most fundamental character.

A Global Peoples Assembly. The articulation of the agenda of global civil society as the foundation for cosmopolitan democracy has encountered great difficulties given the degree to which *representation* of interests and values takes place within a Westphalian structure that with increasingly apparent artificiality confers membership only on states. Transnational social forces and civil society actors have been trying to find "spaces" within this structure that allow some expression of views that are not statist in character. Among the most effective of these improvisations was establishing a strong presence at major conferences held under United Nations auspices on global policy issues such as the environment, women, population, and social well-being. The media increasingly acknowledged such people-oriented perspectives, and their agitation was welcomed by some governments seeking to increase their own impact on the plan of action and declaratory documents that come at the end of such proceedings.

This process of participation reached a climax in a series of such conferences in the early and mid-1990s, and suggested the vitality of these exploratory moves in the direction of accommodating the demands of cosmopolitan democrats. Such a dynamic was so successful from this democratizing perspective that it generated a statist backlash designed to close off such avenues of populist participation. Leading states defended their turf with such lame arguments as the waste of money associated with UN conferences that were derided as "talkfests" and "spectacles." Earlier, these same governments welcomed civil society participation, mainly because of their expected co-opting effect on grassroots criticism, hopefully making these actors part of the process as a way of muting their opposition. But this governmental effort was frustrated by the militancy and effectiveness of these transnational civic presences that were clear about their own goals, which often contradicted the objectives of the most powerful states. By essentially ending the sponsorship of such conferences, this avenue of societal transnational participation has been closed off, at least for the present.

An alternative line of participation that has emerged late in the 1990s has been more militant, taking the form of protest demonstrations in the streets of cities that are the scene of high-visibility, intergovernmental meetings concerned with the functioning of the world economy. These demonstrations have been particularly directed at the institutional manifestations of corporate globalization, and have occurred in relation to meetings of the WTO, IMF, and World Bank, as well as such occasions fashioned by market forces as the meetings of the G-8 and Davos annual sessions of the World Economic Forum. Such expressions of resistance have been effective in stimulating a debate about the shortcomings of globalization, including its regressive distributive patterns and the antidemocratic operating modalities of its institutional support structure.

The result has been calls for more participation and transparency, as well as a demand that social and equity concerns of a distributive character be given weight alongside the priority accorded trade expansion and capital efficiency. Yet, the ad hoc character of demonstrations and activism as methods of achieving participation and influence are not satisfactory means for achieving global democracy in any sustained way. The calls for reform are often misunderstood by most of the public and misrepresented in the media, and are easily deflected because of their episodic expression, the focus on encounters with the police, and the inevitable incoherence of objectives among the demonstrators with diverse, even antagonistic, agendas. Instead of concentrating on the substantive issues at stake, the media, especially TV, treat these events as actual or potential spectacles of violence, despite the fact that well over 90 percent of the demonstrators themselves reject violence as a tactic and seek to express their militancy by symbolic and persuasive means alone. Focusing on the violence also allows the governmental and business/finance elites to deflect criticism and concentrate on arranging their future meetings in a manner that poses obstacles for those organizing popular demonstrations. One idea being considered by G-8 leaders after the explosive 2001 Genoa G-8 and the stormy Gothenberg European Union meetings is to hold future such events in remote rural settings that can be more easily sealed off from demonstrators and media.

What these populist efforts to penetrate the Westphalian edifice in its globalization phase disclose is the need for more durable and institutionalized forms of participatory opportunity for the voices of civil society to be heard, and to not be as easily deflected as only expressions of negative energy. It would seem beneficial to establish a parliamentary organ representative of the peoples of the world as a constructive step at this stage, preferably taken within the formal UN System, but not necessarily so. There are many complexities and obstacles associated with the establishment, operations, and funding of such a parliament or assembly.[42] These can be overcome in practice. The experience over time of the European Parliament (EP) is exemplary and even inspirational in this regard. As with the proposal for a Global Peoples Assembly (GPA), the EP too was dismissed for decades as frivolous. Only recently has the EP taken its place as a vital element in the overall structure of the European Union, and assumed the role of indispensable guarantor of its democratic commitment to the peoples of Europe. The legitimacy and political acceptability of the EU evolution is certainly helped by having a functioning parliamentary organ of governance.[43]

A more substantive confirmation of the value of this recommended initiative has been demonstrated by the experience of the Assembly of the Peoples of the United Nations organized on a grassroots basis and held every second year in Perugia during the last decade. Delegates come from many countries, financed by a large number of Italian urban communities, and discuss salient global and local issues for several days, and then make a dramatic march of solidarity to the nearby spiritually renowned town of Assisi. While the selection of delegates who come to Perugia is presently unsystematic and there is a certain chaotic quality pertaining to the mode of discussion and recommendations, there is an exciting and compelling quality about the establishment and conduct of such a forum that more than offsets these deficiencies. A significantly different political discourse emerges from that associated with meetings of intergovernmental and economistic elites, with a strikingly distinct hierarchy of priorities and expectations. In this sense a GPA would, at the very least, help fashion creative tension between the perspectives associated with corporate globalization and those emanating from the various elements composing globalization-from-below, including those of reactionary character.

As with any expression of democratic sentiment, there can be no guaranty that the forms taken by the process will be substantively beneficial and progressive. There are risks and uncertainties, but the whole movement of progressive politics since the French Revolution has been to endow the people as citizens with increasing authority in shaping the dynamics of governance. An experiment with some type of GPA should be thought about in this spirit, and conceived as an indispensable step in the construction of global democracy.

The International Rule of Law. A positive post-Westphalian world order would upgrade the role of law in structuring relations among participants in international life, thereby diminishing the influence of unequal power, wealth, and capabilities. It would also provide for far greater reliance on third-party procedures for dispute settlement and conflict resolution. The spread of international tribunals in such specialized areas as trade, oceans, and human rights is already suggestive of a trend in this direction that partly reflects growing normativity, but so far these innovations are best understood as mere functional adjustments to growing complexity and interactivity. Such tendencies toward legalization should not be overstated, but at the same time impressive and unanticipated outcomes can arise from humble beginnings.[44] The relevance of geopolitics and militarism will almost certainly remain central to the structuring of security policy as pursued by leading states for the next decade or so, although even here the resonance of the global security discourse is suggestive of discomfort with the old paradigmatic enclosures based on "national security."

September 11: Disruption or Derailment?

It is too early to assess the depth of the impact of the September 11 attacks and the American response on the prospects for the sorts of global reform that would raise hopes that the world order sequel to Westphalia would take the form of humane global governance. In the immediate aftermath, it seems evident that these occurrences were deeply disruptive and have put on hold the encouraging normative trends of the 1990s that led to the strengthening of human rights and democracy in so many parts of the world. What is highly uncertain and speculative is whether this disruption is a temporary phenomenon that will be overcome in the years ahead, or represents a more or less permanent derailment, giving way to the struggle for and against global empire. The antecedent conditions of deepening globalization and the rise of global civil society seemed to be based on the influence of powerful social forces that will make every effort to resume the complex process of negotiating a legitimated post-Westphalian world order, and in so doing, marginalize the U.S. insistence that security priorities be given precedence.

Whether this expectation is likely to be realized depends on how credible the persisting al Qaeda threat appears to be in coming years, and how much resistance to American imperial pursuits takes hold. It remains within the realm of possibility that al Qaeda as a persisting danger will be seen in due course as no more tangible in its harmful future capabilities than Y2K turned out to be. The September 11 attacks may mercifully turn out to be a one-time-only-death spasm of this sort of megaterrorist extremism. But this does end the uncertainty. The Iraq War and its aftermath, with some intimations of further "antiterrorist wars," poses the possibility that war/peace issues will dominate the international agenda even if the terrorist menace subsides or disappears. There is also the substantial danger that aggressive war-making directed at weak countries, especially in the Third World, will generate new and devastating waves of nonstate political violence as the only seemingly viable option of resistance to the American project of global empire.

Achieving Humane Regionalism[45]

In important respects, Westphalian world order was a European regional system for most of its operative period, gradually developing a global outreach that attained its climax in the immediate aftermath of the colonial era. Indeed, the regionality of world order began its decline after World War I with the rise of the United States and Russia to positions of prominence and influence that eclipsed Europe as an independent geopolitical force after World War II. This type of Eurocentric regionality lost almost all of its relevance as a description of the overall Westphalian reality with the collapse of colonialism, the emergence of Japan, at least temporarily, as an Asian financial superpower, and the more recent pronounced rise of China as a world power. The universality of statist participation in the United Nations, as well as constitutive rules that make membership an exclusive prerogative of states, embodies the formal idea of a Westphalian world.

The erosion of this world has been increasingly acknowledged by current Secretary General Kofi Annan, who has associated his leadership of the UN with the central idea of enlisting in the organization the meaningful participation of corporate and civil society actors, and arguing that only by weakening its statist character can the UN hope to retain its relevance to a globalizing world order. Significantly, by appealing to global civil society and to global market forces, Annan has understated the relevance of regional actors to the sort of neo-Westphalian United Nations that he seems to be intent upon crafting during his period of tenure as its leader. Perhaps this is less an oversight than a recognition that regionalism is an uneven force in human affairs at this time if region-to-region realities are taken into account. But is such regional unevenness greater than the disparities that exist among states, or in relation to the leverage of civil society or business/finance actors?

Without question the boldest, most successful international institution-building process has taken place over the last five decades, within the European setting, outdoing in important respects both the growth of the United Nations System and of Global Economic Governance (the combined operations of the IMF, WB, and WTO, as coordinated with treasury officials of leading economies).[46] Such a process has the intriguing feature of arising from the relation among the states that generated and dominated most of the Westphalian era, inventing and structuring Eurocentric patterns of ideological, political, economic, and cultural control. Indeed, their loss of dominance due to the results of two world wars, the weakening and collapse of overseas empires, the overshadowing power of the United States and Russia, and the self-destructive bloodshed of intra-European cycles of warfare were among the factors that led several notable European visionaries to embrace the regional idea in its more modest and literal form as integrative for Europe and as a hedge against future war-making.

The initial benefits of European regionalism were perceived in mainly intraregional terms as facilitating postwar reconstruction and as a means to weaken interstate rivalries that had led in the past to the recurrence of large-scale destructive wars. More recently, this European embrace has also been advocated as a way of both competing with and resisting the adverse impacts of economic and cultural globalization. It has proceeded so far as to give rise to various analogies to state-building precursors and to anticipations of an emergent European polity operating within a constitutional framework, engendering loyalty and political identity. Europe, in this phase of constitution-building and common currency, is being likened to America in its early confederalist phase.

The outcome in Europe and its wider relationships to other regionalism remains uncertain and is likely to remain so for several more decades. Nevertheless, to the extent that European regionalism is perceived elsewhere as a success, it is likely to be replicated to varying degrees, although with dramatic adjustments taking account of the particularities of culture, geography, stage of development, styles of governance, and policy priorities. Regionalism presupposes the will and capacity of states to engage cooperatively, and thus involves some minimum degree of mutual respect and the perception of sharing benefits and burdens equivalently. With the spread of human rights and democratic forms of governance, these preconditions are being met.

Also, with globalization being perceived as posing a threat to cultural identity and as a vehicle for Westernization (and even Americanization), and with a more militarist challenge of an American global empire, enhanced regionalism presents itself as a line of resistance. It aggregates the capabilities of distinct states engaged in bilateral relations and in collective efforts to insulate such civilizational groupings from unwanted extraregional encroachments. The assertive side of regionalism posits "Asian values" or "Islam" as sites of transnational bonding that validates and intensifies regional claims of identity, and underpins calls for a dialogue of civilizations. From a hegemonic perspective, such regionalism is seen as antagonistic, leading to a "clash of civilizations" and an era of "culture wars." Beyond these differing lines of interpretation, regionalist understandings move beyond Westphalian categories by positing the significance and potentialities of nonstatist criteria as essential to the construction of our image of world order. Their prominence is itself evidence of a post-Westphalian emergence.

However, as Björn Hettne helpfully suggests, drawing on Karl Polanyi, part of the regionalist impulse needs to be seen in the historical shadow being cast by globalization, especially its weakening of the territorial autonomy of the state and diminished social expectations relating to the capacity of the state to promote the well-being of its own citizenry.[46] This internationalization of the state, converting it primarily into a nonterritorial instrument facilitating the expansion of the world market, gives rise to an effort to recover a territorial base for autonomous action that can better relate governance to people. Regionalism in Europe, and even in Asia and Latin America, is achieving and may in the future achieve more impressive results. And in more extreme settings of Africa and the Caribbean, even without the juggernaught of globalization, regionalism offers some aggregation of influence to mitigate the extreme weakness of the states constituting "the region."

Yet regionalism is not unconditionally beneficial. It could be the prelude to the establishment of enclaves of reaction in the world that reject the universalizing influence of the main human rights discourse. Such possibilities definitely seem to cast a shadow over Asian regionalism, which in other respects seems promising. But the insulation of China from criticism, the "constructive engagement" of Burma, and the opposition to UN efforts to mount justifiable humanitarian interventions as in the Balkans suggests that regionalism can operate in a reactionary manner with respect to the pursuit of normative goals.

Regionalism may produce new dangerous forms of conflict and withdraw energies and resources from the United Nations system. It may also excuse the richer countries from duties toward poorer regions that are experiencing a variety of humanitarian catastrophes, particularly Africa. As such, regionalism works against the sort of human solidarity needed to take on such global challenges as global warming, ocean pollution, and the militarization of space.

It should be appreciated that the linear growth of regionalism, even in Europe, cannot be assumed. A reversal of trends is quite possible, particularly if the world economy performs poorly, if regionalization does not seem to benefit a particular country, and if nationalistic sentiments grow stronger as a backlash to immigration, other unwanted developments attributable to regionalism and globalization, and threats posed by transnational terrorism. In this regard, it may be too soon to dismiss the possibility of a return to a more decidedly Westphalian framework, even within the wider context of globalization, which unlike regionalism, does not seem reversible. There are presently indications that regionalism is far more popular in Europe among elites than with the citizenry of the respective countries. European regionalism is being currently tested by the introduction of ambitious programs of monetary and fiscal unification, especially by the replacement of national currencies with the Euro. If this succeeds, as seems to be the case, it is likely to provide the foundation for strengthening other dimensions of European regionalism, and of influencing non-European regionalisms to move ahead — but if it should fail, the dampening effect in Europe and elsewhere could be quite dramatic.

Europe currently offers the best arena within which to assess the historical and normative relevance of regionalism as a post-Westphalian enhancement of world order. The protection of human rights, the provision of safety nets to address issues of poverty and unemployment, the experience of ethnic autonomy for minorities that supersedes their secessionist demands, the mobility of labor as more comparable to the mobility of capital, the formation of a citizenry that is multiethnic and multinational while retaining its statist and nationalist bonds of primary affiliation, and a prosperous peace system are among the yardsticks by which to assess whether Europe lives up to its promise, or even exceeds what it now seems to be its positive effects.

A Concluding Note

A definite post-Westphalian scenario is now likely to take shape within the next decade or so, and thus the contours of a new emergent world order are likely to change dramatically as the structure and dynamics of globalization evolve in the years ahead — unless the global empire option is successfully implemented. The global setting is very unstable due to the impact of dramatic technological shifts and the volatility of market forces in an underregulated world economy. In this regard, the immediate situation calls upon us to acknowledge the double reality of a neo-Westphalian world order of the sort described above and of a more distant emergent post-Westphalian world order that could move in either positive or negative directions (as appraised from the perspective of humane global governance).

For the classical framing of international relations in Westphalian terms, what seems the least likely future is to be regarded as providing satisfactory guidance for either policymaking or academic circles. The pace and direction of transition to a post-Westphalian world will depend upon many factors: the degree to which elites can legitimize globalization-from-above, the extent to which the antiglobalization movement can collaborate with governmental forces that are dissatisfied with the manner in which the world economy is functioning, the creativity of reformist and transformative politics within regional and global arenas, and the extent to which the state can demonstrate its problem-solving competence in response to a variety of global challenges (such as global warming, transnational crime, genocide, illegal immigration and refugees, and transnational political extremism).

The agents of positive change are in the process of formation. There are in the background the well-established transnational NGOs that have been active and effective with respect to human rights (especially, on civil liberties, racial discrimination, and gender issues) and environment. In the foreground are more amorphous civil society actors that have been on the front lines of the struggle against various manifestations of corporate globalization, whether in local efforts to oppose large dams and power plants or with respect to global policymaking arenas such as the gathering points for the G-8 or the World Economic Forum. The potency and impact of this activism cannot now be discerned in any clear way. The success of these efforts will largely depend on the ability to form collaborative and durable relationships with those governments that share a commitment to the establishment of humane global governance. It will also depend on the capacity to shape a consensus in global civil society that is dedicated to democratization and nonviolent politics.

What seems likely to persist in various formats is the struggle to deepen and extend democratic practices and procedures. This struggle is likely to consist of a series of rather divergent regional and global initiatives and experiments involving the specific interplay of state, market, region, and world. These divergencies will reflect varying cultural, economic, and political circumstances that are freighted with a range of historical memories and increasingly agitated by a revival of religious influence in different guises that are often closely linked to nationalist and civilizational revivalism. Also of importance are the perceived impacts of environmental tendencies and technological breakthroughs, especially with respect to the adequacy of prevailing regulatory frameworks to protect short- and intermediate-term human health and well-being, and with respect to identifying the limiting conditions of humanity (such as through cloning, robots).

A main argument here is that Westphalian modes of regulatory authority are already insufficient in relation to many issues and will turn out to be more so in the future, but that Westphalian resistance to direct adjustments by the leading centers of state power will remain formidable, blocking creative innovations. In the face of this reality, the movement for humane global governance (the preferred post-Westphalian scenario) is likely to grow stronger at a grassroots level, but may be inclined to aim for and accept neo-Westphalian modifications of statism that realize the normative (ethical, legal, and spiritual) potential of the statist world. This reformist prospect will in turn be strengthened and guided by the existence of a lively and plausible, if visionary, understanding of a post-Westphalian architecture constructed by reference to the premises of humane global governance. Indeed, such world order inconclusiveness is an insignia of this era!

September 11 and its aftermath have greatly complicated this assessment of the Westphalia/post-Westphalia interface, both seeming to revive a statist preoccupation with global security and to posit additional post-Westphalian alternative imperial forms of global governance. At present, from the standpoint of humane global governance as a normative goal, these prospects are all troublesome, or worse. Megaterrorism undermines the state by its ability to exploit in spectacular fashion the vulnerabilities of modernity, but the hegemonic backlash controlled by the United States is validated, and to some extent supported, by governments around the world because it seems like the only viable means to restore security for states in general.

But the clash of September 11 is essentially between two opposed universalist conceptions of world order that are both deeply at odds with the

Westphalian ethos of pluralism based on the sovereignty of territorial political communities. Osama bin Laden has projected a universalizing Islam that regards the Islamic world as corrupted by fragmentation brought about by superseding the caliphate based on unity with the corrupting establishment of sovereign states. George W. Bush, a reactionary visionary, has articulated the American response as one of global military dominance, including the authority to wage preemptive war against those political communities that pose any sort of threat to such an imperial blueprint. From the normative perspective developed to consider post-Westphalian prospects, the September 11 impact has been decidedly dysuptopic up to this point, combining the most destructive features of Westphalia with the most dismal conceptions of an emergent historical sequel involving extremist resistance politics and grandiose imperial schemes of law and order. Whether this impact will be overcome, or shifted in emphasis, in the years ahead is impossible to discern at present. Perhaps we should take heart that the worst, even if given a measure of temporary plausibility, has been evaded in recent world history: The Cold War heightened geopolitical tensions for more than four decades without inducing World War III or the use of nuclear weapons; the Y2K scare proved to be a will of the wisp; and so far, despite prophesies of doom, pollution and environmental decay have not led to ecological collapse.

The inquiry into the future of world order will depend on the degree to which democratic energies arise in sufficiently robust forms to redirect the response to September 11 in more positive directions, addressing legitimate grievances of the peoples of the world and building security around the values and institutions of humane global governance. Relating this prospect to the central themes of this book, the future can evolve positively either as a new stage of a fundamentally Westphalian world of sovereign states or as "the moment" when regionalism and globalism provide political communities with their security and identity to such an extent that it would be appropriate to label as post-Westphalian the new reality.

End notes

1. For illuminating interpretations of Westphalian multidimensionality, see Charles W. Kegley and Gregory A. Raymond, *Exorcising the Ghost of Westphalia: Building World Order in the New Millennium* (Upper Saddle River, N.J.: Prentice Hall, 2002); G. John Ikenberry, *After Victory: Institutions, Strategic Restraint, and the Rebuilding of Order after Major Wars* (Princeton, N.J.: Princeton University, 2001).
2. On the emergence of the sovereign state and states system as the dominant form of political organization, see Hedrick Spruyt, *The Sovereign State and Its Competitors* (Princeton, N.J.: Princeton University Press, 1994). For an assessment of its prospects under conditions of intensifying interdependence and declining capacity, see Joseph A. Camilleri and Jim Falk, *The End of Sovereignty? The Politics of a Shrinking and Fragmenting World* (Hants, UK: Edward Elgar, 1992).

3. For a severe critique of the role of the United Nations in the Balkans and Rwanda during the height of peacekeeping diplomacy in the 1990s, see David Rieff, *Slaughterhouse* (New York: Simon & Schuster, 1995); L. R. Malvern, *A People Betrayed: The Role of the West in Rwanda's Genocide* (London, UK: Zed, 2000). As Malvern makes particularly clear, the UN must be understood as an agent of the main Western states, especially the United States.

4. See Hedley Bull, *The Anarchical Society: A Study of Order in World Politics* (London, UK: Macmillan, 2d ed., 1995); Robert Gilpin, *War and Change in World Politics* (Cambridge, UK: Cambridge University Press, 1981). For influential formulations, a more recent distinguished addition to this literature of statist endorsement is Robert Jackson, *The Global Covenant: Human Conduct in a World of States* (Oxford, UK: Oxford University Press, 2000).

4a. See Michael W. Doyle, *Empires* (Ithaca, NY: Cornell, 1986).

5. See Jan Lodal, *The Price of Dominance* (New York: The Council on Foreign Relations, 2001).

6. For an analysis along these lines, see Richard Falk, "The Critical Realist Tradition and the Demystification of Interstate Power," in Stephen Gill and James H. Mittelman, eds., *Innovation and Transformation in International Studies* (Cambridge, UK: Cambridge University Press, 1997), 39–55.

7. Perhaps most clearly articulated by Bull in "The Grotian Conception of International Society" in Herbert Butterfield and Martin Wight, eds., *Diplomatic Investigations* (Cambridge, MA: Harvard, 1968) 50–73; also Raymond Aron, *Peace and War: A Theory of International Relations* (London, UK: Weidenfeld & Nicolson, 1966); Robert W. Cox with Timothy J. Sinclair, *Approaches to World Order* (Cambridge, UK: Cambridge University Press, 1996).

8. See Kenneth Waltz for the most rigorous argument to this effect in *Theory of International Politics* (New York: McGraw-Hill, 1979).

9. Prominent partial and nonutopian advocates of a global peace system include Czar Alexander, Woodrow Wilson, Franklin Roosevelt, and more recently Olaf Palme, Mikhail Gorbachev, and Nelson Mandela. Wilson can be regarded as "utopian" in the important sense of proposing a mechanism that lacked the capability to achieve the proclaimed goal — that is, the League of Nations as constituted did not have the authority or the capacity to supplant a balance-of-power approach by institutionalizing collective security.

10. For Bull's views on Hobbes, see his essay, "Hobbes and the International Anarchy," reprinted in Kai Alderson and Andrew Hurrell, eds., *Hedley Bull on International Society* (New York: St. Martin's Press, 2000), 188–205.

11. In the Clinton presidency, this idea was formalized as the doctrine of "enlargement," seeking to expand the domain of constitutional democracy as a strategy for extending "peace" to the peoples of the world. In the Clinton formulations, "constitutional democracy" was understood as implying the existence of "a market economy."

12. Of course, there is also the America of Jesse Helms and George W. Bush that prides itself on anti-internationalism, isolationism, and an affirmation of strong sovereign rights, while still insisting upon its moral exceptionalism in world politics. Increasingly, others regard these claims with suspicion in the period since the end of the Cold War, viewing the United States as a typically arrogant, domineering, and self-seeking dominant state whose unilateralism undermines respect for international law and the United Nations.

13. For an influential interpretation that argues against the alleged Wilsonian legacy of moralism, see Henry Kissinger, *Diplomacy* (New York: Simon & Schuster, 1994), 218–45, 762–835. On Wilson's views on world peace and related diplomacy after World War I, see Thomas J. Knock, *To End All Wars: Woodrow Wilson and the Quest for a New World Order* (New York: Oxford University Press, 1992). For an illuminating presentation of the Wilsonian strand in American foreign policy, see Walter Russell Mead, *Special Providence: American Foreign Policy and How It Changed the World* (New York: Knopf, 2001).

14. The contrast here is with "exclusive forms" that emphasize special access to truth and salvation, and regard those without such access as evil or as infidels. This distinction and its relation to contemporary patterns of world order is the main theme of Falk, *Religion and Humane Global Governance* (New York: Palgrave, 2001).

15. For mainly skeptical assessments of supranationalizing claims, see Gene Lyons and Michael Mastanduno, eds., *Beyond Westphalia? State Sovereignty and International Intervention* (Baltimore, Md.: Johns Hopkins University Press, 1995).

16. The controversy about the proper limits of the right of self-determination in the postcolonial era is far from resolved. It has flared up in the concrete circumstances of bloody encounters in such diverse settings as Kosovo, Chechnya, Kashmir, and Palestine. For views expressive of the range of claims, see Y. N. Kly and D. Kly, eds., *The Right to Self-Determination* (Collected Papers & Proceedings of the First International Conference on the Right to Self-Determination & the United Nations, Geneva, 2000) (Atlanta, Ga.: Clarity Press, 2001). For a more cautious set of views about the scope of the right of self-determination, see Wolfgang Danspreckgruber with Arthur Watts, eds., *Self-Dermination and Self-Administration: A Sourcebook* (Boulder, Colo.: Lynne Rienner, 1997).

17. Ken Booth has vividly conceptualized this critique of the Westphalian impact on human well-being in "Human Wrongs and International Relations," *Journal of International Affairs* 71 (1995): 103–26; for a series of essays exploring the relevance of this critique by Booth, see Tim Dunne and Nicholas J. Wheeler, eds., *Human Rights in Global Politics* (Cambridge, UK: Cambridge University Press, 1999).

17a. See Jacinta O'Hagen's fine study, *Conceptualizing the West in International Relations: From Spengler to Said* (New York: Palgrave, 2002).

18. Unconditional territorial sovereignty never did, except as an "ideal type." See Stephen D. Krasner, *Sovereignty: Organized Hypocrisy* (Princeton, N.J.: Princeton University Press, 1999). See also Sohail H. Hashmi, ed., *State Sovereignty: Change and Persistence in International Relations* (University Park, Pa.: Penn State University Press, 1997).

19. It is for this reason that I have elsewhere referred to this period of hybridity and transition as "a Grotian moment" in which the old order persists, yet is increasingly challenged by an emergent new order; it was a truly great achievement of Grotius to provide a synthesis that created conceptual and political space for the new without requiring a repudiation of the old. For my assessment, see Falk, *Law in an Emerging Global Village* (Ardsley, N.Y.: Transnational, N.Y., 1999), 3–31.

20. Although statist views predominated in international relations, there has been a macrohistorical tradition that regarded civilizational units as the basic constitutive force in world affairs. Leading examples of this tradition include Oswald Spengler, *Decline of the West* (New York: Knopf, 1926–1928); Arnold Toynbee, *A Study of History* (Osford, UK: Oxford University Press, 12 vols., 1934–1961); Fernand Braudel, *On History* (Chicago: University of Chicago Press, 1980); William H. McNeill, *The Rise of the West: A History of the Human Community* (Chicago: University of Chicago Press, 1963). A recent example of this genre is the fine study of Jacques Barzun, *From Dawn to Decadence: 1500 to the Present* (New York: HarperCollins, 2000). Important as a corrective to the Western preoccupations of this macrohistorical work is Edward Said's *Culture and Imperialism* (New York: Knopf, 1993). A perceptive overview of the civilizational approach as it relates to international relations is Jacinta O'Hagen, *Conceptualizing the West in International Relations: From Spengler to Said* (New York: Palgrave, 2002).

21. These awkward words are used here to get away from such heavily freighted alternatives as "globalization" and "regionalism."

22. This provocative interpretation of international relations is set forth fully in Samuel P. Huntington, *The Clash of Civilizations and the Remaking of World Order* (New York: Simon & Schuster, 1996). Huntington's geopolitical approach distracted commentators from the innovative side of his assessment of the future of international relations, centering upon a shift in the main axes of significance from statism to civilizationalism. In this respect, Huntington's outlook can be understood as one type of post-Westphalian scenario.

23. For an overview, see Sylvester John Hemleben, *Plans for Peace through Six Centuries* (Chicago: University of Chicago Press, 1943); for more recent visionary thinking, see Wesley T. Wooley, *Alternatives to Anarchy: American Supranationalism since World War II* (Bloomington, Ind.: Indiana University Press, 1968).

24. (Cambridge, Mass.: Harvard University Press, 3d ed., 1966); for a recent proposal along similar lines, see James A. Yunker, *World Union on the Horizon* (Lanham, Md.: University Press of America, 1993).

25. Saul H. Mendlovitz, ed., *On the Creation of a Just World Order* (New York: Free Press, 1975) provides a summary of the diverse models of preferred futures for the 1990s.

26. Take note of cynicism in the face of genocide: Khmer Rouge was exempted for geopolitical reasons associated with "China card," while Rhodesia was "overlooked" because the country was seen as without strategic concern. See Glenda Cooper, "U.S. Memos Reveal Delay on Rwanda," *Washington Post*, August 8, 2001, A20; see also Malvern, note 3, and the report of the International Commission on State Sovereignty and Intervention, "The Responsibility to Protect" (Ottawa, Canada: International Development Research Centre, 2001)

27. See several fine books on these themes, such as Gary Jonathan Bass, *To Stay the Hand of Vengeance: The Politics of War Crimes Tribunals* Princeton, NJ: Princeton, 2001). Martha Minow, *Between Vengeance and Forgiveness* (Boston: Beacon, 1998); Elazar Barkan, *The Guilt of Nations: Restitution and Negotiating Historical Injustices* (New York: Norton, 2000).

28. A coherent presentation along these lines can be found in Herman E. Daly and John B. Cobb, Jr., *For the Common Good: Redirecting the Economy Toward Communtiy, the Environmnet, and a Sustainable Future* (Boston: Beacon, 1989).

29. My initial reliance on this distinction can be found in Falk, "The Making of Global Citizenship," in Jeremy Brecher, John Brown Childs, and Jill Cutler, eds., *Global Visions: Beyond the New World Order* (Boston: South End Press, 1993), 418–31.

30. This theme is developed in Falk, "State of Seige: Will Globalization Win Out?" *International Affairs* 73, 1 (1997): 123–36.

31. See Thomas Risse-Kappen, ed., *Bringing Transnational Relations Back In: Non-State Actors, Domestic Structures, and International Institutions* (Cambridge, UK: Cambridge University Press, 1995).

32. This is counterintuitive because previous thinking on global reform had consistently regarded states and sovereignty as obstacles to the establishment of more humane world order.

33. For elaboration, see Mendlovitz, note 25.

34. See Mehdi Mozaffari, "Mega Civilization: Global Capital and New Standard of Civilization," in Mozalferi, ed., *Globalizations and Civilizations* (London: Routledge, 2001) Aarhus University, Aarhus, Denmark, 1999. For a critique, see David Korten, *When Corporations Rule the World*, 2d ed. (Bloomfield, Ct.: Kumarian Press: 2001); Richard J. Barnet and John Cavanagh, *Global Dreams: Imperial Corporations and the New World Order* (New York: Simon & Schuster, 1994).

35. See Jonathan Schell, *The Fate of the Earth* (New York: Knopf, 1982); see also references cited in note 24.

36. For the most comprehensive account, see Manuel Castels' *The Rise of the Network Society*, 3 vols. (Oxford, UK: Blackwell, 1996–1998); Mark Dery, *Escape Velocity: Cyberculture at the End of the Century* (London, UK: Hodder & Stoughton, 1996); Kevin A. Hall and John E. Hughes, *Cyberpolitics: Citizen Activism in the Age of the Internet* (Lanham, Md.: Rowman & Littlefield, 1998); Gregory S. Paul and Earl D. Cox, *Beyond Humanity: CyberEvolution and Future Minds* (Rockland, Mass.: Charles River Media, 1996); Douglas S. Robertson, *The New Renaissance: Computers and the Next Level of Civilization* (Oxford, UK: Oxford University Press, 1998).

37. The more normatively, less technocratically grounded image of "global neighborhood" seems similarly out of touch with the predatory elements of the main currents of globalization in lethal interaction with neoliberal ideas and hegemonic geopolitics. See report of the Commission on Global Governance, *Our Global Neighborhood* (New York: Oxford, 1995); Falk, *Predatory Globalization: A Critique* (Cambridge, UK: Polity, 1999). I have preferred the terminology of "humane global governance" as goal and ideal, as well as potentiality, but without the implication that such a phrase is descriptive of current world order or the most probable future.

38. There are some complexities present, as "strong states" are needed to resist the predatory aspects of globalization, and the transformation of the state would involve its greater responsiveness to normative demands, including the effort to commit a higher proportion of the national budget to the financing of global public goods. See generally Inge Kaul, Isabelle Grunberg, and Marc A. Stern, eds., *Global Public Goods: International Cooperation in the Twenty-First Century* (New York: Oxford University Press, 1999).

39. See Daniele Archibugi and David Held, eds., *Cosmopolitan Democracy: An Agenda for a New World Order* (Cambridge, UK: Polity, 1995); Daniele Archibugi, David Held, and Martin Köhler, eds., *Re-imagining Political Community: Studies in Cosmopolitan Democracy* (Cambridge, UK: Polity, 1998).

40. See references in note 27.
41. Guidelines for national courts to proceed with the indictment and prosecution of individuals accused of crimes against humanity, genocide, and other serious crimes of state are contained in the brochure "The Princeton Principles on Universal Jurisdiction" published by Program in Law and Public Affairs, Princeton University, 2001. "The Princeton Principles" is the product of discussion and analysis by a group of international law specialists and practitioners.
42. The case for GPA is elaborated by Richard Falk and Andrew Strauss, "On the Creation of a Global Peoples Assembly: Legitimacy and the Power of Popular Sovereignty," *Stanford Journal of International Law* 36, 2 (2000): 191–219; Falk and Strauss, "Toward Global Parliament," *Foreign Affairs* 80, 1 (2001): 212–20.
43. For elaboration of this point, see Falk, "Meeting the Challenge of Multilateralism," in Thomas H. Henriksen, ed., *Foreign Policy for America in the Twenty-first Century: Alternative Perspectives* (Stanford, Calif.: Hoover Institution Press, 2001), 33–47.
44. On "legalization," see Judith Goldstein, Miles Kahler, Robert O. Keohane, and Anne-Marie Slaughter, "Legalization and World Poltics," *International Organization* 54, 3: 385–89.
45. My thinking here is influenced by Björn Hettne, especially "Globalization and the New Regionalism: The Second Great Transformation," in Hettne, András Inotai, and Osvaldo Sunkel, eds., *Globalism and the New Regionalism* (New York: St. Martin's, 1999), 1–24.
46. See Karl Polanyi, *The Great Transformation* (Boston: Beacon, 1957).

Chapter 2
Regionalism

This chapter assesses the actual and potential contributions of regionalism to the achievement of such widely affirmed world order values as peace, social justice, human rights, democracy, and ecological sustainability (Falk, 1975, 1992, 1995a). This assessment proceeds by way of introducing several main features of the global setting that have achieved prominence, initially in the immediate aftermath of the Cold War, and have now been modified by the American-led response to the September 11 attacks as combined with the trials and tribulations of world capitalism of recent years.

The conceptual framework used seeks to clarify the regional dimensions of world order in a manner sensitive to the unfolding historical situation. Necessarily, such an effort is both provisional, subject to revision as political actors make use of regionalist approaches to achieve their goals, and normative, distinguishing those aspects of regionalism that are negative (to be avoided or overcome) from those that are positive (to be achieved or enhanced). Regionalism is thus evaluated in relation to the quest for humane global governance as a desirable frame of political life for the peoples of the world based on the widely endorsed goals embodied in leading human rights instruments and other important statements of aspiration (Falk, 1995a).

Background Considerations

Many of the fundamental tendencies reshaping world order were derived from the Cold War, especially the complex dynamics of globalization. However, the preoccupations of the Cold War, its East/West axis of interpretative logic, made it more difficult to appreciate fully the impact of globalization, including the backlash generated. In November 1989 the Berlin

Wall, the ultrastable and symbolically resonant geopolitical scaffolding provided by bipolarity, especially with respect to Europe since World War II, disintegrated before our eyes. The immediate reaction to this undeniably epochal event was to exaggerate the discontinuity that resulted, thereby neglecting underlying forces for change that were having a transforming impact in any event, such as weaponry of mass destruction, technological innovation, environmental decay, economic integration, a global communications net, and, perhaps most of all, the rise of networking as a potent form of nonterritorial organization (Castels, 1996).

The cumulative effect of these global trends seemed to be eroding the functional competence and drawing into question the normative self-sufficiency (that is, the capacity to confer public goods on citizens and residents) of most sovereign states (Falk, 1995a; Falk, 1997; but see Mearsheimer, 1990). To a superficial extent, September 11 reversed these trends, seemingly returning world politics to its more traditional concerns with global security, warfare, and the domineering role of leading states. This revival of the more familiar concerns of the Westphalia era may be deceptive and short lived, as the new parameters of global struggle cannot be clearly associated with a rivalry between antagonistic states. While the most powerful states have recovered a sense of primacy in relation to market forces, the overall viability of sovereignty may be further undermined as neither the megaterrorist side (al Qaeda) nor the counterterrorist response (the United States) shows fundamental respect for either the sovereign rights of states or the constraints on the use of force embedded in international law (Falk, 2003).

Globalization and Regionalism: After the Cold War and September 11

The end of the Cold War definitely encouraged a greater emphasis on globalization (especially its implications for the world economy) and later on such adverse reactions and contradictory trends as fundamentalism (a vehicle for religious and ethnic extremism) and on the grassroots antiglobalization movement ("globalization-from-below") (Mittelman, 2000). How regionalism of varying attributes fits within evolving globalization is a central world order concern for which evidence and interpretation is currently inconclusive, with assessments subject to continuous reappraisal. This uncertainty is magnified by the unevenness of different regional settings and of the varying degrees to which economic, political, and cultural life has been regionalized. Almost any generalization about regionalism seems suspect and must be qualified, reconsidered, contextualized region by region, and frequently updated to take account of changing conditions. The traumatic impact, especially in the United States after the September 11 attacks, refocused the global agenda in such a way as to draw attention away from the preoccupations of the 1990s, including speculation on how regionalism fit into economic and cultural globalization.

There is one important exception to these admonitions of conceptual caution. It is persuasive to claim that regionalism as a perspective in this historical period is a promising focus for both empirical and normative inquiry, that regionalism identifies emergent trends and structures and clarifies a distinct array of prescriptions and strategies. Following Hettne's assessment, in the near future, hegemonic state actors of a traditional character will likely no longer manage world order to nearly the same extent as during the Cold War (Hettne, 1994, 2002; Gilpin, 1981). What appears to be emerging in its place is a new type of world order shaped from above by a single dominant state with imperial ambitions, resembling more than anything else Pax Britannica at the height of the British Empire; but more aptly discerned, the American Empire is a unique imperial phenomenon still in the process of formation.

The overall trend toward a general weakening of the state is producing adverse types of societal vulnerability to the integrative tendencies in the global economy; it is also partly responsible for the intensity and incidence of pathological forms of anarchy that are dramatically different than the type of structural anarchy Hedley Bull has so influentially depicted as a favorable world order solution (Bull, 1977; Rosenau, 1990; Falk, 1998). This menacing type of anarchism arises from the fusion of networking organizational forms with transnational visionary politics in a tactically explosive manner that appears to have uncovered the vulnerability of the most powerful territorial actors, generating a response that both feeds and hides the empire-building ambitions of the United States, the main target of megaterrorism. From all sides, normal territorial states (and possibly regions) are squeezed, their autonomy diminished, and they find their destinies enmeshed with this emerging postmodern geopolitics in which the central drama is not among states, but between a solitary hegemonic state and a global terrorist network (Falk, 2003). This is an encounter without borders, and between nonterritorial adversaries — each seemingly dedicated to the futile objective of exterminating the other.

Thus, in terms of the quality of world order, the regional alternative to statism, networking, and empire-building seems potentially compensatory for both the erosion of hegemonic balance (as it played out in the cold war decades) and the more acute forms of pathology afflicting both weak and failed states. These background conditions are linked to the end of the Cold War and the rise of megaterrorism in the twenty-first century — especially the collapse of bipolarity, the loss of a capacity to maintain order within bloc limits, and the recalculation of power relations in a postmodern geopolitics in which the dominant state is deeply challenged by a concealed multistate terrorist network, and at the same time finds itself unchallenged and undeterred by rival states. This new set of circumstances makes unipolarity plausible as a sequel to bipolarity, at least in the domain of security, but paradoxically not nearly as effective in sustaining stability and avoiding warfare. Polarities are measures that presuppose territorial states as the parties to conflict, and thus are subject to deterrence, containment, and defense. Such reasoning does not apply to the al Qaeda network, and thus unipolarity is not capable of delivering postmodern global security, and cannot even protect the homeland of the imperial overlord of the system.

Unipolarity was initially disappointing to its advocates, partly as a result of a perception by political leaders in the 1990s of a greatly diminished domain of strategic interests. The ineffectuality of the unipolar actor also reflected the internal pressures exerted by the American citizenry on its government to address domestic priorities, as well as a wariness about global engagements, as in nation-building, that could be costly and yet earned few material dividends. Briefly, the Gulf War (1991) epitomized the early post–Cold War perception of the persistence of hegemonic stability; after all, here was a successful geopolitical undertaking that proceeded by fully instrumentalizing the UN, and in the process even generating universalistic claims of "a new world order" legitimized through collective security mechanisms. Soon after the victory over Iraq in 1991, it became evident that *this* "unipolar moment" was to be brief, and that the idealistic commitment to collective security under UN auspices that had been so loudly proclaimed a few months earlier was abandoned without even a whimper of explanation (Krauthammer, 1990–1991). The Gulf War was a conflict subject to the modernist logic of a world of sovereign states, wherein weight of unipolarity, especially in relation to military capabilities, could be exerted to control the political outcome.

In the Bush II presidency, abandoning the positive achievements of the 1990s has become doctrinal and accompanied by a seemingly perverse effort to undo many of the most promising initiatives of the prior decade — these include enhancing human rights, protecting peoples facing severe abuse from their own government, and supporting criminal accountability for leaders who commit crimes against humanity and other international crimes, and who breach general frameworks of multilateral diplomacy in relation to weaponry of mass destruction and environmental protection. Seemingly, September 11 has generated a second unipolar moment, one focused on the war/peace dimension of international society — which, in some unresolved fashion, seems to pit both al Qaeda and the United States against the rest of international society, but in a postmodern framework that cannot be understood by reference to conflict resolution as it proceeded in the modern period of statist geopolitics.

Why were the 1990s crises in Somalia, Bosnia, Haiti, and Rwanda treated as so much less deserving of a response from the global community than was the Iraqi invasion of Kuwait (Weiss, 1994; Barnett, 2002; Melvern, 2000)? The paramount explanations are, of course, oil and civilizational identities, but also the supposed regional security threat posed by a militant Iraq, likely to possess nuclear weapons within years, to a strategic ally, namely Israel, as well as to a strategic region, the Middle East. It is unlikely that the Gulf Crisis would have erupted in the bipolar world of the Cold War, the dynamics of mutual deterrence inducing greater prudence with respect to obvious strategic interests, as well as a reluctance of either side to challenge the geopolitical status quo. Such restraint was operationalized during the Cold War by the capacity of the superpowers to exert effective control to prevent unwanted initiatives undertaken by secondary states such as Iraq, as well as by the high stakes of a loss of control associated with risks of warfare conducted with nuclear weaponry (Wallerstein, 2002). But it is also unlikely that the internal tensions in Bosnia and Somalia would have spiraled out of governmental control as each country was of strategic importance within a cold war setting — that is, warranting the expenditure of lives and resources by superpowers to maintain a given alignment.

At the same time, the causal significance of the absence of the Cold War is by no means uniform with respect to the collapse of minimum internal order. Lebanon had spiraled dangerously out of geopolitical control in the decade following the outbreak of civil strife in 1975, and superpower interventions failed miserably in the major test cases of Vietnam and Afghanistan, arguably because the character of the conflict was one in which the logic of statism no longer worked in interventionary settings, given the rise of indigenous nationalism associated with the global anticolonial movement. There is some temptation to exaggerate the ordering achievements of bipolarity and deterrence during the cold war era, given the range of security problems that have emerged since 1990. These achievements did seem considerable in Europe and in relation to the non-use of nuclear weaponry, but not otherwise, at least if war prevention is treated as the main test of success. It is also true that bipolarity did produce an overall East/West stalemate, although fragile and periodically bloody, with respect to major challenges posed for the geopolitical status quo outside of Europe, as in Korea and China. The outcome in Vietnam was an exception to this pattern, first confirming the French defeat in an anticolonial war of independence and a later American setback in trying to uphold the geopolitical status quo of a divided Vietnam in the face of intense Vietnamese nationalist resistance. Arguably, the shifts in ideological alignment of Cuba and Yugoslavia also strengthened one side at the expense of the other, if measured against the then-prevailing cold war yardstick of success and failure.

Post–Cold War Strategic Interests

What is somewhat different, however, is the circumscribing of the domain of strategic interests on the part of intervening states in the North, particularly the United States. The outcome in Somalia, and even Haiti and Bosnia, has been widely regarded as a matter of virtual indifference, so long as the external effects of these conflicts are minimized. These external effects are associated with "containment" in the post–Cold War sense — that is, not discouraging the expansion of the rival superpower/ideology, but the spread of disorder and violence via a wider war (Bosnia) or the massive generation of refugees (Bosnia again, but Haiti more centrally, where the prospects of even a relatively small number of black Haitian refugees coming to the United States was regarded for domestic political reasons as unacceptable) (Mandelbaum, 1994; Falk, 1995a).

The UN has been reinstrumentalized since its moment of prominence in the Gulf during 1990–1991, resuming its role as marginal player, while being somewhat unfairly accused of "failing." Unlike the Cold War, when failure was explained as a consequence of stalemate, it is now more damagingly seen as the expression of a feeble "political will" on the part of its principal members, or more recently, on the inability of the United States to translate its global preeminence into a political consensus within the Security Council. In reaction to these trends, enhanced roles for regional actors seem increasingly attractive, this possibility highlighted, although ambiguously, by NATO coming to replace the UN in the Balkans as the principal agency of peacekeeping. This more assertive NATO role was made manifest in the Kosovo War of 1999 and the postconflict peacekeeping sequel (Kosovo Report, 2000). This NATO initiative is best interpreted as partly a matter of regional security, partly a belated humanitarian response to the dismal UN experience in Bosnia, and partly an expression of U.S. foreign policy (reasserting the primacy of the U.S. in sustaining European security, even absent any external threat of the sort posed by the Soviet Union). Despite these varied aspects, the prominence of NATO suggested a new reliance on regional peacekeeping as a geopolitical option.

But security concerns are not the only world order dimension. At least until September 11, the play of economic forces seemed at least as important, if not as visually captivating in a media sense. The transnational economic calculus was reshaped by the triumph of world capitalism, which quickly led to weakening alliances and bloc ties. Such a temporary decline in the globalization of security arrangements made regional security and political economy factors generally more significant, yet not in a uniform manner. This decline was offset in a contradictory manner by the rising globalization of the world economy, stimulating tactics for participation and protection, both types of reaction bearing on regionalist prospects in this period. The patterns of differing influences and perceptions bearing on the role of regionalism are complex and confusing. This role is further complicated by the aftermath of September 11, which has combined the divergent goals of a wide range of states collaborating in the struggle against megaterrorism, while at the same time acting to avoid the consolidation of the American empire-building project.

Europe, North America, and Asia/Pacific, as well as Africa and Latin America, are currently the critical arenas for assessing the world order roles of regionalist configurations. In Europe, the collapse of the blocs, a variety of economic troubles, and the widening of Europe have definitely slowed the deepening of the European Union, and have possibly deferred political integration indefinitely. So many factors are at work that causal inferences will always seem argumentative and inconclusive. Yet there are important differences between Europe and Asia with respect to regionalist developments. In Asia, the U.S. was not nearly as involved during the Cold War, allowing economic priorities to gain precedence, especially in the face of growing feelings of cultural sensitivity about Western influence and Asian identity (Funabashi, 1993). Similarly, the United States was no longer concerned with geopolitical alignments, emphasizing instead favorable trading and investment relations, which in turn produced post–Cold War tensions that encouraged Asian interests in defensive regional and bloc approaches. Whether this process was setting the stage for "the clash of civilizations" is doubtful, but it was shifting economic and political concerns from the old geopolitics of Westphalia to a new geopolitics of interregional relationships as mediated by the Group of Seven (reconstituted at Naples in 1994 as the Group of Eight, adding Russia to their ranks) (Huntington, 1993).

African regionalism may eventually benefit from its remoteness in relation to the world economy, the war against global terror, and the deficiencies of postcolonial state-building. Ambitious regional ideas are currently under consideration in Africa, including the promising NEPAD (New Partnership for Africa's Development) and the possibility of a functioning regional parliament. Africa, neglected in so many respects, may yet surprise the world by establishing a new identity as world order innovator and creator of a viable regional governance structure. There is a long way to go, especially given the depth of the AIDS crisis, but even the fashioning of such an African vision deserves notice.

A focus on strategic considerations as explanatory ignores the complex and concealed politics of instrumentalization: Who is instrumentalizing whom in relation to what? The Westphalian model of world order assumes that states are, more or less, the exclusive agents of instrumentalization. In a globalized world economy, states are themselves increasingly instrumentalized by concealed, external forces such as markets, profit margins, and money laundering, and sustained by a spectrum of nonaccountable criminal and quasi-legal transnational networks and the instrumentalization of states as expressed by way of the weakening of commitments to such foreign policy goals as human rights and environmental protection. This reorientation of policy by states is accentuated by the weakening of organized labor as a domestic and transnational factor and by the discrediting of socialism (and its main operating modes) as an ethical and political challenge to capitalism. Such an analysis supported an argument in favor of "resituating the state" — that is, strengthening its capacity to mediate between market drives and populist social forces (Falk, 1997). The relevance of regional actors is clear, but far from being consistent or self-evident: What is most uncertain can be phrased by reference to the theme of instrumentalization. Formal regional structures are still constituted overwhelmingly by state actors as members, but to what extent are the regional approaches taken by states themselves as the unacknowledged secondary effects of their instrumentalization by the global marketplace or in relation to global empire-building priorities. Within regional frameworks, secondary hegemonic relations of varying sorts can be established, as seems the case with respect to Germany in Northern and Eastern Europe, and certainly on the part of the United States in the setting of NAFTA, and to a degree, in Latin America.

The extent to which these global trends have been disrupted by September 11 remains difficult to assess. The dominant state finds itself under attack, which has shaped a captivatingly dramatic mission of retaliation, waging all out war against its networked adversary. Security concerns take precedence, subordinating market factors, although linkages and concealed economic motives make such generalizations quite suspect. There are, for instance, numerous conjectures that the United States is waging the war against megaterrorism in a manner that promotes its strategic interests in controlling Central Asian and Middle Eastern energy reserves and extending its network of military bases.

Positive and Negative Regionalism

Many dimensions of regionalism are worthy of exploration and analysis at this time: five in particular seem to illuminate the character of the unfolding, yet still inchoate, post–Cold War world order and its more recent shift of emphasis arising from megaterrorism. In discussing these world order dimensions, a distinction between "positive" and "negative" is used to assess global and regional configurations of influence and authority. Positive refers to desired objectives such as reducing political violence, attaining economic well-being, promoting human rights and benevolent governance, protecting ecological diversity and sustainability, and safeguarding health and renewable resources. Negative refers to the negation of these goals by way of warfare, poverty, racism, ecological decay, oppression, chaos, and criminality. In reality, positive and negative aspects are intertwined and give rise to contradictory perceptions; and a given set of conditions associated, say, with global market forces or authoritarian government may generate both positiveand negative outcomes and be controversially interpreted from diverse perspectives. Economic growth, even if it generates a nonsustainable consumerist ethos, may also in the short run alleviate poverty and despair, as softer forms of authoritarianism, while cruel to opponents, may nevertheless provide effective governance at the level of the state.

This evaluation of the regional dimension of world order identifies five patterns of interaction that seem most worthy of attention.

1. *Clarifying the main links between regionalism and the "containment" of negative globalism.* Negative globalism refers, as just suggested, to the conjuncture of largely nonaccountable power and influence exerted by multinational corporations, transnational banks, financial arenas, and their collaborators — espousing an ideology of consumerism and a development ethos weighted almost entirely toward returns on capital achieved by maximizing growth (no matter how often qualified, yet predominantly rhetorically, by the modifier "sustainable" or "equitable"); It is also increasingly important to take into account crime and terrorism of global reach; in essence, the main regionalist tendencies are simultaneously both reinforcing this drift toward negative globalism and creating resistance and alternative mitigating options, including the promotion of positive globalism (promoted by democratizing global institutions, creating accountability and responsiveness to more democratic social forces, and establishing procedures for wider participation by representatives of diverse peoples; also relevant here is the promotion of human rights, including economic and social rights, and a capability by the United Nations and other international institutions to contribute more effectively to global security than what is predicated upon a consensus among currently ascendant geopolitical and geoeconomic forces). It should be acknowledged that the neoliberal ideology informing global market forces disseminates constructive ideas about freedom and the rule of law, as well as destructive notions about greed, extreme individualism, and materialism.

2. *Containing the American project to establish a nonterritorial global empire.* Containing an American-led empire that would control the security of the planet has assumed a new salience after September 11. It is exhibited in several quite distinct contexts: pursuing counterterrorism in essential disregard of international law and the sovereign rights of states; waging a struggle against "rogue states," relabeled "axis of evil" countries; administering the nonproliferation regime by coercive diplomacy and, possibly most consequential of all, by the militarization of space under exclusive U.S. control. This American project draws political energy away from political regionalism, and over time, may lead to a regional geopolitics of resistance that significantly relies on regional solidarity as more effective than nationalism in safeguarding the autonomy of those peoples living outside the orbit of direct American control.

3. *Strengthening regional frameworks to help meet the challenges posed by several manifestations of pathological anarchism.* Pathological

anarchism arises from breakdowns of order associated with political normalcy and effective patterns of governance, leading to sustained violence that includes genocidal outbreaks and other crimes against humanity, as well as chaotic conditions that produce havens for global terrorism and massive displacements of people from their traditional habitats.

A new type of pathological anarchism, with serious implications for regionalism, arises from the potent use of multinational networking to challenge hegemonic patterns of control, especially in the Middle East. The al Qaeda recourse to megaterrorism can be understood as a pathological drive to achieve regional autonomy under extremist Islamic governance that eliminates the American presence, condemns those governments in the region that have collaborated with the United States and with globalization, and seeks to replace the statist divisions of the Islamic world with a unified political community organized along religious lines that implement *sharia* (Islamic law governing social relations normally administered by religious tribunals) strictly.

4. *Facilitating a renewal of positive globalism as a world order project through the medium of enhanced regionalism.* As indicated, "positive regionalism" refers to regionalizing tendencies that promote such widely shared world order values as peace, equity, human rights, and enviornmental protection. The implications of the first three issues are essentially negative and can, to some extent, be diminished or redirected by certain forms of regionalization. Positive globalism conceives of the world's governance structure as aspirational in character — a structure that promotes sustainability, human rights, development (especially in relation to poverty and other forms of deprivation), accountability of leaders, the rule of law, and demilitarization (reducing warfare, arms races and sales, and eliminating weaponry of mass destruction). Given concerns about the homogenization of identities, cultural diversity, and excessive centralization, the encouragement of stronger regional institutions might operate both as an alternative to and complement of positive globalism, thereby providing the peoples of the world with a vision of a desirable world order.

5. *Considering the normative achievements of regionalism in terms of its contributions to the well-being of the peoples living within its framework.* This conception of *positive regionalism* as an end in itself is quite distinct from the evaluation of regionalism as a constituent element in a structure of global governance. It has been most fully explored, of course, in the setting of Europe, especially by the

encounter between Eurocrats of various hue and Euroskeptics, but it is also relevant to visions of a better future in Africa, Latin America, and Asia (Sidjanski, 1992). Due to the focus on the regional/global interface, as well as space constraints, the regionalisms of Africa and Latin America are not discussed here.

Containing Negative Globalism via Regionalism

Negative globalism refers to the adverse effects of economic, political, and cultural integration at the global level (Mander and Goldsmith, 1996). The integrative dynamic is not inherently negative, but it is having a series of adverse effects given the context of the current world order. These effects arise primarily from a hegemonic ideology that validates high levels of insensitivity to human suffering, insufficient attention to ecological sustainability, tendencies toward polarization (widening gaps between and within countries, and among regions) and marginalization (virtual exclusion of countries, regions, and ethnic minorities from developmental progress).

Negative globalism also instrumentalizes the state by promoting elites who espouse the appropriate ideas and by mounting a variety of pressures to conform to globalizing priorities that give governments little political space within which to explore alternative strategies relating to the production and distribution of public goods. Most states are either co-opted or subordinated, weakening impulses to regulate on behalf of even the national common good, much less furthering the global public good. In this regard, the world economy, as a totality but with wide variations in practice, somewhat resembles the early capitalist period when market forces prevailed to the extent that labor was exploited in a variety of ways (such as long hours, low wages, unsafe conditions, no job security, and no protection in old age or in the event of emergencies). At the state level, social movements have helped many societies create a better equilibrium between state and market, corporate and banking power being balanced to differing degrees by the outlook and leverage of organized labor and by the survival of socialist policies. Of course, the evaluation of this equilibrium was controversial, diverse, and dynamic, and varied among countries and over time.

The state in democratic societies mediated between market and social forces until this role was partially superseded by the imperatives of "competitiveness" in the wider settings of the regionalization and globalization of economic life. This process was complex, cyclical, and contextual, and reflected many factors, including the relative efficiency and productivity of labor force and managerial methods, the extent to which labor protection was entrenched, the degree to which competition for markets was being mounted by low wage societies, the overall impact of the Soviet collapse on the socialist option, and the shifting class and ideological composition of civil society.

Three factors underpin negative globalism: (1) the opposition of market forces to the establishment of any global regulatory authority designed to mitigate the socially harmful effects of transnational patterns of trade, investment, and finance; (2) the tension between market forces, especially the efficient use of capital to produce short-run profits and the provision of public goods, including environmental protection, economic and social human rights, and the provision of humane governance; and (3) the assertion of security imperatives that override other world order values, including respect for sovereign rights, self-determination, and efforts to achieve war prevention.

Regionalism has not yet emerged as a coherent counter to negative globalism (Ohmae, 1992). On the contrary, its main drive to date has been facilitating increasingly effective participation on a global level, either by protectionist policies or by achieving export competitiveness. The impact may again result in some levelling down of well-being and environmental standards, at least on an intraregional basis. While preparing for its participation in the European Union, Sweden rolled back aspects of its exemplary welfare system, reducing taxes and cutting some services. Regionalism has helped Europe aggregate capital and maintain technological parity with the United States and Japan, and therefore avoid the fate of moderate marginalization in relation to the globalized market.

The economic achievements of regional arrangements of different sorts are impressive in many respects, but *not* in relation to the containment of negative globalism, at least not yet. Indeed, the contrary conclusion is more illuminating, that regional formations, especially with respect to the three main trading/investing blocs, have served to consolidate the negative features of global economic integration. This consolidating role has been played out by removing economic policy from the realm of domestic politics, an aspect of weakening the state as a mediating actor between specifically territorial concerns, especially of those being marginalized, and global market forces. It is confirmatory, as well, that regionalism has not taken hold in those settings most marginalized by the world economy, and further that religious extremism and political alienation in several Islamic countries has produced a partly voluntary, partly involuntary delinking from the world economy, as seen in Iran, Libya, Sudan, and Saddam's Iraq.

Containing Empire-Building

The challenge posed by the American project to establish the first empire of global scope is an important development that cannot be adequately addressed in this chapter (Lemann, 2002; Brooks and Wohlforth, 2002; cf. Wallerstein, 2002). This empire seeks dominion, but not formal territorial authority, which will be left mainly in the hands of states and regional organizations. The preliminary experience with this emergent empire does not yet reveal its impact on regionalism, whether it will mean that regional actors will remain passive supporters of this American claim to provide security for the constructive forces on the planet, or whether it will result in new patterns of conflict-formation based, in part, on regional refusals to subordinate their autonomy to policies directed from Washington. Much will depend on whether the threat of megaterrorism dissipates with time or intensifies, as well as whether the U.S. economy can rebound from its current troubles. It will also depend on the flow of domestic politics within the United States, particularly whether the Bush leadership and worldview are endorsed or repudiated by the American electorate. The empire-building project at present hangs in the balance on the drawing board of leading Washington policy-makers, but is subject to an abrupt cancellation, especially if the currently unresolved political future casts a dark shadow across the war against Iraq, producing a quagmire of continuing casualties, an expensive, prolonged occupation, and a political outcome that is either imposed on or hostile to the proclaimed American war aims.

Mitigating Pathological Anarchism

Labeling internal deformations of state power as "pathological" implies a conception of normalcy in the relations of state and society that has broken down; to associate this normalcy with the anarchy of international relations is to stress the structural point that institutions of global governance are very weak (Aron, 1966; Bull, 1977). Pathological anarchism refers to acute political disorder: genocide, severe crimes against humanity, large-scale famine, and substantial breakdowns of government. Since September 11, it also refers to the backlash against American hegemonic intrusions upon the Islamic world by way of megaterrorism as actualized by a concealed transnational network presence in sixty or more states.

In the long Westphalia period of international relations, pathological anarchism was essentially ignored unless the strategic interests of leading states were seriously threatened. Such threats rarely were perceived unless the governmental actor in question embarked upon expansion at the expense of the existing distribution of power informing world order. The responses to Nazi Germany and Stalinist Soviet Union are paradigmatic in both respects: appeasement or, at most, containment, with respect to the pathological behaviour, but a willingness by rival states to risk everything to prevent territorial expansions that seek to revise the hierarchy of relations that inform the arrangement of power among states as a particular period in world history. It is not that the pathological dimension is irrelevant. Indeed, especially in relation to democratic societies, the pathological character of a rival state is relied on to mobilize resources and public support, and to sustain the commitments needed to conduct warfare or to practice containment credibly.

The corollary point is that if the pathology does not pose external threats, it will be generally tolerated (Booth, 1995; but see Murphy, 1996;

Moore, 1998). This again has been demonstrated even in the period immediately following the end of the Cold War during the high watermark of humanitarian diplomacy. The much-discussed instances of Somalia, Bosnia, Haiti, and Rwanda exhibit the weakness of the humanitarian impulse as a rationale for the exercise of state power. Perhaps the situation is more ambiguous: the historical memory of the Holocaust has encouraged the sentiment of "never again," particularly in Europe, and this generated strong interventionary pressures in relation to Bosnia in the early 1990s; the CNN factor selectively lifts the veil of ignorance from the occurrence of acute distress and induces public support for constructive responses; and the entrenchment of human rights in international law has eroded the sovereignty arguments that abuses within states are of no concern externally. As a result, there have been responses to the recent instances of pathological anarchism, but of a half-hearted character as compared to the response mounted to reverse Iraq's aggression against Kuwait or to impose an international protectorate upon Kosovo, much less as compared to the post–September 11 geopolitical posture. These responses, collaborations between the UN and leading states, especially the United States, have provided a measure of relief for elements of the afflicted populations, but have not challenged the core pathologies. Diplomacy, sanctions, relief operations, and pinprick assertions of military power have been relied on. Considering this experience of the 1990s, the sum of these humanitarian efforts seems *less* than its parts!

The extent to which responses grew more seriously committed has resulted from boundary-transcending impacts and the displacement of humanitarian arguments by strategic considerations: the prospects of a wider war in the Balkans and the outflow of refugees causing destabilizing effects in important state actors (such as the United States, Germany, and France). These possible developments convert pathological anarchism into an occasion of strategic concern (justifying large allocations of resources and risks of loss of life), raising the stakes in the event that containment fails. Also, in relation to refugees, the alternatives of repatriation or deterrence may both fail, leaving only the option of military intervention. Such an interpretation of the situation in Haiti during the summer of 1994 and Kosovo in 1999 has made some commentators describe intervention as "inevitable."

Enter regionalism: Both states and the UN have failed to address pathological anarchism effectively. Could this failure be overcome, in some circumstances, by the empowerment of regional institutions? Could NATO act in the former Yugoslavia to challenge Serbian "aggression," restoring order and a unified, multiethnic Bosnia? Could the Organization of American States bring constitutional democracy to Haiti? Could the Organization of African Unity act in relation to Somalia, Rwanda, Burundi, Sudan, and Liberia? Kosovo provides one answer that can be interpreted in various ways, as an evasion of Charter controls on the use of force, as an expedient effective protection of a beleaguered population.

The major conclusion to be drawn is that regional communities have not evolved to the point where their institutional ethos or capabilities can sufficiently address pathological anarchism in a manner comparable to the efforts made by competent and constitutionally moderate states in relation to pathologies embedded within their own polities. States, too, are not always effective — sometimes accommodating, containing, and collaborating, but sometimes instrumentalized from below by the pathology or even put in the position where this pathology can capture their legitimate power (as Hitler did in Germany in 1933). Should regional actors be encouraged to take on these ordering tasks as part of the mixture of a commitment to implement human rights and to maintain regional peace and justice, especially protecting those most victimized by pathological anarchism? The effort to prevent weak states from being used as territorial havens for terrorist networks creates major strategic incentives to establish viable states that can exert effective control over their sovereign space.

The dilemma posed here seems quite fundamental: to be effective and autonomous (that is, noninstrumentalized), regional institutions would have to become cohesive and capable of commanding loyalty, thereby coming to resemble in certain respects a federated state of Westphalian lineage. Such an evolution, however, would seem likely to stimulate inter-regional conflict on a global level among regions of greatly different resource bases and civilizational identities, making it more credible that "a clash of civilizations" would indeed ensue as the sequel to the Cold War. This course of development seems less likely in the immediate future, given the degree of global mobilization around a revised global security agenda, this time pitting a coalition of states against a dispersed nonterritorial network seeking to establish its own radical vision of global governance.

Promoting Positive Globalism

There are two intersecting traditions at work. First, the anxiety that *effective global governance cannot prevent encroachments on human freedom unless it avoids centralism.* A regionalized world order is one approach to reconciling the quest for global governance with a concern for constitutional equilibrium, and to a lesser extent with the preservation of cultural diversity (Hutchins et al., 1948). The overriding goals in this outlook are so ambitious — transforming statism, ignoring globalization — in relation to the flow of events and horizons of aspiration that academic circles have rarely considered the serious evolution of this possibility. A more moderate expression of this view is somewhat more influential in the form of an *advocacy of "subsidiarity" via regional institutions* as a way of allocating downward from the UN, particularly with respect to security issues other than megaterrorism, and thus in the context of delimiting the UN role. Such an emphasis on subsidiarity borrows from the European experience, which in turn borrows from a Vatican doctrinal tradition. Such an approach is meaningful, of course, only to the extent that robust regional institutions exist, which is not the case — with the possible exception of Europe, and in extremely limited respects, Central and South America and Africa (Knight, 1994).

The second approach here is to view *regional institutions as complementary and subordinate tools of global governance*, being shaped within the UN, contributing in various settings to either effectiveness or legitimacy or some combination of the two (Knight, 1994). The UN Charter in Chapter VIII seems to envisage such a relationship. Those disposed toward more law-governed modes of governance have viewed regional governance with suspicion because it has so often in international history meant interventionary diplomacy by a hegemonic state, and thus geopolitical manipulation. The revival of the practice and advocacy of spheres of influence suggests a post–Cold War pattern that acknowledges the failures of the UN in the setting of pathological anarchism, but it can hardly be properly identified as a variant of "positive globalism." Conservatives give some credibility to the view that international institutions add elements of constitutional moderation to traditional modes of interventionism and discretionary geopolitics, conceiving of recourse to the UN or a regional actor as confusing, hypocritical, and superfluous from the perspectives of ultrarealist worldviews (Krauthammer, 1991).

At this point, it is difficult to credit regionalism with being more than an occasional instrument for the assertion of hegemonic control that, depending on circumstances, can be viewed as either legitimated by collective procedures or not. The U.S. intervention in Panama in 1989 was carried out despite the refusal to accord it legitimacy at either the regional or UN level, whereas a protective intervention in Haiti enjoyed both regional and UN blessings. There are important differences between these two cases, yet in both contexts intervention is essentially a hegemonic initiative (as it is shaped in Washington with respect to time, goals, modalities, and battlefield control).

Regionalism in relation to the emergence of positive globalism remains a latent potentiality. The Charter gives ample space for complementary regional roles in peacekeeping settings, and in Article 52(3) expresses a favorable disposition toward resolution of disputes at a regional level, thereby seeming to endorse subsidiarity. Again, context matters; Castro's Cuba is under far more intense hegemonic pressures as a regional pariah than it is in the UN setting. It would seem that the virtues of regionalism in relation to positive globalism are, at present, mainly speculative. Its more serious relevance would arise as a derivation from the emergence of positive globalism, not currently in the offing, and especially backgrounded in light of the geopolitical response to September 11 that has accentuated militarist approaches to global security and conflict resolution.

Promoting Positive Regionalism

Regionalism has achieved positive results in relation to specified world order values in several substantive sectors and various geographic settings, most significantly, of course, in Europe, but also in Asia/Pacific, Latin America, Africa, and the Middle East. (Hettne, 1994, 2002). The most impressive of these achievements involves the promotion of human rights, including revolutionary sovereignty-eroding procedures, as embodied in the European framework, and to a lesser extent within the inter-American setting (Held, 1989, esp. pp. 212–42); mitigation and resolution of conflicts via diplomacy, mediation, and regional linkages; promotion of environmentalism; innovations in transnational cooperation and institutionalisation; experimentation by way of the Maastricht Treaty with innovative extensions of political identity by way of the conferral of European citizenship (van Steenbergen, 1994; Clarke, 1994).

European regionalism has demonstrated that it is possible to extend the rule of law beyond the state and often promote further human rights gains within generally democratic states by asserting grievances at a regional level. This has been impressively demonstrated with reference to the extension of gay and lesbian rights, which provides a model for other concerns, including the protection of resident refugees, access to asylum, and the treatment of foreigners or strangers generally. There is a school of Eurocratic thought, given attention a decade ago by Jacques Delors, that believes further economic integration will succeed only if accompanied by parallel moves to strengthen the political facets of the European Union, and that such momentum needs to be maintained to consolidate the economic results in terms of increased trade and investment so far achieved. Again, grassroot dissatisfactions with the Euro and the general troubles of the world economy cast a dark cloud over prospects for any deepening of the European vision at this point.

Perhaps most significantly, regionalism has protected the peoples of Europe against deteriorating standards of living and the prospects of gradual marginalization in relation to the American project of global empire. This protection has been somewhat controversial because of its tendency to build pressure by way of competitiveness to conform to the requirements imposed by negative globalism. The latter has contributed both to high levels of unemployment and to static, or even falling, real wage levels in Europe and North America. An assessment is not a simple matter. To the degree that regionalism has been instrumentalized by negative globalism, it then forms part of an overall global structure of dominance that is leading to acute marginalization for certain nations and regions, sectors deemed inefficient and uninviting if considered either as producers or consumers. The geographic distribution has some North/South features, but the burdens of marginalization are not so neatly configured, given the rise of South and East Asia and parts of South America. This disregard of marginalization is accentuated by the ideological consensus in support of neoliberal economism in elite circles, and reinforced by the scaling back of socialist and welfare-oriented perspectives by even the leading social democratic parties in Europe. There has been some retreat in recent years from these rigid ideological interpretations of globalization, and more realization, even in Washington, that successful global governance calls for attention and resources devoted to states and regions previously written off as irrelevant, and to such widely endorsed social goals as the struggle against poverty. This global integrationist perspective has been further strengthened by the incentive to avoid converting impoverished populations and countries into potential havens for political extremism and terrorism.

With respect to economic regionalization, the most important recent steps have involved developments in Europe, North America, and Asia/Pacific. The cumulative impact on peoples within and outside these more integrated trading blocs is, as yet, conjectural and intensely contested. Whether the characterization "positive regionalism" is at all appropriate cannot be determined at this time until more evidence on effects has been gathered, including the degree to which American empire-building occupies the center of the global stage. A worst-case assessment would suggest that regionalism is serving as a cover for the reentrenchment of relations of privilege and domination that had been challenged during the revolt against colonialism. A best-case scenario would attribute unevenness in benefits and burdens to the short-run, with a more equitable, sustainable, and democratic global economic order emerging in responses to grassroots and other challenges mounted against negative globalism, which surfaced in 1999 during the Seattle antiglobalization demonstration, and subsequently in the form of a dynamic movement spearheaded by transnational social forces intent on establishing a global civil society, a visionary alternative to either global empire or civilizational enclaves.

In the Asia/Pacific region, the internal dimension of regionalism is to take early, mainly informal, and ad hoc steps toward economic cooperation and coordination, viewing especially ASEAN as possessing potential for expansion and further institutionalisation in the post–Cold War era. These steps are reinforced by a new Asian cultural assertiveness, which both moves toward the affirmation of a regional identity, but also represents a deepening of the decolonization process by its implicit repudiation of Eurocentricism.

In this regard, *Asian/Pacific regionalism* resists any renewal of Western hegemonic projects and helps explain Asian unity with respect to opposing doctrines of humanitarian intervention to correct several abuses of human rights or to remove military rulers from power. As such, Asian/Pacific regionalism, even more than its European counterpart, may be moving toward limiting the Western role, especially the U.S., thereby encouraging a defensive dimension of regionalism. This dynamic of resistance has encountered major obstacles since the Asian Economic Crisis and the initiation of the American war against global terror, which includes establishing a military presence with combat roles in several key Asian countries.

A Concluding Note

More particularistic inquiries may help clarify the impact of regionalism on world order values, especially in light of new global economic troubles and the return of security concerns to the top of the global policy agenda. This chapter has conceptualized several main contexts in which regionalism has seemed dynamic in this post–Cold War period, taking special account of pre–September 11 hegemonic passivity on a global level (the disappearance of strategic, zero-sum rivalry, inducing a shrinking of perceived strategic interests; a rising sense of domestic opposition; and increased realization that power-projection is expensive and often inconclusive in relation to "black hole" challenges), of the disappointing capacity of the United Nations to provide a less hegemonic, yet still effective, world order, and of the overbearing reality of globalization with respect to markets, money, and information. Little ground for optimism has been found with respect to regionalism as either a counterhegemonic democratizing influence or as a source of a new kind of benign hegemonic order (although the trend toward the reactivation of spheres of influence is clearly evident in Russia's effort to provide leadership and exert control over the new states that were formerly Soviet republics; by the United States in relation to the Western Hemisphere, especially Central America; through a reassertion of the Monroe Doctrine as an ingredient of foreign policy; and by France in relation to Francophone countries in North and sub-Saharan Africa; and by India in South Asia).

The post–September 11 modification of this analysis relates to the possibility that the United States, in its superhegemonic role, may selectively promote regionalism in sectors of international society (for example, Africa and Latin America) with weak states unable to prevent their sovereign space being used as base areas for global terrorist activities. Hettne has theorized about this externally promoted regionalism under the rubric of "hegemonic regionalism" (Hettne, 2002).

From a world order perspective, one crucial contribution of regionalism is to help create a new equilibrium in politics that balances the protection of the vulnerable and the interests of humanity as a whole (including future generations) against the integrative, technological dynamic associated with various forms of globalism. Transnational social forces connected with human rights and the environment are promoting one kind of balance, but regionalism could be another. Both phenomena are, in part, reactions to the displacement of the state from without and within and the decline of sovereign territorial space as a domain of unconditional political control. Regionalism, if democratically conditioned, might yet provide, at least for some parts of the whole, a world order compromise between statism and globalism that has indispensable benefits for the circumstances of humanity, as well as some new dangers.

Undecidability is a recurring theme in postmodern thought. A rational grasp on reality does not begin to resolve difficult issues of policy choice. The cynical view is that such a circumstance ensures that narrowly conceived actors' interests will prevail, and there is support for such a reading of the times, particularly given the rise and spread of crime, even the danger of the gangster co-opted state. A more hopeful view is that the tendencies toward democratization and human rights can be focused in the years ahead on the menaces of negative globalism and pathological anarchism, and that regional arenas will be important as sites of struggle and as exemplifications of the interplay of opposed forces.

These lines of speculation have been altered by the faltering world economy, as especially highlighted by the revelations associated with Enron Capitalism, demonstrating that the rosy image of the American economic juggernaut was to a significant degree a gigantic fabrication of misleading accounting practices, an impression accentuated by the earlier bursting of the Silicon Valley high-tech stock market bubble. Even more disconcerting has been the American recourse to a war against megaterrorism that has been generalized to include all nonstate movements engaged in armed struggle, seemingly a war without end that arrays a superpower embodying hypermodernity on one side and the primitive techniques of resistance and innovative backlash by a concealed, networked organizational reality on the other. The resulting encounter can be understood as the first postmodern world war — that is, a war with nonstate actors as strategic adversaries of established statist geopolitics, which were already under severe pressure from the rise of transnational market and civil society forces. How regionalism fits into this context is not likely to be understood for at least another decade.

References

Aron, Raymond. 1966. *Peace and War: A Theory of International Relations*. Trans. Richard Howard and Annette Baker Fox. Garden City, NY: Doubleday.
Barnett, Michael. 2002. *Eyewitness to a Genocide: The United Nations and Rwanda*. Ithaca, N.Y.: Cornell University Press.
Booth, Ken. 1995. "Human Wrongs and International Relations," *International Relations* 71, 1: 103–26.
Brooks, Stephen, and William Wohlforth. 2002. "American Primacy in Perspective," *Foreign Affairs* 81, 4: 20–33.
Bull, Hedley. 1977. *The Anarchical Society: A Study of Order in World Politics*. New York: Columbia University Press.
Carr, E. H. 1939. *The Twenty Years' Crisis: An Introduction to the Study of International Relations*. London: Macmillan.
Castels, Manuel. 1996. *The Rise of the Network Society*. Vol. 1 of The Information Age: Economy, Society, and Culture. New York: Basic Books.
Clarke, Paul Barry, ed. 1994. *Citizenship*. London: Pluto, 188–90.
Doyle, Michael D. 1983. "Kant, Liberal Legacies, and Foreign Affairs," *Philosophy and Public Affairs* 12: 205–35, 323–53.

Falk, Richard. 1975. *A Study of Future Worlds.* New York: Free Press.
Falk, Richard. 1992. *Explorations at the Edge of Time: Prospects for World Order* Philadelphia, Pa.: Temple University Press.
Falk, Richard. 1995a. *On Humane Global Governance: Toward a New Global Politics.* Cambridge, UK: Polity Press.
Falk, Richard. 1995b. "Toward Obsolescence: Sovereignty in the Era of Globalization," *Harvard International Review* 17, 3: 34–35, 75.
Falk, Richard. 1995c. "The Haiti Intervention: A Dangerous World Order Precedent for the United Nations," *Harvard International Law Journal* 36, 2: 14–22.
Falk, Richard. 1997. "State of Siege: Will Globalization Win Out?" *International Affairs* 73, 1: 123–36.
Falk, Richard. 1998. *Law in an Emerging Global Village: A Post-Westphalian Perspective.* Ardsley, N.Y.: Transnational Publishers.
Falk, Richard. 2003. *The Great War on Global Terror.* Northhampton, Mass.: Interlink.
Fedarko, Kevin. 1994. "Back to the USSR," *Time,* July 25, 1994, 40–43.
Funabashi, Yoichi. 1993. "The Asianization of Asia," *Foreign Affairs* 72, 1: 75–85.
Gilpin, Robert. 1981. *War and Change in World Politics.* Cambridge, UK: Cambridge University Press.
Held, David. 1989. *Political Theory and the Modern State.* Stanford, Calif.: Stanford University Press, 214–42.
Hettne, Björn Hettne. 1994. "The New Regionalism: Implications for Development and Peace," Occasional Paper, UNU/WIDER, Helsinki, Finland.
Hettne, Björn Hettne. 2002. "The New Regionalism and the Return of the Political," XIII Nordic Political Association. August 15–17. Aarlbord, Denmark.
Huntington, Samuel P. 1993. "The Clash of Civilizations?" *Foreign Affairs* 72, 1: 22–49.
Hutchins, Robert, et al. 1948. *Preliminary Draft of a World Constitution.* Chicago: University of Chicago Press.
Kissinger, Henry. 1994. *Diplomacy.* New York: Simon & Schuster, 804–35.
Knight, W. Andy. 1994. "Toward a Subsidiarity Model of Global Governance: Making Chapter VIII of the UN Charter Operational." Annual Meeting of Academic Council of the United Nations System. The Hague Netherlands.
Kosovo Report. 2000. *Independent International Commission on Kosovo.* Oxford: Oxford University Press.
Krauthammer, Charles. 1990–1991. "The Unipolar Moment," *Foreign Affairs* 70, 1: 23–33.
Lemann, Nicholas. 2002. "The Next World Order." *The New Yorker,* April 1, 42–48.
Mandelbaum, Michael. 1994. "The Reluctance to Intervene," *Foreign Policy* 95, 1: 3–18.
Mander, Jerry, and Edward Goldsmith, eds. 1996. *The Case against the World Economy: And for a Turn toward the Local.* San Francisco, Calif.: Sierra Club Books.
Maynes, Charles William. 1993–1994. "A Workable Clinton Doctrine," *Foreign Policy* 93: 3–20.
Mearsheimer, John. 1990. "Back to the Future: Instability in Europe after the Cold War," *International Security* 14: 5–41.
Melvern, Linda. 2000. *A People Betrayed: The Role of the West in Rwanda's Genocide.* London: Zed.
Mittelman, James. 2000. *The Globalization Syndrome: Transformation and Resistance.* Princeton: Princeton University Press.
Moore, Jonathan, ed. 1998. *Hard Choices: Moral Dilemmas in Humanitarian Intervention.* (Lanham, Md.: Rowman & Littlefield.
Murphy, Sean D. 1996. *Humanitarian Intervention: The United Nations in an Evolving World Order.* Philadelphia: University of Pennsylvania Press.
Ohmae, Kenichi. 1992. "The Region State," *Foreign Affairs* 72, 1: 78–87.
Rosenau, James. N. 1990. *Turbulence in World Politics: A Theory of Continuity and Change.* Princeton: Princeton University Press.
Russett, Bruce. 1993. *Grasping the Democratic Peace: Principles for a Post-Cold War World.* Princeton: Princeton University Press.
Sidjanski, Dusan. 1992. *L'avenir Federaliste del 'Europe.* Paris: Presse Universitaire de France.
van Steenbergen, Bart. 1994. *The Condition of Citizenship.* London: Sage.
Wallerstein, Immanuel. 2002. "The Incredible Shrinking Eagle," *Foreign Policy* (July/August): 60–68.
Weiss, Thomas. 1994. "UN Responses in the former Yugoslavia: Moral and Operational Choices," *Ethics and International Affairs* 8: 1–21.

Chapter 3
Global Institutions

Identifying the Challenge

It is striking how much of the controversy about U.S. foreign policy in the decade following the end of the Cold War has involved disputes about the proper role of international institutional arrangements. These issues have agitated the entire political spectrum resulting in unexpected convergencies between normally antagonistic parties.

Take, for example, the Kosovo intervention by the North Atlantic Treaty Organization (NATO) in 1999. Both hard-core realists and liberal humanists generally supported the intervention — the former because it indicated a renewed American willingness to use force effectively in the service of national interests, and the latter because it put a stop to Slobodan Milosevic's oppression of the Albanian Kosovars and created de facto independence for Kosovo.

What becomes apparent is that evaluating international institutions is now intimately connected with the foreign policy priorities of major states. These institutions are predominantly instruments of states and the state system, reflecting the interplay of national perceptions and aspirations as well as the prevailing geopolitical structure. It seems most accurate to regard such institutions as neither inherently beneficial nor detrimental to the quality of world order or to their contributions to human well-being. So conceived, neither ideological repudiation nor enthusiasm for international institutions is appropriate as a generalized posture of assessment. What is arguably more useful is to evaluate each dimension of multilateralism in its specific substantive and historical context, which includes a sense of the global setting, the relevant world order challenges, and the ways in which a particular country can best pursue its interests and promote its worldview.

For several decades quickly adjusting such assessments has been necessitated by the rate and scope of technological change, which is beginning to alter our understanding of fundamental aspects of human existence, as well as to compress time and space in dramatic fashion. These developments also increasingly demonstrate the need for effective and beneficial global governance. For the United States, the world order challenge is particularly great, as its leadership role involves framing world order, including the approach taken to the production and distribution of global public goods, but also the pursuit of its strategic and moral purposes under conditions of globalization and the menace of megaterrorism.

The U.S. relationship with international institutions can be explored from three perspectives: (1) institutions of global economic governance, (2) a world of regions, and (3) the United Nations System. The three are listed in order of descending priority. So far in this era of globalization, the world economy constitutes the most important multilateral arena, and this remains the case despite renewed preoccupations with global security since 2001.

However, such an economistic view overlooks a critical yet unappreciated arena of American foreign policy — that is, the national response to the new expressions of regionalism now occurring around the world. Perhaps the most important experiment in world order attempted since the formation of the modern state and the emergence of the state system is Europe's current drive toward regional integration. The European Union is a much more dramatic, fundamental, explicit, and intrusive challenge to the sovereignty of its member states than the United Nations ever has been. Likewise, in the western hemisphere, Latin American countries are either clamoring to become members of the North American Free Trade Association or forming their own subregional groupings that operate without U.S. participation. In Asia, also, a variety of ambitious regional initiatives are being proposed and underway.

Finally, the United States' role in the United Nations needs to be reevaluated. This role has been questioned recently both inside the country, where Congress has reduced the U.S. level of financial support, and outside, where countries are complaining both about U.S. manipulation of the organization and about evading the Charter framework in pursuit of its foreign policy goals. After World War II, and during most of the Cold War, the United States was perceived as the main champion of the United Nations, reflecting commitments to social justice, human rights, and the development of international law. The Soviet Union and its bloc were widely regarded in the West as oppressive and secretive societies that regarded the United Nations as "enemy territory," principally because of their minority status when it came to counting votes. At the start of the Cold War, the United States acted as if it owned the UN, seeking to rely on the organization to reinforce its anti-Soviet stands in the name of preserving international peace and security. But with the decolonization of the

1960s, new voting majorities emerged that reflected the shift of global priorities to third world countries. This shift created tension between the UN and the United States, especially on issues of global economic policy and the Arab/Israeli conflict, and particularly in the institutional context of the General Assembly. In the face of such an evolution, the United States became as eager to limit the role and authority of the General Assembly as the Soviet Union earlier had been to prevent unwanted action by both the Security Council and General Assembly. Thus ensued an unlikely pairing that had the two superpower rivals jointly advocating for quite different reasons a critical and selective approach toward the proper role of the United Nations. Because of their adversary geopolitical stance, these two antagonists opposed one another with respect to whether to encourage or oppose recommended UN initiatives on particular issues. Since the end of the Cold War, the voting configurations have again shifted, with overwhelming authority being associated with the Security Council and the issues associated with whether or not the United States is able to fashion a consensus in support of its approach to a given war/peace issue. The Gulf War of 1991 was an expression of America's greatest success in consensus building, while the inability to overcome divisions during the lead up to the Iraq War represented Washington's greatest diplomatic failure.

The Institutions of Global Economic Governance

Aside from anxiety about a third world war, the greatest concern in 1945 was avoiding the sort of breakdown in the world economy that contributed to the Great Depression in the 1930s. In this spirit, the International Monetary Fund (IMF) and World Bank were established to provide a measure of international financial stability, especially with respect to exchange rates and liquidity. The effort in this period to include an international trade regime was defeated due to the strength of special interests within the United States that were then unwilling to accept even modest degrees of institutionalized control over private sector economic activity and did not want to jeopardize subsidies and special treatment.

Unlike the UN, the IMF and World Bank operated on the basis of weighted voting that reflected the scale of participating states' financial contributions. From the perspective of U.S. foreign policy, this voting system was seen as beneficial, but it also has caused problems in this era of globalization. It ensured American control, epitomized by locating the headquarters of these institutions in Washington, D.C., as well as by the World Bank's continued leadership by a prominent, well-connected American. But this degree of Americanization made these institutions particularly vulnerable to criticism because they were mere creatures of U.S. foreign economic policy rather than genuine agents of the organized world community. Third world governments and civil society actors charged the institutions with having market-oriented, overly interventionist agendas and antidemocratic operating practices that mainly benefited local and foreign elites.

With the formation of the World Trade Organization (WTO) in 1995, this pattern of support and opposition deepened. The U.S. government was the leading sponsor of the negotiations that led to the WTO's establishment, which disturbed those Americans, including many sectors of organized labor, who were opposed to economic internationalism and globalization in an ideological climate of neoliberalism. At the time of its establishment, the WTO was backed by most of the political mainstream, who regarded free trade as the lynchpin of world capitalism in the Information Age, the key to sustaining American prosperity at home, and highly beneficial to multinational corporations and banks — most of which were centered in the United States or its close allies. As a further concession to the anti-UN climate in the U.S. Congress in the late 1980s, the WTO was created as organizationally distinct from the UN. (The IMF and World Bank are formally part of the UN system, although they have been administratively and operationally autonomous throughout their existence.)

Critics of globalization have emphasized various objections to the role of these institutions. The most vigorous objections have been associated with their alleged tendency to favor unsound private sector investments and promote policies that neglect impoverished countries, widen income disparities, and discourage fiscal expenditures on public goods. These institutions are accused of being inattentive to the social and environmental harm caused by their uncritical focus on maximizing economic growth, favoring megaprojects such as large dams and power plants, and closing their eyes to corrupt and incompetent use of funds. The 1997 Asian Economic Crisis, however, and its wider reverberations in Japan, Russia, and several important Latin American countries, shook the confidence of even the most ardent proponents of a self-regulating world economy. Early reactions of alarm included calls for "a new financial architecture" and "globalization with a human face." The IMF's initial response to the crisis was to administer heavy doses of fiscal austerity, while the World Bank blamed the downfall in Asia on "crony capitalism." These responses were widely attacked by civil society actors who contended that the neoliberal ideological bias of these institutions was responsible for further jeopardizing the living standards of the poor in many countries. The World Bank was specifically attacked for giving enthusiastic certifications of approval to Asian economies whose dubious financial practices had contributed to destabilizing forms of currency speculation and collapse of investor confidence. The World Bank tended to deflect criticism of its policies by superficially explaining that the Asian collapses were a result of corruption of the various natural economies, and should not be attributed to the basic economic orthodoxy that had been disseminated in the region and elsewhere in the South by the World Bank approach to loans and credit.

Significant reforms have not followed, although these institutions have taken steps to improve their public relations image, including a proclaimed willingness to listen to the critical grassroots voices of global civil society. The leaders of international financial institutions have missed few opportunities to affirm their dedication to abolishing poverty and safeguarding the environment, while simultaneously pledging a renewed, often contradictory commitment to pro-growth development and fiscal discipline. The United States' official position in this period of international questioning has been to reaffirm the basic soundness of market-oriented approaches and to resist regulatory proposals for reform, including even those that come from procapitalist Western European governments. Americans leaders endorsed the view that the Asian economic failures resulted from corruption and overly dirigiste states rather than structural defects in the world economy and an ideology that downplayed adverse social effects. The leadership of international institutions generally went along with this neoliberal view that the world economy was best off when relying on the efficiency of markets. Wealth disparities were regarded as tolerable in this view, so long as it was possible to point to increases in overall material wealth and to advance some controversial claims on the progress of poverty reduction.

In recent years, and especially in the setting and aftermath of the 1999 WTO demonstrations in Seattle, many activists have emphasized the antidemocratic procedures by which global economic policies are formulated, and charged that the neoliberal ideology that guides these policies is systematically insensitive to the well-being of people. Organized labor in the United States was a visible presence in the streets of Seattle, and was concerned that its wages were being lowered and jobs lost due to the world perspective adopted by proglobalization policy makers. Labor representatives protested against the absence of regulatory authority elsewhere in the world, raising human rights concerns about child labor, poor safety, and low wages in a variety of countries, especially in Asia and Latin America. Territorial concerns over the loss of American jobs due to outsourcing and downward wage pressure created the impression that labor in the North was less concerned about abuses in the South than to uphold its own self-serving material interests. The fundamental issue was whether U.S. policy makers should be more responsive to the well-being of their citizens at home, even if it meant sustaining less efficient economic activities. This call for territorial protection included opposition to policies designed to open national economies to global competition. The American mainstream, with notable bipartisan support, has continued to support globalization despite the growing grassroots resistance. This dominant viewpoint helps explain the Congressional decision to clear China for admission to the WTO despite a variety of well-founded human rights concerns and organized opposition from opponents on both the left and right.

When posing the prescriptive question — How should the United States relate to global economic governance? — it seems evident there are no simple answers. It would be a dangerous political and economic mistake to pull back from full engagement in the world economy because of protectionist territorial pressures. But it would also be a serious mistake to suppose the regime governing the world economy will be automatically accepted by the citizenry of democratic societies. Such acceptance depends on the world economy perceived as both materially beneficial and legitimate by most people. Enhancing the legitimacy of the IMF, World Bank, and the WTO depends on several reforms that can be supported by the U.S. government without altering its embrace of globalization:

- Democratize the operation of these institutions, starting with procedures that assure transparency; all member states should be included in decision-making processes, and those corporate and banking interests receiving financial assistance must be held accountable for losses sustained.
- Encourage codes of conduct and voluntary adherence to labor, human rights, and environmental standards as proposed by the UN secretary general.
- Adopt reforms that generate greater confidence in overseas banking practices; stress anticorruption measures and improved bankruptcy procedures, and end tax haven and money-laundering mechanisms.
- Adopt decision-making processes that give greater voice to representatives of governments in the southern hemisphere, including those that are most economically disadvantaged.
- Examine ways to bridge the traditional ideological divide that pits maximizing economic growth against improving the lot of the economically and socially disadvantaged.
- Encourage formal and informal mechanisms to ensure adequate communication with respect to operations and decisions, with information available to all stakeholders.
- Establish procedures to enable meaningful access and participation for selected civil society representatives.

It is certain that foreign economic policy will be a front burner concern of American foreign policy in the years ahead. The system in place has not yet been tested by serious adversity, although the Asian Economic Crisis provided some idea of the fragility of the world economy when things go bad in a big way. U.S. leaders need to support a series of reforms in order to ensure that these institutions of global economic governance act as members of a *legitimate* world order. These efforts must include an attempt to counteract globalization's current tendency to reap extraordinary rewards for elites while leaving billions in poverty. This trend is sowing the seeds of future conflict by creating wider and wider disparities between the haves and the have-nots as between countries, classes, and regions. The pattern also seems to assign future generations the awesome burden of addressing problems that result from presently relying on overly laissez-faire attitudes toward environmental protection and the conservation of scarce resources.

A World of Regions? A Foreign Policy Calculus

The growth of regionalism in the years since World War II is a complex and exceedingly uneven phenomenon that bears significantly on the global role of the United States and the definition of its geostrategic interests.

To begin with, regionalism in Europe, where by far the most ambitious institutional development has occurred, has contributed significantly to American foreign policy — from its formative decades up through the end of the Cold War. European regionalism helped forge American foreign policy goals in at least four respects: (1) it solidified a united front in Western Europe that greatly facilitated the policy of containment during the Cold War; (2) it built an institutionalized framework of cooperation among the major European states that made the recurrence of intra-European war unlikely, thereby bringing unprecedented stability to an area that was the setting of two catastrophic world wars; (3) it offered a partial solution for the problem of Germany and German nationalism — even though this solution initially rested on the East/West rivalry that produced a divided Germany; and (4) it helped with Western Europe's economic reconstruction, thereby exhibiting the relative superiority of capitalism verses socialism, as well as providing markets for U.S. exports and capital.

With the end of the Cold War, the calculus of benefits shifted somewhat, at least until 2001. In general, aside from the former priority of Soviet containment, many of the same factors are present in Europe; however the former challenges seem less urgent and are offset somewhat by new concerns. The most notable of these is that a united and enlarged Europe, encompassing the whole continent and not just the countries in the West, is a potential rival for global leadership. At the very least, now that Europe is no longer dependent on the American cold war security umbrella, the region has become somewhat bolder in expressing independent views on global issues. In the aftermath of the Kosovo War, Europeans talked rather fancifully of creating their own regional military capability that could address regional issues without being dependent on U.S. participation. Even inside NATO there is increasing dissatisfaction with the extent to which American military leaders have dominated the alliance, and it is notable that the KFOR (international security force for Kosovo) commanders in Kosovo following the war have been Europeans. Even during the Cold War, France periodically bristled at the extent of American influence in Europe, and even withdrew from NATO for a time.

Perhaps more relevant is Europe's current relationship to American foreign economic policy. The Euro is mounting a challenge to the dollar in the international currency market, which has increased European confidence in moving further toward the establishment of a regional polity within an agreed constitutional framework. European positions on agricultural protection, hybrid foods, intellectual property rights, steel subsidies, and cultural issues have been sharply at odds with American positions.

On balance, however, the evolution of European regionalism serves American national interests rather well. The fundamental alliance relationship, embodied in NATO, has persisted, and even expanded to include several former Warsaw Pact countries. This suggests that Europe is still committed to linking much of its security policy to the United States, even at the cost of subordination to Washington. From Washington's perspective, European regionalism is the best assurance of the continent's stability. It is notable that the failure to integrate the South Balkans into the framework of European regionalism partly explains the recent wars in the former Yugoslavia.

Aside from these issues, the larger question for American foreign policy is whether a framework of tightly integrated institutions at the regional level is a beneficial move away from a world of sovereign states. After all, a borderless, prosperous, stable Europe is bound to become a powerful model for other regions in the world, and is already exerting some influence on the shape and depth of multilateral organizations in Asia and Latin America. Each region bears on American interests in its own distinctive fashion. Asia and Latin America tend to regard regionalism as a counterweight to American hegemony — political, economic, and cultural. However, this type of regionalism can also satisfy the important American foreign policy goal of enhancing intraregional security. It can also provide a secular and modernizing alternative to a revival of traditional culture that is more likely to adopt an extremist — and anti-Western — outlook. It would seem, then, that U.S. foreign policy should, at minimum, be respectful toward regional initiatives in various parts of the world, and even encourage and support selected initiatives — such as Africa's attempts to regionalize peacekeeping undertakings.

It would be highly misleading to view regionalism as a panacea for the resolution of international conflict. It is true that in Europe, membership in the European Union provides benefits, relationships, and identities that downplay the importance of the territorial sovereign state, as well as rivalries among states. Possibly, but not assuredly, the sorts of ethnic and religious tensions that have tormented Spain and Northern Ireland for many years might become muted, and eventually disappear, in the setting of "Europe" — on the assumption that the attainment of statehood would seem less important.

In sum, the regional dimension of world politics is gaining in importance and altering the manner in which states fulfill their security, economic, and cultural interests. Regional integration also offers non-

Western countries a means to insulate their societies somewhat against a feared onslaught of American pop culture that is endemic to globalization. The most appropriate U.S. foreign policy posture is to welcome stabilizing regional undertakings and consider responses on a case-by-case basis. In the background is the issue of the character of American global leadership: Should it aim for an "imperial" role that views all impulses toward independence and diversity as a threat to its geopolitical designs, or should it lend its support to efforts that bring stability, prosperity, sustainability, and human rights to a larger proportion of humanity? If the latter, then regionalism may be regarded as a generally positive international development whose further evolution is likely to stabilize global affairs politically and economically, even if it means a reduction in direct American influence. In the era of economic globalization, such influence is somewhat anachronistic and far less important than stable management of international relations. A world of regions might become quite an attractive model for the next phase of international relations, a post-Westphalian world order in which the state continues to be the predominant actor, but shares the stage with regional and global economic institutions.

To some extent, these expectations have been complicated by the overall impacts of the September 11 attacks and the American-led response. The security imperative of the United States is such as to disregard boundaries, including regional ones. The megaterrorist war launched by al Qaeda puts virtually the whole world at risk of being targeted, and creates a common, nonstate enemy. But so far, unlike the Cold War, the acceptance of American leadership has grown recalcitrant with the passage of time, producing a confrontation with old habitual allies during the Iraq Crisis. The present set of circumstances is ambiguous with regard to the future of regionalism. To some extent, regionalism is more valued than earlier to moderate the American quest for a global empire. To some extent, regionalism is less able to establish an autonomous zone for its members because neither side in the Great Terror War is prepared to acknowledge regional authority in the conduct of a postmodern war of global scope. Significantly, the Iraq War controversy split Europe down the middle, with some countries rejecting the American argument and others closing ranks behind American leadership. The combination of enlarging the EU and the absence of consensus with respect to the American grand design, whether packaged as antiterrorism or perceived as empire-building, makes the future of regionalism in Europe quite problematic. And if the regionalist outcome in Europe is problematic, then it is also so for other regions with less regional experience and commitment.

The United Nations: A Crisis of Confidence

Ever since the end of World War I and Woodrow Wilson's call for collective security within an institutional framework of sovereign states, American opinion has swung back and forth on the wisdom of a reformed world order, as well as its own degree of participation. At present, due in large part to unilateralist leadership in the White House, a reactionary U.S. Congress, and the frustrations associated with diplomacy of the Iraq War, there appears to be diminished support for the United Nations. But even such a bland generalization can be quickly undermined, as may be happening in the course of the American occupation of Iraq, which has given rise to increased calls for an expanded UN role in the reconstruction effort. This is unfortunate, casting a shadow across America's leadership of world affairs generally and perpetuating the perception that the United States has abandoned its traditional commitment to making the world more peaceful and equitable. For better and worse, the UN remains the only truly universal political organization in existence, and provides the peoples of the world with a beacon of hope. The degree to which Washington is perceived as trying either to dominate or ignore the organization is directly proportionate to a loss of confidence in U.S. global leadership — this in turn leads to charges that America is acting as an irresponsible "rogue" superpower or hegemon.

This perception should be addressed constructively, but it also needs to be understood. Throughout the cold war years, the UN's weakness with regards to peace and security was attributed to the Soviet Union's obstructionist behavior. When the Security Council reached consensus on the eve of the Gulf War in 1991, American leaders were optimistic that the UN would now be able to consistently serve as a reliable instrument of U.S. foreign security policy. As it happened already with the Gulf War, which was mandated by the UN but managed by Washington, there was widespread concern that the United States was manipulating the organization to suit its will, instead of acting collectively in the spirit of the Charter. Shortly after the Gulf War, when humanitarian disaster struck Somalia, the other problematic side of the United States–UN relationship emerged. What had started out as a pure humanitarian mission in 1992 was gradually transformed into an American attempt to restore governmental authority in Somalia. Somali warlord factions seeking political control fought back with an attack that resulted in the death of eighteen American soldiers. Suddenly, it became clear the military prowess so impressively on display in the Gulf War could not perform successfully in the civil unrest and turmoil of a country such as Somalia. Several key American leaders and much of the media blamed the UN for the outcome and spoke against risking American lives in any such future humanitarian undertakings. The 1992–1995 Bosnia War further decreased confidence in the UN, resulting in a corresponding reliance on more conventional statecraft and U.S.-led alliances of likeminded countries. This downgrading of UN peacekeeping capacities reached its initial point of culmination in the 1999 Kosovo air campaign, which was completely conducted under NATO auspices.

Nevertheless, the UN became the main agent of postwar administration in Kosovo. Similarly, in sub-Saharan Africa, the UN remains indispensable in coping with the worst cases of widespread civil violence and chaos. Although, with today's global awareness, it is impossible to ignore humanitarian catastrophes altogether, the United States does not have to face these challenges alone, or even at all. Despite its shortcomings, the United Nations remains by far the best, and often the only, framework within which to address such challenges — to the extent that they can be addressed at all.

Thus, it would seem desirable for the United States to adopt a more positive and flexible attitude toward the United Nations. Such an attitude could be immediately signaled by no longer wielding its "financial veto." It was never in America's interest to indulge former Senator Jesse Helms to continue playing such an influential role in shaping the U.S. approach to the UN during the 1990s. It involved simultaneously downgrading and insulting the UN, while still having the temerity to demand that the secretary general come to Washington on his knees in a plea for money to keep the organization going.

President George W. Bush has extended this troublesome U.S. relationship into the twenty-first century, initially pursuing a unilateralist diplomacy contemptuous of all forms of international cooperation, and then soliciting unconditional support for the American response to the September 11 attacks. There was a genuine extension of such support in the immediate aftermath of the attacks, even with respect to the Afghanistan War, but this dissipated rapidly as the White House attention shifted to Iraq. Despite its oppressive regime, Iraq was not seen as significantly linked to the al Qaeda threat, and thus recourse to war against Iraq called into question the most fundamental of UN commitments — that is, the outlawry of aggressive war.

It would be beneficial if the next American leader rebuilt the American public's confidence in the United Nations. Such an effort should emphasize the importance of the UN's role in activities related to human rights, the environment, social issues, and the general discussion of such global challenges as AIDS, fresh water scarcity, and transnational crime and illegal migration. The UN is the best available forum for proposing global reforms and considering current grievances. Given the degree to which technological innovation, economic activity, and media presence are creating a "one world" awareness, the UN is needed to reconcile territorial citizenship with wider regional and global realities. Instead of perpetuating the UN's image as a plaything of domestic U.S. politics, it is imperative that American political leaders better explain why we need a strong UN that can serve our people and the peoples of the world in this era of turbulent globalization.

At the same time, it is important not to expect too much from the UN with respect to peacekeeping. Most leading states remain unwilling, by and large, to risk the lives of their citizens for undertakings that do not serve national interests. Even if the United States redefines its interests to include the promotion of democracy and human rights, it is unlikely to fight wars on behalf of humanitarian diplomacy unless its strategic interests also happen to be at stake — as they were to some extent in the Kosovo crises. When genocidal behavior that does not harm national interests occurs, a UN-directed, volunteer initiative may be the only politically viable response, and such a capability should be created at the earliest possible time.

More elusive challenges involve confronting what might be called "the democratic paradox": the U.S. government has been championing the democratization of states around the world, while simultaneously opposing the democratization of the UN system. The U.S. government led the opposition to increasing UN sponsorship of the large conferences on global policy issues that were becoming effective vehicles for the participation by nongovernmental organizations during the 1990s. These conferences provided an excellent laboratory for experiments in global democracy. In today's world, the practice of democracy can no longer be confined to participation in national elections or the internal operations of the state. There needs to be greater openness to human concerns in global arenas of decision.

One mechanism for overcoming the democratic paradox could be the creation of a global parliament as an additional organ of the United Nations. It may seem to be a utopian idea, but the operation and evolution of the European Parliament suggests that such an institution is both feasible and useful as a means of legitimating governance on a regional scale. The mechanics of establishing a global parliament are complicated, but far from insurmountable. Support from the United States for such an institution would restore America's role as a creative and visionary force seeking to improve the international framework.

In essence, the complexity and fragility of the world system in its many dimensions is making a case for effective and democratic global governance. Such governance is likely to be most respected if it draws upon the legitimacy of the United Nations.

A Concluding Note

Considering multilateralism from the perspectives of international financial institutions, regionalism, and the UN leads to some rather clear conclusions. First of all, global economic governance is imperative for the continued growth and stability of the world economy, as well as the regulation of new technology. Although the rationale for global governance is widely accepted, increasing its legitimacy here and abroad is one of the crucial challenges facing U.S. leaders today. The absence of transparency, accountability, and grassroots participation arouses criticism and has already produced widespread and diverse opposition to the Bretton Woods institutions and the WTO.

Second, regionalism is responsive not only to the practical realities of economic and environmental cooperation, but also to the affinities of shared historical and cultural experience. The European experience illustrates the momentum that can build up in support of a regional approach, but also reveals the need to balance integration with national identity. The extension of regionalism to the Western Hemisphere also has intriguing possibilities that should be carefully considered by those who shape American foreign policy in the years ahead. Regionalism also provides a potential barrier to American empire-building, which should be endorsed by American anti-imperialists, as well as by leaders and civil society actors around the world.

And finally, the future of the United Nations needs to be treated as a higher foreign policy priority than in the recent past. The organization has been allowed to drift into the doldrums largely because the United States has not lived up to its responsibilities as its most prominent member, and has exhibited a lack of respect for views opposed to its own. There is a need for a strengthened United Nations that acknowledges the rising prominence of civil society actors and the necessity of extending democratic practices to international institutions. So far, the U.S. position exemplifies the democratic paradox of favoring democracy at the domestic level but resisting its application at the global level. Creative U.S. leadership in the UN over the next decade depends on gradually overcoming this paradox and lending support to institutional innovations and procedures of a democratizing character. In a sense, world order since 2001 underscores the challenge, but also reveals the difficulty of dealing with peace and security in a global setting where key actors are no longer exclusively territorial sovereign states. The rise of nonstate political actors with formidable destructive capabilities, as well as a state with global reach seemingly determined to establish the first truly worldwide empire in human history, both suggest the waning of a statist system of world order.

Chapter 4
Global Civil Society

Engaging the Project

The pursuit of responsible global capitalism needs to be understood, above all, as both a *political* project and an evolving *empirical* process. By this is meant that there must be some attention given to what political scientists call *the problem of agency*, the actors and social forces that are committed to the desired course of change. Such a view is skeptical about reliance on patterns of voluntary adjustment, whether as a result of moral sentiments, the benevolence of those in the private sector whose behavior is under critical scrutiny, or as a pragmatic response to social pressures and economic opportunities. Ideas do matter, and voluntary adjustments can be significant under certain circumstances; but the history of social change confirms the view that very little of lasting significance occurs without threats posed to the established order by those advocates of change sufficiently engaged to mount a struggle, take risks, make sacrifices, and in the end, generate incentives for elites to strike bargains of accommodation. Crudely put, the humanization of industrial capitalism since the mid nineteenth century must be understood predominantly as an outcome of struggle, centering upon the emergence in civil society of a robust labor movement increasingly influenced by radical thought, especially by the Marxist critique of capitalist exploitation combined with revolutionary optimism about the socialist future of humanity.

When the social forces demanding change become "dangerous classes," elites move beyond gestures of compromise to seek negotiated settlements that institutionalize a regulatory regime reflective of a new societal consensus, giving rise to an equilibrium between civil society and the private business sector. The great triumph of capitalism was its willingness to give ground in relation to successive phases of this challenge during the latter part of the nineteenth and until last decade of the twentieth century, to incorporate into its operations a sufficient degree of moral sensitivity, and to overcome by stages the challenge posed by Marxist ideas and labor radicalism, a challenge made also geopolitically formidable by the emergence of Soviet Union after World War I. The Russian Revolution, followed by Soviet ideological and diplomatic pressures, the Great Depression of the 1930s, and the rise of an anticapitalist fascist alternative in Europe mounted a second round of pressures for moral adaptation. Unless the political leaders could address the material, social, and psychological needs of their citizens, capitalism would be discredited to the point where it would likely fall victim to extremisms of left and right. Again, moral adjustments were mainly achieved as a result of pressures, both from within and without, and a sense in the private sector that unless social reforms were accepted, the capitalist system could not survive, and especially could not be combined with political liberalism, which here meant moderation of governmental authority as assured by the rule of law reinforced by constitutionalism. Economists, especially Keynes, gave intellectual respectability to a new and more socially responsible capitalism that pledged full employment, counteracted business cycles, and accorded organized labor an important seat at the tables of government and policy formation.

But the long period of the cold war, with its priorities of national security, the changing nature of capitalist enterprise, and the public dislike of the huge governmental bureaucracy that administered the programs of social democracy created a climate of opinion that over time became antigovernment and antilabor. Such a climate gave rise in the 1980s to the Thatcher/Reagan reorientation of capitalism around a more economistic approach that weakened the weight of moral factors, especially the compassionate elements of welfare capitalism, and substituted in their place an increased reliance on efficiency, the profit motive, and an undisguised hostility toward socialist values and prescriptions. When the Cold War wound down, inducing the collapse of the Soviet Union, the ideological embrace of neoliberalism by the governments and rapidly constituted business elites of the successor states was immediate and abrupt. The Chinese skillful adoption of capitalism coupled with its achievement of a spectacular rate of economic growth provided further testimony that the way to go in development was by an unqualified reliance on capital-guided market factors. Also influential were the impressive records of sustained economic growth by Japan and the so-called emerging market economies, especially in Asia. This ideological consensus was further promoted by the growing influence of international financial institutions, the efforts of the World Economic Forum at its annual meetings at Davos, and the actions taken at the Group of Seven annual economic summits of leading industrial countries. Moreover, neoliberal thinking was increasingly accepted, even by left-leaning political leaders in the Third World. In this end-of-history atmosphere, it seemed as if the global future belonged to this interplay of banks and corporations, helped along by the dominance of neoliberal ideas as promoted by leading governments, by the Internet, and by the waning national and global influence of labor.

It is not surprising that in such a political environment, global capitalism abandoned its earlier moral pretensions associated with governmental responsibility for the production of public goods, and reverted, in spirit if not practice, to the virtually unregulated capitalism of the early industrial revolution. There no longer existed, domestically or internationally, a credible socialist alternative, and it was socialism with its explicit focus on human well-being that all along gave capitalists the practical incentive to achieve moral credibility in the eyes of the public, even at the cost of narrowing profit margins. But if there is no socialist alternative, these incentives disappear, and efficiency and profitability arguments fill the air far more persuasively—although politically it is difficult to roll back welfare features of the social contract between society and the state. The U.S. government was (and remains) the most ardent champion of the neoliberal attention to markets, privatization, and the logic of competitiveness, increasingly shaping its global diplomatic leadership role around the promotion of what it labeled "market-oriented constitutionalism," a phrase echoed in the final declarations of the World Economic (G-7) Summits during the early 1990s.

In the face of these developments, there are abundant reasons to be concerned about the overall effects of economic globalization. In the 1980s and early 1990s, the income gaps between rich and poor within and between societies were widening at an exponential rate while half of the world's population earned less than two dollars per day, and hundreds of millions were without safe drinking water, health facilities, and educational opportunities. Whole regions, especially sub-Saharan Africa and the Caribbean and Central America were excluded from the benefits of global economic growth given unstable investment and trade possibilities. There were resentments associated with the way in which the International Monetary Fund (IMF) and World Bank seemed to be following the lead of Wall Street and Davos without regard to their social effects or moral implications, especially in relation to the more economically disadvantaged countries and the poor generally. It became clear that these global managers of fiscal discipline were often precluding Third World Governments from devoting scarce resources to social priorities and rapid development.

Despite these signs of distress, there was little adverse reaction to globalization until the two shocks of the late 1990s. First, the Asian Economic Crisis, which started in 1997 with volatile currency markets and banking scandals in South Asia, not only canceled overnight the gains of the poorest half of the population in countries such as Indonesia, Thailand, and Malaysia, but burst the bubble of globalization. These regional adversities, in a variety of forms, soon spread to Japan, Russia, Turkey, and elsewhere in succeeding years. Second, there was the dramatic birth of the antiglobalization movement in Seattle during the World Trade Organization (WTO) ministerial meetings at the end of 1999, generating a series of demonstrations around the world whenever and wherever the policymakers of globalization gathered. The movement reached its climax at Genoa almost two years later, where turbulent and large antiglobalization manifestations took place, which were timed to coincide with the annual economic summit of the G-7 (having become by then the G-8, with the inclusion of Russia).

As with earlier efforts of capitalism to achieve wider societal acceptance, these developments posed new threats to the global capitalist order: functional threats associated with the absence of appropriate regulation and normative threats arising from the spreading grassroots perception of globalization as both immoral and antidemocratic. More to the point, these challenges helped shape a double political project — the transformation of globalization by civil society and the legitimation of globalization by business elites and their allies in government. The problem of agency was far from solved, but, at the very least, this combination of chaotic markets and massive street protests shook the champions of globalization out of their mood of complacency at the same time it convinced the core elements of the antiglobalization movement that they were making progress and were onto something big and worthwhile. This interplay between demands for reform from civil society and accommodation and response by the global business world marked a new point of departure for world politics in that it was no longer merely a sequel to the Cold War, but rather represented the beginning of contestation in an era of economic globalization.

The common ground was the need for *normative* (moral, legal, and regulative) adjustment in the actual and perceived workings of the world economy so that economic growth contributed a greater share of the returns on investment and trade revenue to *public goods* (domestically, regionally, and globally), so as to insulate fragile economies from sharp declines. As with the backlash against the abuses of early industrial capitalism almost two centuries ago, it became clear that unbridled market forces lead to corruption, exploitation, and zones of severe deprivation. The humanizing of capitalism is not a self-generating force, but must be achieved by the constant exertion of pressure, both credible challenges from those that claim victimization and responses by those that control economic policy.

Such an evolving set of circumstances was seriously dislocated by the events of September 11 and its aftermath, especially the military campaigns in Afghanistan and Iraq. All at once, the United States was at war — not in a conventional sense of a struggle carried on against another state, but in the form of an undertaking to crush terrorism on a worldwide basis. Such a war, new in the annals of warfare, knows no boundaries of time or space, and its perpetrators on both sides pick their targets without any show of deference to the territorial rights of sovereign states, and do not necessarily differentiate friends from enemies. With the United States as the chief target of the al Qaeda network as well as the leader of the response, the preoccupations of world leaders and the media have for the present shifted away from transnational economic issues and back to traditional strategic geopolitics, with its focus of global security, conflict constellations, and the war/peace agenda. The world economy persists, evolves, and its positive and negative effects are felt in a variety of settings; but at this point it is no longer the focal point of political and public attention. Indeed, it is now unclear whether we are experiencing a temporary diversion in the emergent era of globalization or we are at the early stages of as a second cold war fought along civilizational lines.

The transnational forces of civil society are also in the process of regrouping. To some extent, their attention has also shifted in the direction of war/peace issues and the adoption of priorities associated with the resistance to what is widely and increasingly understood as American empire-building. True, the World Social Forum (modeled as a counterpart to the World Economic Forum) in 2002 and 2003 held successful meetings in Porto Allegro, Brazil, but the momentum for global economic reform and regulation seems to have slowed to a virtual halt. There are some minor countertrends that could in time alter this assessment, such as the acknowledgement that mass impoverishment may act as breeding grounds for terrorists, leading to some attention devoted to poverty reduction and economically deprived states by the United States and other governments. It is probable that the highly publicized African tour devoted to poverty reduction and foreign economic assistance of then U.S. Treasury Secretary Paul O'Neill and U-2 singing star Bono in the spring of 2002 could not have happened without the goad of September 11. Nevertheless, it will take time to redirect the energies of global capitalists and their critics to world economic issues of moral consequences and fairness, and to introduce these concerns into the standard operating procedures of the globalizing world economy.

The Politics of Language

This chapter emphasizes social forces and moral pressures that are responding in politically significant ways to the patterns of behavior associated with the current phase of global capitalism. As a consequence, it seems preferable to frame such activity by reference to "global civil society" rather than to "transnational civil society." Even so, the word "society" is definitely problematic at this stage of global social and political evolution, due to the increasing porousness of natural boundaries and the persisting weakness of social bonds transcending nation, civilization, race, and gender. Such a difficulty exists whether the reference is to "transnational civil society" or to "global civil society." But the transnational referent tends to root the identity of the actors in the subsoil of national consciousness to an extent that often neglects the degree to which the orientation is not one of crossing borders, but of inhabiting and constructing a polity appropriate for the globalizing social order. Such a nascent global polity is already partly extant, yet remains mostly emergent and aspirational (Wapner, 1996).

A similar issue arises when selecting the appropriate terminology to use when identifying the actors. It seems convenient to retain the term "nongovernmental organizations" (NGOs) to designate those actors associated with global civil society because it is accurate and convenient, widely used, and thus easily recognizable. But it is also somewhat misleading and inappropriate in relation to the fundamental hypothesis of a diminishing ordering capability by the sovereign state and states system. To contrast the actors and action of global civil society with the governments of states, as is done by calling them NGOs, is to confer a derivative and subordinate status, and to imply the persistence of a superordinate Westphalian world of sovereign states as the principal constituents of the contemporary world order. Until recently, this hierarchical dualism was justifiable because the preeminence of the state was an empirical reality, reinforced by the absence of any other significant international actors capable of autonomous action and support by a constructivist affirmation of an anarchical society composed exclusively of sovereign states.

To overcome the difficulty of relying on this somewhat anarchronistic statist rhetoric, James Rosenau proposes alternative terminology to that of NGOs by calling such entities "sovereignty free actors" (Rosenau, 1990). Besides being obscure, such a substitute terminology still operates in a Westphalian shadowland in which actor identities are exclusively derived from sovereign actors — namely, states. A comparable problem exists if the reference is to "transnational social forces," although the sense of "transnational" is more flexible and autonomous than "sovereignty free." Marc Nerfin proposed another possibility some years ago (Nerfin, 1986) in the form of a framework that recognizes the social reality of "the third system" (the first system being that of states, the second of market forces or "merchants") from which came civil initiatives of motivated citizens supportive of global public goods.

There is by now a wide and growing literature on "global civil society," especially as related to environmental politics on a global level (Wapner, 1996; Lipschutz, 1996; Global Civil Society Yearbook, 2001). For our purposes, global civil society refers to the field of action and thought occupied by individual and collective citizen initiatives of a voluntary, nonprofit character — both within states and regions and transnationally. These initiatives often proceed from a global orientation, but not necessarily, as local and regional perspectives are also strongly represented within the ranks of civil society. These various patterns of response are, at least in part, reactions to certain globalizing tendencies and effects that are perceived to be partially or totally adverse. At present, most of the global provocation is associated directly or indirectly with market forces and the discipline of regional and global capital. As will be made clear, such a critical stance toward economic globalization does not entail an overall repudiation of an integrated world economy, but it does seek to identify the ways in which its adverse effects can be avoided, to correct social injustices and disruptions (such as recessions and currency volatilities), and to reconcile the management of the world economy with aspirations for global democracy and sustainable development.

To focus this inquiry further, I also propose a distinction that I have relied on previously, although always with some misgivings: that is, the distinction between global market forces identified as "globalization-from-above" and a set of oppositional responses of transnational social activism and global civil society identified as "globalization-from-below" (Falk, 1993, 1995). This distinction may seem unduly polarizing, dyadic, and hierarchical, apparently constructing a dualistic world of good and evil. My intention is neither hierarchical nor moralistic, and there is no illusion that the social forces emanating from global civil society are inherently benevolent while those from the corporate/statist collaboration are necessarily malevolent. Far from it. One of the contentions of the chapter is that there are dangerous chauvinistic and extremist societal energies released by one series of ultranationalist responses to globalization-from-above that are threatening the achievements of the modern secular world — achievements that have been based on the normative side of the evolution of an anarchic society of states in the cumulative direction of humane governance (Bull, 1977). It is no less important to acknowledge that there are strong positive effects and potentialities arising from the various aspects of globalization-from-above (Hirst and Thompson, 1996; Held and McGrew, 1999). At the same time, the historic role of globalization-from-below is to challenge, resist, and transform the negative features of globalization-from-above, both by providing alternative ideological and political space to that currently occupied by market-oriented and statist outlooks and by offering opposition to the excesses and distortions that can be properly attributed to globalization in its current phase. That is, globalization-from-below is not dogmatically opposed to globalization-from-above, but addresses itself to the avoidance of adverse effects, and to providing an overall counterweight to the essentially unchecked influence currently exerted by business and finance on the process of decision making at the level of the state and beyond.

In the context of seeking responsible global capitalism, I believe that it is global civil society, as embodied by the idea of globalization-from-below, that offers such a vision and provides the most credible — indeed, possibly the only — significant answer to the challenge of agency. These social forces remain weak and divided, but compared to considering socialist political parties and organized labor as alternative agents of change and reform, it is globalization-from-below that alone seems capable of raising doubts in a politically relevant manner about the various irresponsibilities of dominant operating modes of global capitalism. Of course, to raise doubts is not to solve the agency problem; it is a foundation upon which to build further, especially by gaining support from such largely superseded oppositional forces of the industrial phase of global capitalism, and even from states that feel hostile, or at least ambivalent, about the drift of the world economy. So, at this point, the most useful designation for the new wave of opposition to post–Cold War global capitalism is probably best understood as "globalization-from-below and allies."

Responding to Economic Globalization

There have been various failed responses to economic globalization, conceived of as the capitalist portion of the world economy. Without actually assessing these failures, it is worth noticing that the efforts of both Soviet-style socialism and Maoism, especially during the period of the Cultural Revolution in China (to avoid the perceived deforming effects of global capitalism) were dramatic, drastic, and ended in disaster. By contrast, despite the difficulties, China's act of subsequently embracing the market under the rubric of "modernization" and even Russia (and the former members of the Soviet empire) in the form of the capitalist path has been generally successful. The same is true for many Third World countries that have forged a middle path between socialism and capitalism, and in doing so have relied on the state as a major player in the economy, particularly with respect to market-facilitating support services, public utilities, and energy. For most of these countries, as well, the change from defensive hostility toward the world market to a position of enthusiastic accommodation has been generally treated by domestic elites as a blessing.

In the last two decades, the learning experience at the level of the state has been largely one of submission to the discipline of global capitalism as it pertains to the specific conditions of each country. Fashionable ideas of "delinking" and "self-reliance" are in a shambles, as is perhaps best illustrated by the inability of North Korea, the greatest of all champions of a stand-alone, anticapitalist economics, to feed its population. In contrast, its capitalist rival sibling in South Korea has often been observed scaling the peaks of affluence, as well as moving ahead with democratization, despite passing through a rocky passage on its road to economic modernity. Looked at differently, it is the geopolitical managers of the world economy who use such policies of exclusion and denial as a punishment for supposedly deviant and hostile states, seeking to legitimize such a coercive diplomacy under the rubric of "sanctions" — a policy often widely criticized in this period because of its cruel effects on the civilian population of the target society. Even Castro's Cuba, for so long an impressive holdout, is relying on standard capitalist approaches to attract foreign direct investment, and to partially open its economy to market forces. Fukuyama's notorious insistence on the end of history is superficially correct, at least for now, if understood as limited in its application to the global triumph of capitalism as an uncontested policy paradigm, and not extended to cultural and political life (Fukuyama, 1992; Clark, 1997).

Another response to the hegemonic influence global capitalism has taken is in the negative form of extreme backlash politics. Such a response looks for inspiration either backward toward some premodern traditional framework deemed viable and virtuous (as with religious extremists of varying identity, or of indigenous peoples) or forward by ultraterritorialists who want to construct an economic and political system around the archaic model of protectionism, keeping capital at home and excluding foreigners to whatever extent possible. These responses, aside from those of indigenous peoples, have a rightist flavor because of their intense affirmation of a religious, ethnic, or nationalist community at war with the evil "other" or infidel — identified as secularist or outsider, and more graphically, as Western, Christian, Crusader, American. The most menacing form of such backlash politics is now associated with the al Qaeda efforts to launch an intercivilizational war on September 11. To the extent that these movements have gained control of states, as in Iran since the Islamic Revolution, or even threatened to do so, as in Algeria since 1992, the results have been dismal: economic deterioration, political repression, widespread civil strife, exclusion from world markets, and an alienation of the citizenry. Even more serious, however, is recourse to megaterrorism that has unleashed a global war against terrorism conducted under U.S. leadership on a broad basis that poses its own dangers to all sectors of international society (Falk, 2002).

Specific causes of these backlash phenomena are related to the perceived political and economic failures of global capitalism and its secularist and materialist outlook, and as postcolonial Western or American hegemony. However, the correctives proposed have yet to exhibit a capacity to generate an alternative capable of either successful economic performance or the ability to win genuine democratic consent from relevant political communities. At the same time, at least prior to September 11, the antiglobalization movement was coming of age. One aspect of its growing maturity was its tighter internal discipline and intellectual coherence. Another was its entry into the dialogue of prime time arenas of global capitalism, such as the World Economic Forum and the World Bank; and perhaps most impressive of all, another sign of the maturing antiglobalization movement was its willingness and ability to work in collaboration with governments to promote global reforms, and to express and develop its outlook by reference to a *positive* globalization rather than merely as a negation of corporate globalization.

The predominance of an insufficiently regulated and morally irresponsible phase of global capitalism has also induced a series of attempts by civil society to mitigate the adverse effects of economic globalization. The most effective of these responses have been issue-oriented, often involving local campaigns against a specific project. One of the early attempts to enter the domain of transformative politics more generally was made by the emergence of green parties at the national level throughout Europe during the 1980s. Significantly, this green movement significantly worked *within* the framework of sovereign states rather than at the transnational level. Green activism has often exhibited tactical brilliance and media savvyness in its moves to expose some of the dysfunctionality of national and global capitalist behavior, especially the disregard of the environmental damage that arises from a rush to profits.

The early political success of the greens was less a result of its capacity to mobilize large numbers in support of its specific causes and programs, and had more to do with the extent to which it insisted on placing the environmental challenge high on the policy agenda of states and the international community. But the green movement's attempt to generalize its identity to provide an alternative leadership for all of society — and particularly its younger members — across the full range of governance or to transnationalize its activities to promote global reform met with frustration and internal controversy that fractured green unity, most vividly in Germany, but elsewhere as well. Those who argued for a new radicalism beyond established political parties within a green framework were dismissed as utopian dreamers, while those who opted for influence within the existing framework were often scorned as victims of co-optation, derided as opportunists, and written off as gradualists. The green movement and its political parties have persisted in Europe, but mainly as one more voice in civil society. Occasionally as in Germany they have played prominent roles in government, forming a coalition with Social Democrats, but, in general, they are no longer widely perceived as a vehicle for an alternative worldview to that provided by global capitalism; nor are they possessed of a sufficiently loyal and united constituency to pose a threat to mainstream economic or political thought. Because of its initial creative focus on the environmental agenda, both conservatives and progressives were drawn to green politics on political economy issues, giving the perspective of originality, but at the cost of being unable to broaden its appeal to major constituencies whose policy priorities were only incidentally related to the environment. In particular, greens were unable to convey a coherent position on global capitalism as their ranks were split between socialists and free marketers, which both limited their growth and made it difficult for the green movement to be an effective contributor to antiglobalization politics.

Local grassroots politics has been another type of response directed at the siting of a nuclear power reactor or large dam, mobilizing residents of an area facing displacement and loss of traditional livelihood, and sometimes involving others from the society and beyond, who identify with the poor, the displaced, and with issues relating to the protection of nature and cultural heritage. These struggles have had some notable successes. But these are reactions to symptomatic disorders associated with the choice of developmental shortcuts, either motivated by glory-seeking national leaders, greedy investors, international financial institutions thinking mainly of aggregate economic growth, and most often by some combination of these factors. Such local forms of resistance can be effective, and over the years, have led the World Bank, and more generally the investment community, to be more sensitive to the human, environmental, and health effects of large-scale development projects. As a consequence, the whole process of conceiving large-scale developmental projects has evolved to the point that it does fulfill many of the mandates of responsible global capitalism, although continual public vigilance is needed to monitor specific undertakings. The temptation to cut corners at the expense of the environment and local, essentially disenfranchised poor people is always a live possibility, as indeed is the willingness to be guided by experts far from the scene of societal and ecological disruption who generate advice by abstract theorizing, sometimes even expressed by algebraic formulae (Roy, 2001). The World Commission on Dams brought together stakeholders of dams, development, and capitalism to forge a policy consensus, reflecting both the growing influence of the global civil society perspective and its own nonconfrontational evolution. Its report gives a snapshot of the play of these contesting perspectives (Dubash et al., 2002).

Closely related to the above issues have been a variety of activist attempts by elements of global civil society to protect the global commons against the more predatory dimensions of globalization (Shiva, 1987; Rich, 1994; Keck and Sikkink, 1999). Here Greenpeace has had a pioneering, distinguished record of activist successes. For instance, by exhibiting an imaginative and courageous willingness to challenge entrenched military and commercial forces by direct action, it has had dramatic impacts on public consciousness and has helped reshape market behavior in the process. Examples include its campaigns to outlaw commercial whaling, to oppose the plan of Shell Oil to dispose of the oil rig Brent Spar in the North Sea, to mobilize global support for a fifty year moratorium on mineral development in Antarctica, and, perhaps most significantly, although focused on the behavior of governments rather than market forces, its resistance for many years to nuclear testing in the Pacific (Prins and Sellwood, 1998).

Rachel Carson's lyrical environmentalism and Jacques Cousteau's extraordinarily intense dedication to saving the oceans suggest the extent to which even single, gifted individuals can exert powerful countertendencies to the most destructive sides of an insufficiently regulated market or of governments that put military activities ahead of all other concerns. But these efforts, although plugging some of the holes in the dikes, are not based on a coherent critique or alternative ideology. As a consequence, they only operate at the level of the symptom and in given situations, while neglecting the disorders embedded in the dynamics of globalization.

There is no effort to build a movement that focuses a large portion of its energies on monitoring or reshaping the outlook and operational ethos of global capitalism.

Some other global civil society initiatives, especially in the 1970s, promoted awareness of the cumulative dangers associated with further unregulated economic growth in a setting of a continuing expansion in world population. One of the earliest such initiatives was promoted by the Club of Rome, a transnational association of individuals prominent in business, science, and society that led the famous study *The Limits to Growth* (Meadows, 1972). The study relied on a rather elaborate, yet in the end misleading, computer program, which purported to measure the interplay of trends in population growth, pollution, resource scarcity, and food supply. It concluded that industrialization as then practiced on a global scale was not sustainable, but tended toward imminent catastrophe for the entire world. Around the same time, a group of distinguished scientists from various countries working with the British journal *The Ecologist* issued their own warning, but with a redeeming vision, under the title *Blueprint for Survival* (Goldsmith, 1972). These alarms stimulated a debate and led to some temporary adjustments, but the resilience of the world capitalist system at the time was such that no fundamental changes occurred, and the warnings issued as signals soon faded into the background. Neither a sense of alternative nor a movement of protest and opposition took hold. There existed no organized transnational social forces back in the 1970s: The Cold War was still dominating political consciousness, and the most that was achieved was the birth of a global environmental protection movement that enlisted the support to varying degrees of many governments. Socialism was then still a formidable force; there was no disposition to indict capitalism because of its wider geopolitical role, principally the economic containment of the Soviet Union; and the minimal international consensus that existed was devoted to such issues as reducing fertility rates in poor Third World countries, resource conservation, and seeking more regulatory authority at the global level (Falk, 1972).

The World Order Models Project (WOMP), which started its work in the late 1960s, illustrates a somewhat more far-reaching and comprehensive effort to challenge the existing world order and find alternatives through the medium of diagnosis and prescription by a transnational group of independent academicians. The efforts of this group have been confined to the margins of academic reflection on world conditions. Also, until recently, the policy focus and animating preoccupation of governmental decision makers has been centered on war, and only recently has it been broadened to include environmental dangers. Although WOMP has produced overall assessments of the world situation, its background and the interests of its participants made the work less sensitive to the distinctive challenges and contributions of economic globalization than to the dangers to global security associated with the nuclear arms race, and the general problems of overcoming mass poverty in Third World countries through rapid and sustainable economic development (Mendlovitz, 1975). As such, the emphasis of WOMP on war and the war-making sovereign state did not come to terms with either the durability of the state or the need to avoid its *instrumentalization* by global market forces. These efforts failed to address systematically the issue of reforming global capitalism. WOMP also failed to appreciate that the principal world order danger is no longer the unconditional security claims of the sovereign state, but rather the inability of the state to protect its own citizenry, especially those who are most vulnerable, in relation to the economic and social downsides of global market forces. This refocused concern that held the political imagination in the 1990s, that is, after the Cold War, has itself been temporarily eclipsed by the renewed priority accorded to the security role of the state in the aftermath of September 11.

A better connected and more recent effort to address overall global issues was attempted by the Commission on Global Governance — an initiative inspired by Willy Brandt and the earlier work of the Brandt Commissions on North/South relations, as expressed in its main report, *Our Global Neighborhood* (Global Governance, 1995). This venture, claiming authority and credibility on the basis of the eminence of its membership drawn from the leading ranks of society, including past and present government ministers, seemed too farsighted for existing power structures and yet too timid to engage the imagination of the more activist and militant actors in civil society. The commission's report failed to arouse any widespread or sustained interest, despite the comprehensiveness and thoughtfulness of its proposals. As an intellectual tool it was also disappointing. It failed, for example, to clarify the challenge of globalization that existed in the early 1990s. It ignored the then especially troublesome character of Bretton Woods approaches to world economic policy, and it exempted the operations of global capitalism from critical scrutiny. As a result, the commission's efforts to anchor an argument for global reform around an argument for "global governance" seemed more likely to consolidate globalization-from-above than to promote a creative equilibrium based on the struggle that was beginning to be associated with the still disparate activities and perspectives grouped beneath the rubric of globalization-from-below.

In part, the timing of the commission's efforts was unfortunate, as they began their work in the aftermath of the Gulf War when attention and hopes were centered on the future of the United Nations, and finished at a time when the UN was being harshly, if somewhat unfairly, blamed for its attempts to resolve conflicts and protect the populations in Somalia, Bosnia, and Rwanda in the period between 1992 and 1994. But this was not the fundamental problem with the approach taken: This was more a failure of nerve to address clearly and explicitly the adverse consequence of globalization, a focus that would have put such a commission on a collision course with the then reigning adherents of the neoliberal economistic world picture. Given the claims of "eminence" and "independent funding" that characterized the commission, it is not to be expected that it would be willing or able to address the structural and ideological deficiencies attributable to the prevailing world order framework. This inevitably means that, despite the best efforts of its membership to make a contribution to global policy making, the actual impact of its work and report was to confirm a sense of pessimism about finding an alternative world picture to that provided by the existing neoliberal prism on global capitalism, which, in the context of this chapter, was tantamount to giving up on the search for a responsible global capitalism.

What is being argued, then, is that the various challenges arising from global capitalism in its postindustrial phase have not, as yet, engendered a sufficient response in two related respects. First, there is an absence of an ideological alternative to what is offered by the various renditions of neoliberalism, which could provide the social forces associated with globalization-from-below with a common theoretical framework, political language, and program. Second, there is a need for a clear expression of a critique of globalization-from-above that seeks to meet the basic challenges associated with poverty, social marginalization, and environmental decay, while preserving the economic benefits derived from capitalism in its present form. The political imperatives of globalization-from-below are thus at once *both* drastic and reformist, accepting the global capitalist framing of economic choice, but believing that ethical and ecological factors should be brought to bear more systematically — in effect, an abandonment of neoliberalism in the search for a more socially and politically regulated framework for this latest phase of global capitalism.

It is central to the position taken here to realize that the world order outcomes arising from the impact of economic globalization are far from settled, and in no sense predetermined by either the current ideological consensus or by geopolitical pressures. The forces of globalization-from-above have assumed major control of corporate globalization and are pushing it in an economistic direction that is influencing the state to adopt a compliant set of attitudes and policies — that is, privatization, free trade, fiscal austerity, competitiveness, and above all, growth. But there are other options and policy objectives, such as "sustainable development," "global welfare," and "cybernetic libertarianism." The further evolution of global capitalism is likely to reflect increasingly the play of these diverse perspectives and priorities. The perspectives and priorities of globalization-from-above are being challenged in various ways, but activist resistance has been mainly piecemeal and critical. Important, also, is the effort directed at the mobilization of the now disparate forces of globalization-from-below in the direction of greater solidity and political weight, as well as reviving discussions about how to achieve a responsible global capitalism in the new setting of warfare in world affairs that has once again pushed economic policy concerns into the background. Preoccupations with global security arise not only from the megaterrorist threats of the post–September 11 atmosphere, but also from the threats of catastrophic regional wars fought with weaponry of mass destruction, as illustrated by the India/Pakistan confrontation in 2002 over Kashmir, and the still recurrent threat of a renewal of warfare on the Korean peninsula. It is my conviction that such a mobilization is most likely to occur beneath the banner of a reformed and deepening sense of democracy, which becomes more and more responsive to the basic aspirations of peoples everywhere to participate in the processes that are shaping their lives, and with growing attention given to security factors and nonmaterial values, including the control of crime and the resolution of political grievances (the roots of terrorism) that exist around the world. In effect, the next phase of the antiglobalization movement, as it regains its focus in the first decade of the twenty-first century, will almost certainly become more concerned with the "political" aspects of a socially acceptable and humane political economy for this era of globalization. In the 1990s the preoccupation of global civil society mirrored the economistic musings of those who were fashioning neoliberal global designs at Davos, the board rooms of world corporations and banks, and brainstorming sessions held at the World Bank and the IMF.

The purpose of the next section of this chapter is mainly to clarify what is meant by "democracy" and "politics" in relation to the analysis of the world economy given the confusing relevance of the global war on terrorism.

Toward Responsible Global Capitalism: A Plea for Normative Democracy

It will not be possible to attain a responsible global capitalism unless there is a more transparent and supportive form of global governance than what currently exists; and this will not be achieved without continuous and robust pressure exerted by global civil society, reinforced by a coherent and feasible sense of alternative policy options and worldview. For this reason, I place great emphasis and invest my hopes on efforts to overcome the current global democratic deficit. As earlier indicated, this quest would have been simpler and more easily attainable without the disruptive effects of September 11, the ensuing war on global terror, and the menace of large-scale regional warfare. Whether these disruptions are temporary is difficult to assess at present, but however long they do last, the importance of democratizing global governance structures remains a political imperative that is linked directly to the presence or absence of a responsible global capitalism.

To introduce the idea of "normative democracy" is to put forward a proposal for a unifying ideology capable of both mobilizing and giving coherence to the disparate social forces that constitute global civil society, and providing the political energy necessary to advance the quest for a greater moral responsiveness within the wide orbit of global market activities. The specification of normative democracy adopted here is influenced strongly by David Held's work on democratic theory and practice, particularly his formulations of "cosmopolitan democracy" (Held, 1995). However, it offers a slightly different terminology so as to emphasize the agency role of global civil society with its range of engagements that go from the local and grassroots to the most encompassing arenas of decision (Held, 1995; Archibugi and Held, 1995). Normative democracy as an outlook also draws upon Walden Bello's call for "substantive democracy," set forth as a more progressive movement alternative to the more limited embrace of "constitutional democracy" (Bello, 1997). I prefer the concept of normative to that of substantive democracy because it highlights ethical and legal norms, and in so doing, reconnects politics with moral purpose and values, and underscores the moral emptiness of neoliberalism, consumerism, and most forms of secularism. There is also a practical reason: to create alternatives to the current appeal of religious extremists as the sole politically relevant source of an ethical response to the inequities and materialism of contemporary global capitalism. At the same time, it is important to recognize the indispensable role of moral purpose and spiritual concerns in the renewal of progressive politics (Falk, 2001).

Contrary to widespread claims in the West, there is no empirical basis for the argument that the economic performance of a country is necessarily tied to constitutional democracy and human rights. Several countries in the Asia/Pacific region, most significantly China, have combined an outstanding macroeconomic record with harsh authoritarian rule. Globalization-from-above is not an assured vehicle for the achievement of Western-style constitutional democracy, including the protection of individual and group rights. But democracy, as such, is the essence of a meaningful form of political action on the part of global civil society, especially to the extent that such action, even when radical in its goals, refrains from and repudiates violent means. In this regard, there is an emergent, as yet implicit, convergence of ends and means on the part of several distinct tendencies in civil society: these include issue-oriented movements, nonviolent democracy movements, and the emergence of governmental elites that minimize their links to geopolitical structures. This convergence presents several intriguing opportunities for coalition building and a greater ideological coherence among the various institutions and interest groups seeking to achieve a responsible global capitalism. Against this background, normative democracy seems like an attractive umbrella for theorizing, not dogmatically, but to exhibit affinities.

Normative democracy adopts a comprehensive view of the fundamental ideas associated with the secular modern state. Security is conceived as extending to environmental protection and to the defense of economic viability (Malaysia, 1997; but see Soros, 2002). Human rights are conceived as encompassing the social and economic rights of individuals, as well as such collective rights as the right to development, the right to peace, and the right of self-determination. Democracy is conceived as extending beyond constitutional and free, periodic elections to include an array of other assurances that governance is oriented toward human well-being and ecological sustainability, and that citizens have access to the various arenas of decision making.

The elements of normative democracy can be enumerated, but their content and behavioral applications will require amplification and adaptation in varied, specific settings. This enumeration reflects the dominant orientations and outlook of the political actors that make up the constructivist category of a substantive profile of normative democracy. This enumeration is not a wish list, but rather is descriptive and explanatory of an embedded consensus with respect to political reform. The elements of this consensus are as follows:

1. *Consent of citizenry:* Some periodic indication that the permanent population of the relevant community is represented by the institutions of governance, which confer legitimacy through the expression of freely expressed consent in the context of meaningful choice. Elections are the established modalities for territorial communities to confer legitimacy on government, but referenda and rights of petition and recall may be more appropriate for other types of political community, especially those of regional or global scope. Direct democracy may be most meaningful for the governance of local political activity.

2. *Rule of law:* All modes of governance should be subject to the discipline of the law as a way of imposing effective limits on authority and of assuring some form of checks and balances as between legislative, executive, judicial, and administrative processes. An independent and respected judiciary plays an indispensable role in fulfilling expectations about a rule-governed society that is also responsive to considerations of equity and justice. Also, there is a need for sensitivity to the normative claims of civil initiatives associated with codes of conduct, conference declarations, and societal institutions (for instance, the Permanent Peoples Tribunal in Rome).

3. *Human rights:* Taking account of differing cultural, economic, and political settings and priorities, the establishment of mechanisms for the impartial and effective implementation of human rights by global, regional, state, and transnational civil sources of authority. Human rights are conceived by reference to the elements of human dignity. They encompass economic, social, and cultural rights, as well as civil and political rights, with a concern for both individual and collective conceptions of rights, emphasizing tolerance toward differ-

ence and fundamental community sentiments, and sensitivity to valued legacies of the past and the life prospects of future generations.

4. *Participation:* Effective and meaningful modes of participation in the political life of the society, centered upon the processes of government, but extending to all forms of social governance, including the workplace and home. Participation may be direct or indirect, that is, representational, but it enables the expression of views and influence upon the processes of decision making on the basis of an ideal of equality of access. Creativity is needed to find methods in addition to elections through which to ensure full participation.

5. *Accountability:* Implying the existence of suitable mechanisms for challenging the exercise of authority by those occupying official positions at the level of the state, but also with respect to the functioning of the market and of international institutions. Establishing an international criminal court in 2002 provided one mechanism for assuring accountability by those in powerful positions who have been traditionally treated as exempt from the rule of law, provided the reach of this institution is respected by the powerful actors in world society, which is now only a distant prospect.

6. *Public goods:* A restored social agenda that corrects the growing imbalance, varying in seriousness from country to country, between private and public goods. Such an imbalance exists with respect to relieving poverty and improving health, education, housing, the conservation of scarce resources, and basic human needs, but also in relation to support for environmental protection, regulation of economic globalization, innovative cultural activity, and infrastructural development for governance at the regional and global levels. In these regards, a gradual depoliticalization of funding either by a use or transaction tax imposed on financial flows, global air travel, or some form of reliable and equitable means to fund public goods of local, national, regional, and global scope is worth serious consideration.

7. *Transparency:* An openness with respect to knowledge and information that builds trust between the institutions of governance and the citizenry at various levels of social interaction. In effect, establishing the right to information as an aspect of constitutionalism, including a strong bias against public sector secrecy and covert operations, and criminalizing government lies such as the sort revealed in connection with CIA lies about alleged "UFO sightings" so as protect the secrecy of U.S. Air Force spy missions. Internationally, transparency is particularly important with respect to military expenditures and arms transfers. The priority given to counterterrorist activities of the government provides a sweepingly dangerous rationalization for governmental secrecy, especially in the wake of September 11 anxieties.

8. *Nonviolence:* Underpinning globalization-from-below and the promotion of substantive democracy is a conditional commitment to nonviolent politics and conflict resolution. Such a commitment does not nullify all rights of self-defense as protected in international law, strictly and narrowly construed. Nor does it necessarily invalidate a limited recourse to violence by oppressed peoples when peaceful methods to achieve change and rights have been frustrated and met with repressive responses. However, this ethos of nonviolence clearly imposes on governments an obligation to renounce weaponry of mass destruction and to negotiate actively phased disarmament arrangements. It also demands commitments dedicated to demilitarizing approaches to peace and security at all levels of social interaction, including peace and security at the level of city and neighborhood.

Globalization-from-Below and the State: A Decisive Battle

Without entering into a detailed discussion, it seems that different versions of neoliberal ideology have exerted a defining influence on the orientation of political elites governing sovereign states. Of course, there are many variations reflecting conditions and personalities in each particular state and region, but the generalization holds without important exception (Sakamoto, 1994; Falk, 1997). Even China, despite adherence to its ideology of state socialism, has implemented by state decree, and with impressive results, an extreme market-oriented approach to economic policy. This suggests that the state can remain authoritarian in relation to its citizenry without necessarily jeopardizing its economic performance — and indeed advancing its competitiveness — so long as it adheres, more or less, to the discipline of global capitalism. In these respects, neoliberalism as a *global* ideology is a contingent source of policy guidance and is purely economistic in character, and certainly does not imply a commitment to democratic governance in even the minimal sense of periodic fair elections. Order and stability plus a high degree of receptivity to foreign investment and trade are all that is currently *necessary* to be a successful and accepted global economic player, as evidenced by China's admission to the World Trade Organization in 2001. Of course, where geopolitics intrudes, exclusions without an economic rationale may take place, as when the United States takes the lead in sanctioning a wide variety of governments it deems hostile to its interests. Sometimes, as with the case of Cuba, the exclusion is mainly justified by reference to deficiencies of human rights, but such an argument is mounted so selectively as to appear arbitrary.

Globalization-from-below, in addition to a multitude of local struggles, is also a vehicle for the transnational promotion of substantive democracy, an ideological counterweight to neoliberalism, and a partial program for a responsible global capitalism. It provides an alternative, or series of convergent alternatives, that has not yet been posited as a coherent body of theory and practice, but nevertheless offers the tacit common ground of an emergent global civil society. Normative democracy, unlike backlash politics or the coercive diplomacy of sanctions that closes off borders and hardens identities, seeks to promote a politics of reconciliation that maintains much of the openness and dynamism associated with globalization-from-above, but counters its pressures to privatize and marketize the production of public goods. In effect, the quest of normative democracy is to establish a social equilibrium that takes full account of the realities of globalization in its various aspects. Such a process cannot succeed on a country-by-country basis, as the partial rollback of welfare in Scandinavia suggests, but must proceed within regional and global settings. The state remains both the instrument of policy and decision making that most affects the lives of peoples and the primary link to regional and global institutions. In the last two decades, the state has been instrumentalized to a considerable degree by the ideology and influences associated with globalization-from-above. This has resulted in declining support for public goods despite a period of strong, sustained economic growth. It has also produced a polarization of the distribution of the wealth, leading to incredible wealth for the winners and acute suffering for the losers. An immediate goal of those disparate social forces that constitute globalization-from-below is to reinstrumentalize the state to the extent that it redefines its role as mediating between the logic of capitalism and the priorities of its peoples, including their short- and long-term goals. Of course, this support for a strong state is associated with its social capabilities and responsibilities, and not with the sort of security prerogatives that have indeed let the state again take command over the course of global policy formation.

Evidence of this instrumentalization of the state on behalf of the claims of global civil society is present in relation to global conferences on broad policy issues that had been organized under UN auspices. Transnational citizens' campaigns for global reform were beginning to make an impact on the public consciousness and behavioral standards in the 1990s. These UN conferences increasingly attracted an array of social forces associated with global civil society and gave rise to a variety of coalitions and oppositions between state, market, and militant citizens that were organized to promote substantive goals (e.g., human rights, environmental protection, and economic equity and development). These UN conferences became arenas of political participation that were operating beyond the confines of state control, and were regarded as provocative and threatening by the established order, which consisted of a coalition between market forces and geopolitical leaders. One effect is for reactionary forces associated with status quo globalization and geopolitics to withdraw support for such UN activities, pushing the organization to the sidelines on global policy issues as part of a process of augmenting geopolitical control over its agenda and orientation. Such a reaction represents a setback for globalization-from-below, but it also shows that the social forces associated with promoting normative democracy have become sufficiently formidable adversaries.

Such a process of reinstrumentalization could also influence the future role and identity of regional and global mechanisms of governance, especially as these may add to the regulatory mandates directed toward market forces and the normative mandates with respect to the protection of the global commons, promoting demilitarization, and the overall support for public goods. However, presently in the foreground are preoccupations with megaterrorist threats to security, especially in the United States and its new array of close allies, as well as the global campaign that has been directed at combating terrorism generally, which is intertwined with the diplomatic emphasis on regional war prevention.

Conclusion

In this chapter I have argued that the positive prospects for global civil society depend very much on two interrelated developments: (1) achieving consensus on "normative democracy" as the foundation of coherent theory and practice, and (2) waging a struggle for the outlook and orientation of institutions of governance with respect to the framing of global economic policy. The state remains the critical focus of this latter struggle, although it is not, even now, a matter of intrinsic opposition between the state as instrument of globalization-from-above and social movements as instrument of globalization-from-below. In many specific settings, coalitions between states and social movements are emerging, as is evident in relation to many questions of the environment, economic development, and human rights. It may even come to pass that transnational corporations and banks adopt a long-term view of their own interests; and by seeking to influence the policy content of globalization-from-above, they may heal relations with their critics and improve their image as constructive global citizens with the preferences of global civil society. The recent popularity of codes of conduct and other voluntary programs suggest an eagerness on the part of the managers of global capitalism to improve their image as ethically sensitive and humanly constructive players in the world economy (Broad, 2002). It is also helpful to remember that such an unanticipated convergence of previously opposed social forces led to the sort of consensus that produced "social democracy" and "the welfare state" over the course of the nineteenth and twentieth centuries. There is no evident reason to preclude such comparable convergencies on regional and global levels as a way of resolving some of the tensions caused by the manner in which globalization is *currently* enacted.

Even September 11 gives rise to movements in these directions, as well as its major diversionary impact. The acceptance by even the Bush administration of an enhanced commitment to poverty reduction by way of foreign economic assistance and reducing the debt burden of poor countries could not have occurred without the growing realization that "failed states" have become dangerous for the rich and powerful. Such a climate of awareness may yet push global capitalism to seek legitimacy by affirming a stakeholder ethos that includes the poor, workers, future generations, and environmental protection. The UN Secretary General has been encouraging such a voluntary process of engagement on the part of the business sector by creating a "global compact" within the UN System that publicly formalizes corporate commitments to these goals, which certainly moves away from the spirit and substance of neoliberal and irresponsible global capitalism. Whether such initiatives are more than gestures will depend on whether the vigilance of global civil society assumes a sufficiently potent form in the years and decades ahead.

References

Archibugi, D., and D. Held, eds. 1995. *Cosmopolitan Democracy: An Agenda for a New World Order* (Cambridge, UK: Polity Press, 1995).

Bello, W. 1997. "Alternate Security Systems in the Asia-Pacific," Bangkok Conference of Focus Asia, March 27–30.

Broad, R. 2002. *Global Backlash: Citizen Initiatives for a Just World Economy* (Lanham, Md.: Rowman & Littlefield).

Bull, H. 1977. *The Anarchical Society: A Study of Order in World Politics* (New York, N.Y.: Columbia University Press).

Clark, I. 1997. *Globalization and Fragmentation: International Relations in the Twentieth Century* (Oxford, UK: Oxford University Press).

Dubash, N. K., M. Dupar, S. Kothari, and T. Lissu. 2001. *A Watershed in Global Governance? An Independent Assessment of the World Commission on Dams* (Lokayan, India: World Resources Institute).

Falk, R. 1972. *This Endangered Planet: Proposals and Prospects for Human Survival* (New York, N.Y.: Random House).

———. 1993. "The Making of Global Citizenship," in J. Brecher, J. B. Childs, and J. Cutler, eds., *Global Visions: Beyond the New World Order* (Boston, Mass.: South End Press).

———. 1995. *On Humane Global Governance: Toward a New Global Politics* (Cambridge, UK: Polity Press).

———. 1997. "State of Siege: Will Globalization Win Out?" *International Affairs* 73: 123–36.

———. 1998. "Global Civil Society: Perspectives, Initiatives, and Movements," *Oxford Development Studies* 26, 1: 99–110.

———. 2001. *Religion and Humane Global Governance* (New York, N.Y.: Palgrave).

———. 2002. *Winning (and Losing) the War against Global Terror* (Northampton, Mass.: Interlink).

Fukuyama, F. 1992. *The End of History and the Last Man* (New York: Free Press).

Global Civil Society Yearbook. 2001. (Oxford, UK: Oxford University Press).

Global Governance, Commission on. 1995. (Oxford, UK: Oxford University Press).

Goldsmith, E., et al. 1972. *Blueprint for Survival* (Boston, Mass.: Houghton Mifflin).

Held, D. 1995. *Democracy and the Global Order: From the Modern State to Cosmopolitan Governance* (Cambridge, UK: Cambridge University Press, 1995).

Held, D., A. McGrew, et al. 1999. *Global Transformations* (Cambridge, UK: Polity).

Hirst, P., and G. Thompson. 1996. *Globalization in Question* (Cambridge, UK: Polity Press) 1–17, 170–94.

Keck, M. and K. Sikkink. 1998. *Activists beyond Borders: Advocacy Networks beyond Borders* (Ithaca, N.Y.: Cornell University Press).

Lipschutz, R. D. 1996. *Global Civil Society and Global Environmental Governance* (Albany, N.Y.: State University of New York).

Malaysia. 1997. "Malaysia PM Mulls Action against Speculators," *Turkish Daily News* (July 29, 1997).

Meadows, D., et al. 1972. *The Limits to Growth* (New York, N.Y.: Free Press).

Mendlovitz, S. 1975. *On the Creation of a Just World Order* (New York: Free Press).

Nerfin, M. 1986. "Neither Prince nor Merchant: Citizen — An Introduction to the Third System," *IFDA Dossier* 56: 3–29.

Prins, G., and E. Sellwood. 1998. "Global Security Problems and the Challenge to Democratic Process," in D. Archibugi, D. Held, and M. Kohler, eds., *Re-imagining Political Community: Studies in Cosmopolitan Democracy* (Cambridge, UK: Polity), 252–72.

Rich, B. 1994. *Mortgaging the Earth: The World Bank, Environmental Impoverishment, and the Crisis of Development* (Boston, Mass.: Beacon Press)

Rosenau, J. N. 1990. *Turbulence in World Politics: A Theory of Change and Continuity* (Princeton, N.J.: Princeton University Press).

Roy, A. 2001. *Power Politics* (Boston, Mass.: South End Press).

Sakamoto, Y. 1994. *Global Transformation: Challenges to the State System* (Tokyo, United Nations University).

Shiva, V. 1987. "People's Ecology: The Chipko Movement," in R. B. J. Walker and Mendlovitz, eds., *Towards a Just World Peace: Perspectives from Social Movements* (London: Butterworths), 253–70.

Soros, G. 2002. *George Soros on Globalization* (New York: Public Affairs).

Wapner, P. 1996. "The Social Construction of Global Governance," paper presented at annual meeting, American Political Science Association, August 28–31, 1996.

Part Two
Normative Contours

Chapter 5
Toward Global Justice

The Changing Global Context

Major changes in the global setting over the course of the last few decades have produced significant trends in support of the pursuit of global justice. The American-led response to the al Qaeda attacks of September 11 seems likely to halt this progress, at least temporarily, but if a longer time horizon is adopted, it seems likely that the positive trends will resume. If winning the global war against terrorism depends on addressing the deep roots of such political violence embedded in the terrain of deprivation and grievance, then the indirect effect of the attacks could even be to strengthen an awareness that the promotion of justice is pragmatically integral to global security. So conceived, global justice is no longer understood as an expression of an altruistic spirit, but rather reflecting changing societal values and the benefits of cooperative nonviolent approaches to conflict resolution and dispute settlement.

At the same time, diverting attention from the global justice agenda reflects pressures additional to those associated with worries about transnational terrorism on a large scale. It would appear that American leaders have seized the occasion to promote an empire-building grand strategy either because only such a structure of authority can quell the megaterrorist threat or because the terrorist menace mobilizes domestic support in the United States for this project of global dominance. However understood, such a project works against the struggles for global justice, both by focusing attention on war/peace issues and giving rise to resistance and peace movements that challenge the imperial design at home and abroad.

The Afghanistan War, as initiated and waged, seemed at first reasonably related to the antiterrorism war, although its aftermath aroused a variety of doubts about American goals, intentions, and capabilities. But the shifting focus of global security attention has given rise to growing skepticism about whether the worldview of the Bush White House has any coherent understanding of how to deal with megaterrorism. There are also related concerns that "antiterrorism" performs as a cover for "empire-building."

The "axis of evil" phrase in President George Bush's 2002 State of the Union Address immediately set off alarm bells, raising anxieties around the world about the American definition of a wider war zone than that produced by the September 11 attacks, one that has neither an obvious end point nor any discernible spatial boundaries. The debate on Iraq policy leading to the Iraq War initiated without any approval by the UN Security Council and in direct violation of the Charter exemplifies the view that there exists widespread political opposition to the way the U.S. government is managing global security issues. The persistence of Iraqi opposition to the American occupation of the country reinforces these concerns, and leaves an acute uncertainty as to the political outcome of the Iraq War. Perhaps the major unanticipated costs of the imperial grand design will lead domestic forces in the United States to reconsider its security policy, and repudiate by elections and grassroots opposition the sort of extremist views that had been earlier uncritically accepted by the American people, seemingly lulled into a submissive condition by the September 11 experience, a climate of opinion falsely praised as "patriotism." (See Chapter 10.) Whether or not this change of mood occurs in the United States, it is more important than ever to remind ourselves of how much progress had been made during the 1990s with respect to global justice.

In this spirit, it is helpful to take account of six notable developments that encouraged the pursuit of global justice in the 1990s. As with corporate globalization, the end of the Cold War opened a political space that made it more feasible to adopt global justice initiatives. Several features of the global setting combined to give rise to the first normative revolution in the history of international relations: (1) the end of the ideological rivalry that accompanied the Cold War; (2) the focus of attention on world economic policy within a market-oriented framework; (3) the crucial role of international human rights standards and ethos in a series of peaceful transitions from authoritarian rule to constitutional democracy; (4) the heightened influence of transnational social forces and networks of activists in a wide array of normative (ethical, legal, social) arenas of decision; (5) the anticolonial movement and its sequel resting on an implementation of rights of self-determination; and (6) the geopolitics of ambivalence with respect to the conduct of humanitarian diplomacy either under the auspices of the UN or on some other basis. Each of these developments deserves some brief explanation.

End of the Cold War. The strategic rivalry between East and West between 1945 and the late 1980s tended to give an ideological edge to all discussions of normative issues, including human rights and matters of international accountability for criminality on the part of representatives of sovereign states. Despite this atmosphere of tension and conflict in the realm of values and ideas, remarkable progress was made during the Cold War in establishing an impressive foundation for human rights in international law. The United Nations provided the auspices for this notable achievement, realized principally through the medium of a series of intergovernmental negotiated texts that evolved from legal documents encompassing human rights as a whole to a focus on such specific sectors of concern as racial discrimination, the treatment of women and children, and the prohibition of torture.

After the fall of the Berlin Wall in 1989, these developments were largely freed from their polemical roles as instruments of international propaganda. From this time forward, failures by governments to respect fundamental human rights, especially in the civil and political domain, increasingly eroded the underpinnings of political legitimacy of a government. A consensus emerged among leading states that legitimate governance at the national level depended upon a minimal constitutionalism, a robust private sector, and at least nominal respect for human rights, including especially property rights and reasonably free contested elections to determine political leadership. Of course, this consensus was somewhat hypocritical as the behavior of many governments in "good standing" exhibited little respect for even such minimal human rights standards as the prohibition on torture.

In this regard, it is important to take account of changes in the development approaches of countries in the South. With disappointments associated with foreign economic assistance, the collapse of the hitherto leading socialist country, the impressive success of the East Asian market-oriented economies, the Chinese triumphant entry into the world market, and the failure of the 1970s movement for a New International Economic Order, there was a widespread abandonment by countries in the South of Marxist-oriented, and even distinctively "Third World" development perspectives. One expression of this new climate of opinion was a shift in emphasis by capital-importing countries from attempts to expropriate and regulate strictly foreign owned properties to ease constraints on profitability as part of a concerted effort to attract maximum private investment, which presupposed the stability of alien property rights, minimal regulation, low rates of taxation, and noninterference with the repatriation of profits. Obviously, the leading international financial institutions played a huge role in promoting this reorientation of national economic policies, including making the availability of capital and credit conducive to the establishment of conditions attractive to private investment, both domestic and international.

Corporate globalization. These factors associated with the disappearance of strategic rivalries, with their recurrent threats of major warfare and periodic competitive interventions, along with a shared preoccupation around the world concerning the dynamics of rapid economic growth, led to a new phase of world politics, most widely labeled as "globalization." An economistic emphasis on GDP growth, especially given the accompanying opposition to interferences with the efficient use of capital, created some of the discontents associated with emergent patterns of neo-liberal global economic governance (Falk 1999).

Part of the enthusiasm for such an unabashed embrace of neoliberal ideas by dominant forces around the world resulted from a new attitude toward the relationship between conditions favoring economic success and preferred political arrangements. At least rhetorically, and to some extent behaviorally, there was a shift in leadership circles involving an abandonment of the view that authoritarian rule, disciplining labor, and protecting entrepreneurial interests, was best for growth and investment. These attitudes were replaced by an endorsement of liberal models of democracy and a show of respect for human rights. This shift mainly focused on establishing conditions allowing free, multiparty elections and rights of political opposition, but was also generally supportive of efforts at the international level to respect human rights. It is important to take note of the transnational support given to the anti-apartheid movement as it related to change in South Africa and to the struggles of the peoples of East Europe to break free from Soviet and domestic oppressive rule. These successful movements to achieve human rights in politically difficult circumstances lent credibility to the overall campaign to promote human rights on a worldwide basis. Establishing an Office of the High Commissioner of Human Rights within the UN System was an institutional recognition in 1993 of the growing role and potential of human rights in international life.

Transitional justice. A closely related development concerned the manner with which constitutional democracy emerged in various national settings that had been previously brutally governed in an authoritarian and abusive manner that deserved repudiation retrospectively. This process of transition raised serious questions about the degree of scrutiny that should be directed at past crimes against humanity, torture, and other crimes associated with the exercise of state power. On the side of maximal scrutiny were those who argued in favor of individual accountability for serious past crimes of the state. On the side of minimal scrutiny were those who were either associated with or supportive of the former government or those who believed as a matter of prudence and "social peace" that it was necessary to give up or at least soften the quest for "justice" so as to sustain the process of democratization. This choice usually reflected pragmatic and subjective calculations, based especially on controversial assessments of the degree to which military and political forces from the old order retained significant influence within the armed forces, security and intelligence services, and other structures of governmental power. The most common formula for compromise in this context was to finesse the issue by opting for "truth" — that is, establishing a truth and reconciliation commission in some form, whose members were respected for their integrity and professional competence. In exchange for such an overt reckoning with the past, insisting on strict accounting and retributive justice relating to the criminality of the old regime was renounced. The widespread adoption of such an approach, especially in Latin America, caused a backlash, particularly among vicitimized communities, which identified and condemned the emergence of a "culture of impunity." In response, supporters of truth and reconciliation commissions in these circumstances generally argued that this reconstruction of the past was as far down the path of legality and deterrence that the political realities would allow. There has been a spirited debate on the appropriateness of diverse adjustments to the challenge of transitional justice under a variety of national circumstances (Hayner, 2000; Rotberg and Thompson, 2000).

As earlier indicated, the change in the global setting of the 1990s opened the way toward more ambitious approaches on these matters. The authority of the United Nations was used to establish special criminal tribunals (such as those in the former Yugoslavia, Rwanda, Sierre Leone, possibly East Timor, Cambodia, and Iraq). In turn, these ad hoc initiatives generated an impressive coalition of governments and nongovernmental organizations (NGOs) seeking to push the world even further in the direction of accountability through establishing an international criminal court as a permanent feature of global governance.

In this respect, the truth commission mechanism gathered material about the criminality of certain governments and their leaders, and thereby implicitly repudiated the misdeeds of the past and the political climate that allowed their occurrence. The commissions also acknowledged and documented the extent of victimization that always turned out to be even more gruesome and widespread than suspected even by the enemies of the old regime. Such an approach also imposed on the new political order an obligation to provide reassurances about its own commitment to the rule of law and the nonrepetition of human rights abuses. But such commissions should not be romanticized. They also fell short of some expectations, and by their nature exhibited an inability and unwillingness to impose accountability on those responsible for even the most unforgivable crimes of the past, or in most instances, even to identify clearly who were the main perpetrators. It is a matter of conjecture among sociologists and psychologists as to whether reconciliation can and should occur in the absence of some retributive mechanism that both punishes the most guilty and takes away ill-gotten gains. Some anthropologists have argued that without this retributive dimension, the disclosures associated with "truth" do not protect the society from a recurrence of violence, especially in settings where past abuses were associated with ethnic cleansing (Borneman, 2002; Rotberg and Thompson, 2000).

Activist networks. The unexpected impact of international human rights came about initially largely through the efforts of voluntary associations of citizens acting on the basis of transnational values and goals. Amnesty International and Human Rights Watch, particularly in relation to civil and political rights, developed surprisingly effective means to exert influence on governments. Environmental organizations such as Greenpeace and Friends of the Earth were also extremely effective, and tactically creative, addressing issues concerned with public health as well as environmental protection. Linkages were established between these transnational NGOs, local activists, and individuals and groups that were the targets of governmental abuse. Information became an instrument of "soft power" as most governments were reluctant to have their image tarnished by the publication of objective reports by respected civil society actors that could not be dismissed as hostile propaganda. Similarly, corporations became increasingly aware of their own vulnerability to well-targeted consumer boycotts in the event of economic behavior that encroached on human rights. This emergent transnational activism has attracted increasing academic attention. (Keck and Sikkink, 1998), as has the emergence of global civil society (Kaldor, 2003).

This activism in civil society has also selectively encouraged governments, especially those of a liberal democratic persuasion, to take human rights more seriously in forming their foreign policy. Western governments also realized during the latter stages of the Cold War that they enjoyed a definite advantage over communist governments with regard to civil and political rights. As a result, Western governments tended to put human rights increasingly on their foreign policy agendas, and gave such issues prominence in East/West negotiations, perhaps most saliently in Europe, especially in the aftermath of the Helsinki Accords of 1975. This agreement that stabilized the borders of Eastern Europe in exchange for an annual accounting of human rights adherence turned out to be historically relevant beyond the wildest expectations of its Western negotiators, both discrediting oppressive regimes and mobilizing domestic opposition in Soviet bloc countries during the 1980s around the assertion of legitimated demands for political freedoms and reforms. In the 1980s, the peaceful transition of Eastern European countries (with the partial and notable exception of Romania) and of the Soviet Union was greatly facilitated by the prior buildup of civic activism that rested its claims on demands for patterns of governance that respected international human rights standards.

Such activism also lent decisive international weight to the anti-apartheid movement, and especially led such governments as the United States and Great Britain to abandon their support of the South African government as a strategic ally in the Cold War and as a beneficial private sector arena. This movement also involved the whole of the United Nations in a concerted effort that overcame geopolitical tensions to exert pressure via sanctions and collective delegitimation on the racist regime in South Africa. The success of these pressures in producing a multiracial democracy without accompanying bloodshed was one of the political miracles of the 1990s, and demonstrated the degree to which grassroots activism when effectively linked to intergovernmental pressures can help produce dramatic societal changes. The impact of such activism should not be exaggerated. The indigenous struggle of the victims of apartheid was the most essential source of pressure, and provided the political and moral underpinning of the international movement.

Of course, it is notable, and a matter of controversy, that "human rights" in this activist transnational sense gave almost no attention to economic, social, and cultural rights. There have been recent attempts in both the North and South to rectify this imbalance. The Center for Economic and Social Rights, founded by a group of young American law school graduates in the mid-1990s, is an NGO of transnational scope that is explicitly dedicated to the implementation of these neglected international standards. Initiatives associated with opposition to certain aspects of corporate globalization, including resistance to the imposition of structural adjustment programs and antidebt coalitions, have moved even Western public opinion toward the gradual acknowledgement that economic and social rights often are accorded primacy by activists, and deserve at least a status of equivalence in the life experience of economically disadvantaged countries seeking to cope with the poverty and severe economic distress of a significant portion of their populations, often a substantial majority.

Recent problems associated with ethnic violence and encroachments on the survival of indigenous peoples have called attention to the importance of cultural rights (Lam, 2000). The terrorist attacks of September 11, including their apparent fanatical expression of religious extremism, is a further dramatic indication of the relevance of cultural rights for the agendas of transnational activist networks. The concern takes on an urgency in this new global context, giving sudden priority to cultural rights as part of the struggle to avoid "the war against global terrorism" escalating by either side into "a clash of civilizations" that would destructively widen the scope and add to the intensity of this new core conflict configuration.

The emergence of such networks has evolved to the point where it is plausible to posit the emergence of "global civil society" as a constituency of networks committed in various ways to the promotion and attainment of global justice across a wide range of issues. (See Chapter 4.) The strength of this new dimension of world politics has been augmented by a flexible capacity to enter into collaborative relationships with governments in the pursuit of shared goals with respect to global public goods. The most successful expressions of this collaborative process to date are the Anti-Personnel Landmines Treaty and the Rome Treaty leading the establishment of the International Criminal Court. But such collaboration has long been a formal and informal aspect of UN global conferences on such matters as environmental protection, women, and the resources of the oceans. It has also forged new identities that reshape citizenship and loyalties in deterritorializing ways that challenge the exclusivity of nationalist allegiances as administered by sovereign states, as well as traditional ideas of national patriotism. Such emergent patterns of citizenship are not anti-state, but are giving rise to multiple bonds of affiliation and identity associated with activist networks, regional and civilizational affinities, and a sense of global or planetary solidarity. There are also contradictory trends evident that threaten political fragmentation, a variety of ethnic and religious movements, and an assortment of micronationalisms producing turmoil and bloodshed in many parts of the world.

The anticolonial movement. A momentous change in the climate of opinion accompanied the movement of decolonization, bringing into global policy arenas normative ideas about fairness and justice, and of course, the right of self-determination given a historic role in restructuring international society. Increasingly, the legitimation of nationalist struggles against colonialism rested on overwhelming UN support for the right of self-determination available to all colonized peoples (provided that the exercise of the right did not result in the dismemberment of existing states, or even altering colonial boundaries, however artificial and ethnically divisive).

There are two relevant considerations. The first was the acceptance of a right of self-determination as a fundamental human right, which under favorable political circumstances at the end of the Cold War was extended beyond colonial and statist settings to reinforce secessionist movements following the breakup of the Soviet Union and in relation to the disintegration of the former Yugoslavia. The second involved the participation in world politics of a large number of non-Western states with demands for global reform, especially in the economic and political spheres, raising questions about the nature and priorities of global justice.

Geopolitics of ambivalence. In the 1990s there arose a new sense that the UN might find the authority and political support to act even with respect to civil strife and breakdowns of internal order resulting from impending or unfolding humanitarian catastrophes. The new phase of this process began in relation to famine and disease in Somalia during 1992, generating both an active effort under the UN to alleviate the suffering of the Somalis and a subsequent, clumsy American-led state-rebuilding initiative to overcome warlordism that aroused fierce indigenous political resistance to the international presence. This effort to consolidate political control in Somalia at the level of the state produced a backlash that led to lethal attacks on UN peacekeepers; eighteen American soldiers (and as many as a thousand Somalis) died in an urban firefight with forces in Somalia opposed to the political dimensions of the American presence, an incident popularized by the movie "Black Hawk Down."

The political difficulties associated with such undertakings combined with the vulnerability of peacekeeping forces to indigenous resistance led to a reluctance by leading states to rethink the scope and character of humanitarian interventions under UN auspices. This reluctance was particularly exhibited in relation to sub-Saharan African conflicts where costly interventions could not be explained and justified by governments from the perspective of their strategic interests. Such a Western unwillingness to get involved whatever the circumstance was painfully evident in the course of the refusal by the international community to do what it could to prevent genocide in Rwanda during 1994. Important UN members resisted taking even small steps that might have saved many lives, perhaps hundreds of thousands, in the face of the onslaught underway (Melvern, 2000). This post-Somalia mood also deeply altered the early stages of the UN response to ethnic cleansing in Bosnia, a process of Serb-led ethnic cleansing that reached its gruesome climax with the massacres of some seven thousand male Muslims that took place within a UN "safe haven" at Srebrenica in 1995 (Rieff, 1995). Against this background, it was surprising, although not entirely fair, that the UN was discredited and later progressively bypassed in the context of an impending humanitarian catastrophe in Kosovo, inducing "a coalition of the willing" to wage war in 1999 within the NATO framework to achieve effective protection for the increasingly vulnerable and abused Albanian Kosovar majority population. Such a process attained effectiveness as expressed by the departure of Serb military and police forces, but at the expense of international legality, opening up an undesirable gap between what is permissible according to international law and what is morally and politically legitimate by reference to fundamental human rights, including the prohibition on ethnic cleansing (Independent International Commission on Kosovo, 2001).

A further counterintuitive point is that many states' ambivalence in response to these extreme sets of circumstances produced some unexpected outcomes beneficial for the normative order. Such responses were meant partly to camouflage the unwillingness of major states to take risks or pay the costs of an effective humanitarian intervention, and partly to deflect public pressures as mediated through "the CNN factor" to protect the victims of oppressive state policies. The most important of these initiatives was the decision by the UN Security Council in 1993 first to establish and fund ad hoc international criminal tribunals for the prosecution of severe crimes of state associated with the breakup of Yugoslavia, and later to deal with genocide in Rwanda. Such an initiative allowed the UN and its members to regain some of the high moral ground without making any controversial commitment to intervene directly in a peacekeeping mode. Geoffrey Robertson describes the climate of opinion that led to the establishment of the Yugoslav tribunal as "a fig leaf to cover the UN's early reluctance to intervene in the Balkans" (Robertson, 2001, xvii–xviii). Such a step also revived the Nuremberg idea in the post–Cold War setting on the basis of a half century of legal development with respect to international humanitarian law and in view of human rights law generally. The momentum of this revival has persisted into the new century, heightened by the indictment, apprehension, and prosecution of Slobodan Milosevic, the individual viewed most responsible for inflaming Serb nationalism and presiding over its policies of ethnic criminality in Bosnia and Kosovo (Bass, 2000).

This revival in response to the Balkan turmoil triggered further impressive efforts throughout global civil society to establish a permanent international criminal court (ICC). This project enlisted the support of many governments and produced the major effort that resulted in the Rome Treaty of 1998. The ICC as agreed upon in the treaty is a product of many compromises, but even with restricted authority, it represents a potential institutional leap forward with regard to individual accountability for severe crimes of state and the extension of the rule of law in a manner that overrides earlier prerogatives of sovereignty. In this ironic regard, it is possible to conclude that in the 1990s this geopolitics of ambivalence relating to humanitarian peacekeeping led to a failure of the organized international community to both protect several peoples exposed to extreme threats and harm and to make the perpetrators of such abuse more likely than ever before to be brought to justice in some form.

In effect, the reluctance of leading states to regard humanitarian goals as worthy of the sacrifice of their citizens' lives or receiving a major commitment of resources, while at the same time responding to pressures to put a moral face on foreign policy, has had strange and contradictory effects. Among these has been to lend support and credibility to civil society pressures to impose accountability on leaders for crimes of state and to take rather ambitious steps to institutionalize the process. It always has been questionable whether the ICC would be accepted in practice by the most powerful states, especially, of course, the United States. This was the case before September 11, and is even more so since then.

The September 11 Attacks

The impacts of the megaterrorist attacks of September 11 on the global context and its normative order is uncertain at this point, but it is likely to cause an eclipse, at least temporarily, of efforts to carry forward earlier initiatives relating to global justice and kindred preoccupations with the equitable dimensions of global governance and the regulation of the world economy. The most immediate effect of mobilizing governments to engage in a war against global terrorism is displacing and redirecting economic and normative concerns, and again allowing security issues and geopolitical pragmatism to dominate the global policy agenda. Cooperative relations among governments to carry on "the global war against terrorism" necessarily leads to opportunistic diplomacy that overlooks instances of domestic oppression and human rights abuses in exchange for cooperation in pursuing "terrorists." The unilateralism of the American definition of legitimate wartime goals, especially in the aftermath of the Iraq War, suggests a period of turmoil and violence throughout international society that will pose insurmountable obstacles in the path of reformers and reform movements. At the same time, the anxiety generated by a new global setting of warfare is likely to produce strong countermovements by states and transnational social forces.

The analysis here suggests that the complexity and interconnectivity of the world order as a result of technological innovations is likely to make this eclipse of global justice a temporary phenomenon. Such an anticipation is also reinforced by the extent to which transnational activism is likely to reassert its demands for legitimate forms of global governance, which includes the extension of the rule of law and the institutionalization of procedures for accountability at national, regional, and global levels. Furthermore, there may even be unexpected outcomes, including a willingness by countries to participate in the establishment of accountability mechanisms and law enforcement procedures relating to terrorism in exchange for comparable commitments with respect to crimes against humanity, genocide, and international humanitarian law.

Without acknowledgement, and for reasons of strategic self-interest, rich countries are likely to adopt a new sense of resolve to address issues of poverty and development among the more economically distressed parts of the world. Such an outcome is not at all assured, as some counterterrorist analysts have been quick to point out that there has been little or no global terrorism emanating from the most disadvantaged of all parts of the world, sub-Saharan Africa. The more persuasive approach to this issue is to note that certain conditions, widespread poverty, despair, and humiliation give rise to extremist politics, and that such conditions have currently affected large portions of the Islamic world to the detriment of world peace and human well-being.

Implementing Accountability Norms: Options and Mechanisms

As suggested, the global context created favorable and diverse conditions, especially during most of the decade of the 1990s, for the pursuit of transnational justice. This pursuit was not only directed toward the rectification of present grievances. It also focused, perhaps to a greater, unprecedented extent, on the redress of historic wrongs. This focus can be described as a multifaceted worldwide phenomenon of responding to perceived examples of acute injustice previously inflicted on persecuted and victimized collective identities (such as race, religion, nationality, or gender). A useful overview of the range of restitution claims has been made by Elazar Barkan (Barkan, 2000).

In gaining an understanding of this pursuit of justice, it is useful to consider both the substantive type of injustices that have given rise to the perceived grievance and the mechanism of rectification that is invoked in response. Finally, it will be helpful to consider institutional and doctrinal

developments intended to regularize the process by which victimized col-
lectivities can be protected, either by their own initiative or through the
operations of global law enforcement mechanisms.

Several accounts of the emergence of this global justice movement need
to be delineated. First, a series of stages is evident that proceeds from the
evolution of human rights to their internationalization, and then further, a
range of moves to promote their enforcement have been taken. This
emphasis on the centrality of human rights is effectively argued by such
authors as Michael Ignatieff and Geoffrey Robertson (Ignatieff, 2001, Robertson, 2001; also Falk, 2000). Second, the willingness of private sector
actors (banks and corporations) and governments to acknowledge some
responsibility by offering substantial compensation for past wrongs, what
might be described as a restitution ethic can be noted; Barkan regards this
path of restitution as "a potentially new international morality ... a new
globalism" (Barkan, 2000, ix; Rickman, 1999). Third, a more synthetic
view of this dramatic heightening of global justice draws on a rights discourse, a restitution and accountability ethos, and various impulses to stabilize and legitimize world order (either to soften criticism of corporate
globalization or, more recently, as a contribution to waging war against
global terrorism). This article proceeds on the basis that this third view of
the transnational justice movement gives the best overall account. It
should be noted that none of these overviews very convincingly answers
the question of timing raised in the early part of this paper: Why the dramatic emphasis on global justice in the decade of the 1990s? Why not earlier? And why the prediction now of a temporary eclipse?

The Role and Nature of Historic Injustices

The purpose here is to identify the most salient injustices that have been
the source of initiatives designed to mitigate their bad memory and give
various forms of relief to victims and their representatives. Often, if not
invariably, the dynamic of redress is pursued relentlessly by a particular
community of victims, challenging the opposite dynamic of denial that is
embraced often unwittingly by the wider societal community, and certainly by the perpetrators and their supporters.

The Centrality of the Holocaust. Survivors of the Holocaust that
occurred in Nazi Germany had been very active and effective since 1945 in
efforts to secure various forms of relief. The magnitude of the crimes committed, particularly against the Jewish people in Europe, exerted a formative impact on the entire post–World War II imagination, especially in
combination with the guilt felt by the victorious liberal democracies of
Western Europe and North America. Such an interaction to varying
degrees was responsible for the Nuremberg Judgment, the criminalization
of genocide by treaty, the internationalization of human rights, the global

pursuit of Nazi era perpetrators of Nuremberg crimes, a variety of efforts to reverse the confiscation of Jewish property, and, more controversially, the establishment of the state of Israel. In this regard, the Asian victims of Japanese injustice and exploitation from the World War II era received far less attention, with the Tokyo Trials of Japanese leaders accused of war crimes receiving scant notice at the time and subsequently. It remains difficult to obtain the documentary record of the outcomes of these trials, and Japan was never placed under pressure comparable to Germany to renounce its past and restructure its future. As a result, and in the setting of a far less individualistic political culture, Asian victims of injustice have been far slower in the pursuit of their rights than were their European counterparts. The story is complex, and the explanation of the salience of the Holocaust contested, but the importance of Holocaust-related efforts to rectify Nazi criminality cannot be doubted.

After the years immediately following World War II, this activism associated with the victims of the Holocaust also was generally overtaken by the global preoccupations of the Cold War. But there were exceptions, the most notable of which was the overseas abduction and subsequent 1961 trial and execution of Adolph Eichmann in Israel. By this undertaking, Israel established an international precedent affirming the right of national courts to prosecute crimes against humanity wherever and whenever they occur, providing the foundation for what has later come to be known as "universal jurisdiction." There were other prosecutions under varying circumstances in several European countries associated with punishing those associated with Holocaust crimes. In his authoritative study, Gary Jonathan Bass argues that these post-Nuremberg trials were more effective in focusing on the Holocaust crimes, as Nuremberg had devoted its main attention to crimes against the peace committed by the expansionism of Nazi regime (Bass, 2000).

In the 1990s, however, the unfinished economic business of Holocaust claimants gained notoriety, achieving significant success in a number of areas: the recovery of so-called Holocaust gold and bank deposits from Swiss and other banks; the pursuit of proceeds from insurance policies issued on the lives of Holocaust victims but never paid; the recovery of stolen art treasures; and compensation for various categories of "slave labor" performed for the benefit of private German corporations. Billions of dollars were transferred to victims and their representatives, either on an individual basis or through lump sum arrangements. Criticisms were voiced about the monetization of suffering, alleging even the emergence of "a Holocaust industry." Also, lawyers were criticized for their large fees and many complaints were voiced about the differential success of various categories of victims. Those from Eastern Europe fared less well, as did the non-Jewish victims of Nazism, especially the Roma people, than their Jewish counterparts from Western Europe.

Despite such criticisms, these movements toward redress did accomplish a number of results that are significant in relation to the overall pursuit of global justice: validating and, to a degree, vindicating the rights of victims, even after the passage of years, to obtain economic redress for the violation of their property rights, including the right to receive compensation for work performed under abusive conditions; inspiring other non-Holocaust claimants to seek comparable forms of redress, especially those victimized by Japanese imperial policies in a manner discussed in the following section. The pressures for redress in relation to the Holocaust ordeal were not solely, or perhaps predominantly, associated with the vindication of legal rights. Moral suasion and the reputation of governments and private sector actors were also important factors, suggesting both the emergence of a climate of opinion that supported some response to claims by such victims and suggested adverse consequences for alleged private and public sector wrongdoers that took legalistic refuge by way of rules of evidence, prevailing practices in the past, and defensive denials of responsibility.

Asia/Pacific Redress. There is no doubt that the Holocaust redress experience inspired efforts by a range of other victim communities, but especially on the part of those that arose out of the experience of Japanese expansionism before and during World War II. In part, such a delayed pursuit of redress in the 1990s was explicitly tied to the primacy of the Holocaust as underscored by the title of Iris Chang's widely read book on the 1937 Nanking massacres, *The Rape of Nanking: The Forgotten Holocaust of World War II* (Chang, 1997; Li, Sabella, and Liu, 2002). Aside from the psychological advantages associated with Eurocentrism and the sheer horror associated with Auschwitz, the Asian/Pacific context was less hospitable to redress: the Japanese government was far less repentant than the German government; in a peace treaty with Japan, the United States had waived all individual claims, a legal obstacle for claimants that did not exist in the Holocaust setting; Japan had made several "voluntary" payments to Asian countries, and in exchange were excused by negotiated bilateral agreements from further legal responsibility; there was less of an Asian tradition supporting individual claims or collective responsibility by governmental or private sector actors than existed in the more rights oriented political culture of the West.

Despite this, Asian/Pacific concerns with redress picked up considerably in the 1990s, but it placed far less emphasis, for reasons just indicated, on legal rights to obtain economic restitution. It concentrated more on exerting an influence on public opinion, seemingly content to achieve symbolic satisfaction in informal arenas where past criminality could be confirmed, and by soliciting formal acknowledgement and repudiation, especially by the Japanese Government. With respect to war crimes in the countries occupied by Japan, public and academic meetings, often with the inclusion of Japanese participants, reconstructed the criminality alleged to have occurred. In effect, redress was sought by the activation of memory, its validation by responsible governmental leaders, and an intangible impression that by bringing such criminality to light it would prevent its recurrence in the future.

Global civil society also contributed to this activation of historical memory, especially in the form of participating in the organization and conduct of "citizens' tribunals" that confirmed allegations and reached conclusions, which included recommendations. The Japanese wartime practice of "sexual slavery" and "comfort women" was made the subject of a highly publicized proceeding in Japan (Chinkin, 2001).

In very recent years, more direct legal efforts to recover some form of compensation from Japan on behalf of various groups of victims, including those forced as prisoners of war into labor that benefited private firms and the Japanese war effort, have not succeeded for reasons earlier suggested. At the same time, the presentation of such claims and associated publicity has greatly heightened awareness of such abusive patterns, which itself seems to have a beneficial effect on the healing process, even after a lapse of decades.

Redress for Indigenous Peoples. Representatives of indigenous peoples have for the past thirty years or so made various efforts to internationalize their struggle to protect the remnants of their traditional prerogatives with respect to land, resources, and ways of life (Lam, 2000). There is great diversity of perspective and strategy, but a consensus as to a broad array of normative demands set forth in the 1994 Declaration of the Rights of Indigenous Peoples, which highlighted a still contested claim of a right of self-determination, and brought the worldview of indigenous peoples into the open for the first time ever. The UN has provided valuable and influential space for the articulation of this consensus in the form of the Informal Working Group on the Rights of Indigenous Populations that met annually for several weeks in Geneva under the auspices of the Committee against all Forms of Discrimination and Persecution.

The redress being sought was diverse, but was mainly future-oriented in the sense of seeking to protect what remained of the patrimony of indigenous peoples against the assaults associated with large-scale, modernizing development projects. There was widespread recognition by governments and by the United Nations that the grievances of indigenous peoples were founded on historic injustices of dramatic proportions, but also of present encroachment, and that some level of response should be encouraged. But what level? And within what framework of rights? Any attempt to rectify the massive past wrongs seemed outside the bounds of political feasibility, and so the focus shifted to preserving the status quo in the face of continuing assaults, which is itself a great undertaking in many specific instances, considering the developmental pressures brought to bear on traditional peoples whose lands and settlements so often stand in the way of large dams and hydroelectrical expansion, of urban and suburban building schemes, and of governmental policies of weapons testing and the licensing of private sector mining ventures and resource development schemes.

Reparations for Slavery. In recent years there have been increasingly more serious efforts by African governments and descendants of slaves in North America to seek reparations for the suffering associated with the institution of slavery and the associated bondage and taint endured by millions of individuals. Prior to the 1990s, such contentions had been dismissed as frivolous, divisive, and not worthy of serious discussion in responsible arenas, but the successful pursuit of Holocaust claims, especially those related to slave labor, lent an aura of plausibility to the contention that the victims of slavery, or their heirs, should be compensated to some extent and given a degree of symbolic satisfaction.

The 2001 UN Conference on Racism held in Durban, which was the target of hostile withdrawal by the U.S. delegation, acknowledged that slavery and the international slave trade were crimes against humanity "and should always have been so." The final declaration of the conference stops short of supporting reparations, and instead puts its emphasis on states "to honor the memory of the victims" and to call for the universal condemnation of slavery and its "reoccurrence prevented."

Political Crimes of State. The idea that even political leaders can be held accountable under international legal standards for crimes against their own citizenry was given its historic impetus at Nuremberg. Such accountability overrode contrary ideas of sovereign immunity, acts of state, and the territorial character of criminal law. After World War II, such standards of accountability were imposed on surviving leaders of Germany and Japan, but the notion of accountability was associated with wartime, and was applied in such a way as to give weight to allegations of "victors' justice." Along these lines, historian Richard Minear wrote a devastating analysis of the Tokyo War Crimes Tribunal (Minear, 1971). Telford Taylor, a respected member of the U.S. team of prosecutors at Nuremberg, wrote a far more positive appraisal of the comparable criminal process in the context of the German trials (Taylor, 1992). Despite serious shortcomings, the imposition of accountability at Nuremberg and Tokyo was based on trials in which the defendant was given an impressive degree of procedural due process. Those convicted and punished were clearly responsible for waging "aggressive war" and were more or less implicated in grossly inhumane practices.

At the same time, the governments that organized these trials and constructed world order after 1945 were not themselves ready to institutionalize what had been an ad hoc and flawed approach to accountability. The Nuremberg Principles were formulated in an authoritative form by the International Law Commission, and then endorsed by way of a UN General Assembly Resolution. In this sense, a normative framework for accountability was incorporated into international customary law in the early 1950s, and theoretically became binding on all states. But no institutional implementation was seriously contemplated until after the Cold War.

To the extent that the Nuremberg idea of accountability was kept alive during the cold war era, it was a result of activist individuals in civil society, and particularly in the United States during the latter stages of the Vietnam War. In this period, various acts of noncooperation with government policy, whether refusing to serve in the armed forces, pay taxes, or other forms of resistance, were justified by the existence of "a Nuremberg obligation." Individuals, it was argued, were obliged to obey international law, not their own government, with respect to fundamental issues relating to recourse to war and its conduct. Such arguments also stimulated antinuclear activists in North America and Western Europe to engage in various forms of nonviolent civil resistance based on the obligation of citizens to defy national law and policy and obey international law.

Notions of accountability resurfaced with a flourish during the 1990s. First of all, before the International Criminal Tribunal for former Yugoslavia there were international trials of individuals arising out of alleged crimes committed in the course of the Balkan Wars. And second, there was the spectacular Spanish indictment and subsequent 1998 British detention of General Augusto Pinochet for the notorious crimes committed during his tenure as head of state in Chile from 1976 through 1989. This incident encouraged wider scrutiny that extended to such controversial figures as Henry Kissinger, Saddam Hussein, Ariel Sharon, and others, especially facilitated by the activation of a revolutionary Belgian law conferring universal jurisdiction on Belgian courts with respect to such crimes of state. These developments also stimulated efforts to provide a more authoritative framework to guide national courts when asked to impose accountability on persons alleged to be responsible for past crimes of state. A collaborative effort of international law experts has produced The Princeton Principles on Universal Jurisdiction, an attempt to set forth guidelines for national judges in addressing issues of universal jurisdiction (Princeton University, 2001). At the same time, the American official line of objections to this upsurge of international efforts to impose criminal accountability has led to a degree of rollback, most dramatically, a diplomatic offensive against the Belgian law and practice with respect to universal jurisdiction that pressured the Belgian government to give up its law enforcement claims unless Belgians were victims of the abuse.

Modalities of Response

As Martha Minow has observed, "a century marked by human slaughter and torture, sadly, is not a unique century in human history. Perhaps more unusual than the facts of genocides and regimes of torture marking this era is the invention of new and distinctive legal forms of response" (Minow, 1998, 1). We need to underscore this realization that unspeakable mass crimes against people is not a departure from history, but the growing resolve to treat such behavior as unacceptable ruptures of the normative order of world society, and as such, acts that need to be formally and effectively repudiated is giving rise to a greater sense of responsibility on the part of international society in the face of such criminality at the level of the state. This repudiation relies on legal mechanisms to render "justice," to avoid endorsing retaliatory and vindictive violence, and to seek an eventual reconciliation through a combination of transparency (documenting the evil), retribution (punishing the perpetrators via a fair procedure), and forgiveness (shared resolve to move forward in a new spirit of reconciliation). As argued, this process gained momentum after the end of the Cold War, exemplified by Nelson Mandela's leadership in the last phases of the anti-apartheid movement, and is now suddenly placed in serious jeopardy, at least temporarily, by the response to events of September 11. This section briefly reviews the main lines of response that have been adopted to fit a wide range of national and global contexts.

If the focus here is on transnational justice, should the role of national institutions in addressing past instances of injustice be included? Given the interpenetration of the national and the global, the distinction has become extremely artificial for many, but not all, purposes. Here, the initiation of some procedure at least to document past criminality has become part of the rehabilitation process, signifying discontinuity with the past, which seeks to restore full legitimacy to a government. But also, an interactive dynamic is working in both directions. The judicial scrutiny of Pinochet in Spanish and, especially, British courts appeared to create a new receptivity to prosecuting Pinochet in Chile, after Pinochet was returned due to the British finding that he was not medically fit to stand trial. The truth and reconciliation process that became so widespread for the past two decades as an integral feature of transitions to democracy at the state level undoubtedly contributed to the willingness of many governments to support the entirely consistent idea of an international criminal court. The statute of such a court, as prefigured by the Rome Treaty, recognized the complementary character of national and international tribunals, while giving priority to national prosecution as an expression of deference to the Westphalian model of global authority.

Criminal Trials: National and International

There is no more dramatic instance of movement toward transnational justice than the indictment and prosecution of those responsible for the perpetration of unforgivable crimes, especially heads of state. This revival of the Nuremberg idea of accountability for violating fundamental international (and national) norms represents part of a wider process of seeking to limit sovereign discretion and to establish "responsible sovereignty" as a condition of membership in good standing of a state in international society. Thus allegations and indictments directed at Pinochet and Milosevic have received worldwide media attention and attract great public interest.

Beyond this, the trial of perpetrators of such international crimes, even if belatedly, achieves a form of retributive justice. Although the punishment can rarely fit the crime, given its character, it helps with the healing of victims and their families. Such trials also generate a documentary record of criminality that contributes to an ethos of prevention.

Of course, there are problematic aspects, as well. The International Criminal Tribunal for former Yugoslavia has been criticized as "politically" motivated. The indictment of Milosevic that occurred in the midst of a NATO attack on his country in 1999 is often mentioned in this regard, and has been stressed by Milosevic in his defense against the charges being brought against him at The Hague. If he was not indicted in relation to the Bosnian War where more severe instances of ethnic cleansing occurred, why did the prosecution seek indictments for his conduct in Kosovo? If it was claimed in reply that only his crimes in Kosovo could be established by available evidence, then why did the Hague Tribunal not wait until the military campaign had ended? Other criticisms related to the failure to give as much attention to Croatian and Bosniac crimes as to Serbian crimes, the slowness of the process, and the lightness of some of the sentences given the gravity of the allegations on which the indictment was based. Why has the parallel tribunal established in Arusha, Tanzania, to examine the crimes associated with the Rwanda mass killings of 1994 received such scant funding and attention? Why did the Hague prosecutorial process whitewash NATO's recourse to war without a UN endorsement, as well as give a clean bill of health to American military tactics, in the Kosovo War, which were widely challenged by independent scholars and journalists?

Invoking principles of universal jurisdiction, the use of national courts to prosecute international crimes committed by non-national governments or military officials has become controversial enough to be politically nonsustainable. The Belgian law that allowed prosecution of crimes against humanity wherever committed stimulated a discussion of judicial activism, but now the law has been amended out of existence as a result of the geopolitical backlash that its application provoked. The International Court of Justice, acting more conservatively in relation to the basic idea of sovereignty, suggested unanimously in a 2002 decision that government officials holding official positions enjoy unconditional diplomatic immunity; they cannot be indicted or prosecuted as long as they are in office. This left open the Pinochet issue of whether such individuals can be prosecuted subsequently for the crimes alleged during their period of government service. Criticism centers on issues of practicality and the unevenness of international society. In a world of states, such impositions of law undoubtedly disrupt diplomacy in some instances, and if applied widely to current leaders could likely generate acute international tensions, as was well illustrated by the Israeli and American reactions to the earlier Belgian initiatives. There exist wide disparities of subjective appreciation as to what constitutes criminality, especially when a government uses violence to deal with radical nationalist movements of self-determination. The processes of transnational justice have not yet come near to attaining the level of expectations associated with the rule of law, where equals are treated equally. Hence, it is an imperfect justice, with the strong treated differently than the weak, but still arguably an advance over widespread circumstances of "immunity" and "impunity."

It remains uncertain whether most leading states will decide to become parties to the International Criminal Court now that it is established. Past efforts to include terrorism among indictable international crimes by an international tribunal have foundered due to a lack of consensus as to whether "terrorism" should be defined to include violence by states against civilians, as to how nationalist and self-determination struggles should be treated, and whether capital punishment should be imposed. Such obstacles do not exist at a national level where states generally legislate their own self-serving definitions of terrorism.

Civil Litigation and Economic Reparations

Domestic legislation in several countries, especially in the federal units that constitute the United States, have facilitated class actions for Holocaust-related economic claims arising from past confiscations and thefts of property, slave labor, and nonperformance of economic duties. Payments in the billions of dollars have resulted; however, due to high legal fees and the large number of claimants, recovery on a per capita basis is still of mainly nominal and symbolic value. The compensation received makes no pretense of full restitution for the losses endured.

Similar initiatives dealing with the economic dimensions of Japan's abuses of fundamental property rights have not succeeded, and seem unlikely to for the reasons mentioned earlier. In part, this is due to the lesser leverage of the claimants, but it is also a result of the treaty waiver of private claims and the continuing support given to this legal defense in American courts in relation to the obligations of the Japanese government and Japanese corporations (accused of using slave labor throughout the Pacific).

American courts have also been used to obtain compensation by recourse to Federal litigation that is based on harms resulting from the commission of international crimes. In the celebrated case *Filartiga*, an American plaintiff was allowed to recover damages for torture endured in Paraguay on the theory that torture was an international crime under a previously ignored old American law, the Federal Tort Claims Act (*Filartiga v. Pena-Irala*, 1980). This promising line of judicial activism has generated a strong negative reaction in the Justice Department of the Bush presidency. The Attorney General, John Ashcroft, has mounted a major campaign to persuade Congress to repeal the law so as to avoid the alleged diplomatic side effects of such prosecutions.

The future role of national courts in implementing international criminal law and human rights standards is very much in doubt at present. If the geopolitical climate shaped by the current American leadership persists, it is likely that national courts will be allotted a greatly diminished role, especially in the United States — except for prosecutions associated with antiterrorism.

Truth and Reconciliation Commissions

As discussed earlier, under certain circumstances of peaceful transition to democracy, the criminality of the prior regime cannot be addressed in a retributive manner for a variety of political reasons. In these settings, the impulse to repudiate the past, to heal the wounds of victims and their families, and to pledge respect for rights in the future, recourse to a truth and reconciliation procedure often provides the most satisfactory and effective mechanism for acknowledgment of past crimes. The parameters of a particular commission are negotiated, reflecting the play of forces in each setting, and in some instances, it is possible that criminal prosecutions may complement the truth and reconciliation procedure. As in the South African instance, where amnesty was conditional on a full disclosure of past conduct, the ideas of truth and reconciliation are directly related to retributive justice. Depending on the particular arrangement, perpetrators may be named, as in the case of El Salvador, or merely the offenses described, as in the case of Chile. (See generally, Hayner, 2000).

Humanitarian Diplomacy

In the 1990s, one of the most important initiatives to protect abused or suffering peoples involved international undertakings of an interventionary character, preferably under UN auspices. Generally discussed under the rubric of "humanitarian intervention," such actions, if involving military force and a mandate to engage in state-building, were and remain controversial and challenge adherence to traditional notions of sovereignty. The main lines of objection were associated with legal arguments based on the UN Charter precluding interventions in matters "essentially within domestic jurisdiction" (Article 2(7)). The fundamental issue here is the balance between international accountability for wrongdoing and sovereign rights to exercise territorial supremacy. Efforts have been made to develop a principled framework by which to strike a balance between these two ordering ideas — implementing international standards to prevent humanitarian catastrophe and respect for territorial sovereignty (Independent International Commission on Kosovo 2001, 191–98; Wheeler, 2000).

The contested practice of humanitarian intervention with and without UN authorization seemed a central issue in the 1990s. The controversy and mixed results of the Kosovo War, together with the shift in priorities after September 11, make the future prospect of humanitarian intervention seem rather remote. At the same time, the global climate could change rapidly in the face of severe instances of suffering and public pressures mounted to intervene in specific places. The blurred domestic/international boundary makes it likely that the challenge of humanitarian intervention, although pushed now toward the background, will reemerge in the years ahead, particularly in Africa where several peacekeeping operations are currently underway that contain varying elements of humanitarian intervention, although not expressed in this language.

The Promise of the Future: Finding Hope

The pursuit of transnational justice was vastly accelerated in the 1990s, but is likely to be sidelined in the early part of the twenty-first century as a result of the new preoccupation with global terrorism. At the same time, the momentum that underlies the development of international human rights and accountability movements is likely to be sustained even in this period by transnational social forces operating within global civil society. The move from normative architecture (framing rights and duties) to implementation and enforcement seems irreversible. In this sense, institutional innovations, together with public opinion, are likely to keep the agenda of transnational justice alive — despite the shift in geopolitical mood. And even this shift may have unanticipated consequences, such as creating a more effective framework for combating transnational crime, including its most virulent expression, antistate terrorism.

The perspective adopted here also takes note of the degree to which the confidence of ordinary people in the justice of international life, especially in developing countries, is currently at a low ebb. This dynamic of demoralization reflects several related concerns: frustration with the fruits of decolonization; widespread conviction that international order is sustained by the imposition of double standards as determined by the rich and powerful countries of the North; perceptions that the benefits and burdens of globalization are spread inequitably, with the most vulnerable peoples, countries, and regions unfairly burdened while the more economically privileged parts of the world benefit disproportionately; a declining commitment to development assistance and debt relief; and an absence of institutional opportunities to express these concerns in an effective manner.

At this stage, the prospects for more humane approaches to global governance will depend principally on the activism and imaginative tactics of civil society and those governments that can see beyond the geopolitical tensions of the post–September 11 world. The concreteness of such an engagement with reform initiatives is likely to be tested in relation to establishing the following initiatives, associated respectively with accountability, self-determination, and global democracy: an International Criminal Court, a Palestinian state in accordance with international law and human rights, and the establishment of a global peoples assembly.

Toward an International Criminal Court

The project to establish a permanent international criminal court was initiated after the World War II trials of the defeated political and military leaders of Germany and Japan. The initial idea was to create institutional regularity for the application of international criminal law, thereby lifting the prospect of individual accountability from beneath the clouds of criticism associated with "victors' justice." As early as 1948, the UN General Assembly instructed the International Law Commission (ILC) to study the issue. But the momentum behind such an initiative was lost, a casualty of the cold war impasse that blocked many initiatives for decades. Then, in mid 1990s in the aftermath of establishing the ad hoc tribunals for former Yugoslavia and Rwanda, the General Assembly asked the ILC to submit a draft statute of an international criminal court. In 1996 the General Assembly carried the process a step further, mandating a diplomatic conference that would seek intergovernmental agreement on the establishment of such a tribunal. The conference was held in Rome in 1998, leading to the adoption in treaty form of the Rome Statute of the International Criminal Court, adopted by a vote of 120-7, with twenty-one abstentions. The Court has been established in 2002 after the UN receives a sixtieth ratification.

The ICC has authority to prosecute the following crimes: genocide, crimes against humanity, war crimes, and the crime of aggression (in the event that the definition and condition of application of this last crime is reached). The exercise of criminal jurisdiction is limited by the acceptance of the complementarity principle by which the ICC can only act if systems of national justice fail to indict and prosecute those alleged to be guilty of such crimes. In this sense, the ICC is a second line of protection, with primary reliance placed on national judicial systems. According to the Rome Statute, prosecution can only be initiated if the state of the victim and the state with custody over the individual have both ratified the treaty. Another contested issue involved the capacity of the Security Council to interfere with the jurisdiction of the ICC. After much debate, a compromise proposal put forward by Singapore was accepted. It allowed the Security Council to halt prosecution for one year, renewable for a further year, provided nine of the fifteen members voted to do so; and a veto cast by one of the permanent members could not block such a vote. Some important countries, including the United States, have indicated a refusal to commit their governments to the treaty in its present form. There is controversy as to whether the ICC can play a constructive role without the participation of leading states.

The establishment of an ICC that is widely ratified is a promising innovation (Shelton, 2000). It provides a measure of legal protection against the worst abuses of state power directed at people. It limits territorial sovereignty by making leaders accountable to external standards. Such accountability may have a deterrent effect. It also provides those victimized by the crimes with vindication and punitive relief. It extends the rule of law to the behavior of the highest officials and to those who act under the color of their authority. By institutionalizing such accountability rather than imposing it on an ad hoc basis, there is great hope equals will begin to be treated equally, and those who are victimized can look to the organized international community for the administration of minimal criminal justice.

If and when the ICC comes into existence, formidable obstacles will remain. At the most elementary level are issues of funding and judicial independence. At a more fundamental level are issues of parity, especially whether the jurisdiction of the ICC can be effectively extended to alleged offenders in the most powerful countries. Also at issue are the practical difficulties of determining whether justice can be consistently and reliably rendered in domestic courts where nationalism is likely to cloud the issue of responsibility. As the Pinochet litigation dramatized, there is also evolving support for the exercise of universal jurisdiction by domestic courts — that is, holding an individual subject to indictment and prosecution for crimes of state wherever and whenever they took place. Such support does not yet exist, as the World Court decision in 2002 on diplomatic immunity disclosed, for extending this responsibility to high government officials while they remain in office.

Toward a Palestinian State

No issue has been more troubling to the peoples of developing countries, especially the Middle East, than the inability of the international community to find a path to Palestinian self-determination. The frustration of Palestinian rights has been widely seen as the most vivid expression of double standards in international life, thereby undermining respect in general for international law and the UN. The fulfillment of such a Palestinian quest could go far in restoring international confidence in the current structure of world order.

As of 2001, there is a broad consensus that the peace process should be renewed, hopefully leading to the establishment of a viable Palestinian state and the normalization of Israel/Palestine relations. The nature of the peace process and the content of viability remain the subject of intense controversy. The suffering endured by the people of Palestine, the ordeal of violence experienced for decades by peoples of both Israel and Palestine, and the instability of the region generated by the unresolved character of the encounter between Israel and the Palestinian people give the international community a strong interest in finding a fair and stable solution. There are concerns that the present framework of relations between the Israelis and Palestinians has reached a tragic impasse for both sides, and that fresh thinking is needed to avoid a continued drift of occupation and terrorism from persisting, if not escalating.

As of 1993, the parties attempted a peace process based on an agreed Oslo framework of principles, with the United States playing a third-party role. These negotiations reached contested results as to whether or not they provided a fair solution that almost secured the assent of both Israel and Palestine (Kapeliouk, 2002; Beilin, 2001; Manley, 2001). One widely endorsed approach is to resume this Oslo Peace Process on the basis of the recommendations of the International Commission chaired by former senator George Mitchell and known as "The Mitchell Report," appointed by Bill Clinton after a Middle East conference of governments in late 2000 seeking to end violence. The report essentially froze the construction of Israeli settlements, established a firm ceasefire based on suppression of militants by the Palestinian National Authority, and resumed negotiations between the two governments on final status arrangements. This approach allows the parties to bargain directly with one another, the bilateral diplomacy being guided or facilitated by the United States. Such a process is, for obvious reasons, shaped by asymmetries of power and is unlikely to yield a fair or stable outcome.

Another approach would be to combine what is currently being proposed to revive the peace process of the 1990s with a commitment to adhere to a framework of international humanitarian law while negotiations proceed, especially the application of the Fourth Geneva Convention on the Protection of Civilians. In practical terms, adherence would prohibit settlements, collective punishments, and targeted assassinations. It would also prohibit terrorism as violence directed at civilians and civilian society in all its forms, whether under the auspices of the state or by armed nonstate organizations.

In addition to international law, deference to UN authority in searching for the content of a fair solution would be an important step forward in seeking Palestinian self-determination and a secure future for both Israelis and Palestinians. Such deference could help identify the contours of a solution of the difficult questions of the status of Jerusalem and the return of Palestinian refugees. It could also give more than rhetorical meaning to the implementation of Security Council resolutions 242 and 338, the mantra of consensus that has been repeated without behavioral consequences for decades — that is, since the end of the 1967 War, which initiated the occupation of the West Bank and Gaza.

The main point here is that a peace process that itself exhibits respect for the relevant guidelines of international humanitarian law would give far greater confidence that any outcome reached would be fair to both sides. This approach would contrast with the Oslo years, during which Palestinian allegations of violations of their legal rights were brushed aside as interferences with the peace process or as matters to be resolved by the negotiations. Israel's argument insisted that Palestinian complaints should not interfere with the design of final status arrangements. Such a pattern allowed "facts on the ground" to double the number of Israeli settlements and change the demographic structure of Jerusalem while the Oslo process unfolded, and enabled an elaborate infrastructure of expensive bypass roads connecting the settlements to pre-1967 Israel to be built in the West Bank, greatly complicating negotiations, encroaching on Palestinian land, and embittering important segments of Palestinian public opinion.

It should be emphasized that a legitimate peace process needs to reflect the initial UN resolve and widespread global consensus to partition the historic mandate of Palestine so that Israeli and Palestinians would each have a homeland sufficient to sustain a fully sovereign state. At this stage, such a vision takes on a sense of urgency that is shared throughout the world. The outcome of a peace process can only result in real peace if both peoples are given independent and secure states that enjoy equivalent, sovereign rights. It needs to be better appreciated by global public opinion that the security of Palestine is no less important and no less precarious than the security of Israel. Such an equivalence of benefits might be best epitomized by the abandonment of a sovereignty-oriented approach in relation to the administration of Jerusalem. The best solution for all concerned is internationalizing this much contested holy city under the auspices of the United Nations, or perhaps under another independent, supranational entity. Such an arrangement could maintain a unity of governance and give expression to the Christian interest, and also affect the inspirational idea that Jerusalem belongs to the peoples of the world.

The key to achieving a solution to the Israel/Palestine conflict is the acceptance by both governments of a process that acknowledges and implements international law and human rights, and treats several important consensus decisions within the United Nations with respect. If the Palestinians are forced to swallow a geopolitical bargain, reflecting the existing inequality of diplomatic, economic, and military capabilities, the results will be unstable and, in the end, nonviable, confronting Israel as well with the disillusioning prospect of renewed hostilities.

Even though the leadership on both sides will likely prove reluctant in considering this reoriented approach, it would be a creative contribution to resolving this endless struggle for the international community to promote a a solution that takes account of the interests of both peoples, of the region, and of the world, and then commit the resources and facilitate the arrangements that would bring such a vision to reality. It would greatly raise confidence in the problem-solving and justice-promoting capacities of the organized international community.

Toward a Global Peoples Assembly

A current deficiency in the structure of international society relates to the issue of representation. Such an issue is sometimes associated with the existence of a global democratic deficit — that is, the insufficiency of institutional arenas and procedures in relation to the effective realization of democratic values. The system of representation embodied in the UN as constituted in 1945 was based on sovereign states. Such a system reflected the values of the day, including the legitimacy of territorial governance premised on antidemocratic principles. But the global setting has changed in crucial respects: although states retain their primacy, the stage of world politics must now be shared with private sector actors and transnational social forces. The UN secretary general has made a number of suggestions in recent years about taking structural account of these changes. One expression of this concern is the Global Compact that was established to create a role for multinational corporations within the UN System, giving these corporate actors a certain status of global citizenship in exchange for their voluntary acceptance of international operating standards relating to the environment, human rights, and labor practices.

Another expression is the Millennial Assembly of Global Civil Society, which convened in 2001. It produced an unprecedented gathering of NGO representatives at the United Nations who articulated a vision of the future based on the aspirations of global civil society. Unfortunately, this historic event was held on the condition that it would not become a recurring feature of UN operations, and was expressly mandated for one time only.

Both of these adaptations significantly retain the vitality and relevance of the UN and align forms of government with the norms of global democracy. The extension of the rule of law helps achieve a reliable and equitable global order based on treating equals equally to a far greater extent than they currently are. A Global Peoples Assembly (GPA) is concerned with enhancing the quality of global dialogue, giving a voice to people unrepresented by government and ensuring that nongovernmental and civil society perspectives enter the global policymaking process in a regular fashion. A prime dimension of any democratic order involves participatory rights, and at present, peoples, citizens associations, and NGOS have no arena of their own within the UN system or at the global level. The regional experience in Europe with the European Parliament illustrates the benefits of such institutions, acquiring stature and influence over the years despite modest beginnings and early dismissive attitudes.

Of course, establishing a GPA would be a formidable challenge. Aside from expecting strong resistance by some states, there are huge, genuine problems of representation and funding. Devising efficient and responsible operating procedures and authority for such a body would also require patience, imagination, and experience. At this stage, it would be a step in the right direction to initiate a discussion on the general issue of global democracy and civic participation, with the project of establishing a GPA as one means of realization (Falk and Strauss, 1997, 1999, 2000, 2001).

Establishing a GPA would also compensate for the reduced availability of UN global conference arenas as opportunities for democratizing participation by transnational social forces representative of global civil society. Such a dynamic did occur in the 1990s, contributing to a sense of popular participation in the global policy process. It also occasioned a statist reaction to such events, derided by some governments as "spectacles" without tangible outcomes, making it unlikely that such events will be held nearly as frequently on the central world order challenges of the day. A GPA could help provide an alternative forum viewed initially as an experiment in the democratizing of world order, and acknowledge that, to retain their legitimacy, the world's authority structures must take active initiatives to incorporate global civil society into their institutions of representation. At the very least, the time to contemplate such moves has arrived, and responds to the sense of many peoples throughout the developing world that their voices, priorities, and vulnerabilities are not heeded, either within the United Nations or in the wider behavioral and political patterns of world politics.

A Concluding Note

The three prescriptive ideas just delineated are illustrative and not meant to be exhaustive. Their common intention is to sustain and revive the momentum of the 1990s in the world after September 11 with respect to trends toward global justice. The renewed stress on "security" needs to be the occasion for a variety of perspectives to enter a global dialogue that includes the advocacy of "human security." In this sense, the security of states is complemented by the security of peoples, and the security of peoples is enhanced by the realization of global justice and democratic practices. Abstractions are not enough. Concrete steps must be taken to restore the confidence of the peoples of the world, especially now amidst what increasingly appears to be a war of global scope combined with a prolonged and deepening world economic recession.

References

Barkan, E. 2000. *The Moral Guilt of Nations: Restitution and Negotiating Historic Injustices*. New York: W.W. Norton.

Bass, G. J. 2000. I. Princeton, N.J.: Princeton University Press.

Beilin, Y. 2001. *A Manual for a Wounded Dove* (in Hebrew). Tel Aviv: Yedioth Ahronoth Books.

Borneman, J. 2002. "Reconciliation after Ethnic Cleansing: Listening, Retribution, and Affliction," *Public Culture* 14: 281–304.

Chang, Iris. 1997. *The Rape of Nanking: The Forgotten Holocaust of World War II*. New York: Penguin Books.

Chinkin, C. M. 2001. "Women's International Tribunal on Japanese Military Sexual Slavery," *American Journal of International Law* 95 (2): 335–41.

Falk, R. 1999. *Predatory Globalization: A Critique*. Cambridge, UK: Polity Press.

Falk, R. 2000. *Human Rights Horizons: The Pursuit of Justice in a Globalizing World*. New York: Routledge.

Falk, R., and A. Strauss. 1997. "For a Global Peoples Assembly," *International Herald Tribune*, Nov. 14, 1997.

Falk, R., and A. Strauss. 1999. "Globalization Needs a Dose of Democracy," *International Herald Tribune*, Oct. 5, 1999.

Falk, R., and A. Strauss. 2000. "On the Creation of a Global Peoples Assembly: Legitimacy and the Power of Popular Sovereignty," *Stanford Journal of International Law* 36, 2: 191–219.

Falk, R., and A. Strauss. 2001. "Toward Global Parliament," *Foreign Affairs* 80, 1, 212–20.

Filartiga v. Pena-Irala. 1980. United States Court of Appeals, 2nd Circuit.

Hayner, P. B. 2000. *Unspeakable Truths: Confronting State Terror and Atrocities*. New York: Routledge.

Ignatieff, M. 2001. *Human Rights as Politics and Idolotry*. Princeton, N.J.: Princeton University Press.

Independent International Commission on Kosovo. 2001. *Kosovo Report: Conflict, Response, Lessons Learned*. Oxford, UK: Oxford University Press.

Kaldor, M. H. 2003. *Global Civil Society: A New Phenomenon*. Cambridge, UK: Polity Press.

Kapeliouk, A. 2002. "A Partner for the Future." *Le Monde Diplomatique*, Feb. 2002.

Keck, M., and K. Sikkink. 1998. *Activists beyond Borders: Advocacy Networks beyond Borders*. Ithaca, N.Y.: Cornell University Press.

Lam, M. C. 2000. *At the Edge of the State: Indigenous Peoples and Self-Determination*. Ardsley, N.Y.: Transnational Publishers.

Li, F. F., R. Sabella, and D. Liu, eds. 2002. *Nanking 1937: Memory and Healing*. Armonk, N.Y.: M. E. Sharpe.

Manley, R., and Hussein Agha. 2001. "Camp David: The Tragedy of Errors." *New York Review of Books*, Aug. 9.

Melvern, L. 2000. *A People Betrayed: The Role of the West in Rwanda's Genocide*. London: Zed.

Minow, M. 1998. *Between Vengeance and Forgiveness: Facing History after Genocide and Mass Violence*. Boston, Mass.: Beacon Press.

Minear, R. H. 1971. *Victors' Justice: The Tokyo War Crimes Trial*. Princeton, N.J.: Princeton University Press.

Princeton University, Law and Public Affairs Program. 2001. *The Princeton Principles on Universal Jurisdiction*. Princeton, N.J.: Princeton University Press.

Rickman, G. J. 1999. *Swiss Banks and Jewish Souls*. New Brunswick, N.J.: Transaction Publishers.

Rieff, David. 1995. *Slaughterhouse*. New York: Simon & Schuster.

Robertson, G. 2001. *Crimes against Humanity: The Struggle for Global Justice*. New York: New Press.

Rotberg, R. and D. Thompson, eds. 2000. *Truth v. Justice: The Morality of Truth Commissions*. Princeton, NJ: Princeton University Press.

Shelton, D., ed. 2000. *International Crimes, Peace, Human Rights: The Role of the International Criminal Court*. Ardsley, N.Y.: Transnational Publishers.

Taylor, Telford. 1992. *The Anatomy of the Nuremberg Trials: A Personal Memoir*. New York: Knopf.

Wheeler, N. J. 2000. *Saving Strangers: Humanitarian Intervention in International Society*. Oxford, UK: Oxford University Press.

Chapter 6
Religious Resurgence

Points of Departure

Even before the September 11 attacks, the relevance of religion to global governance was a subject of controversy and confusion. After the Cold War, it was the energies of Islam that mounted the greatest threat to the sort of world order the West was championing, which rested on a domestic governance model of constitutionalism, a strong private sector economy, and an implicitly secular/scientific worldview. The role of global institutions was mainly a facilitative one, especially with respect to the smooth operations of the world economy, but also served the secondary interests of states and the state system. This vision of a future based on liberal values of moderate states and robust markets was widely promoted as the best path to progress and prosperity, especially as underpinned by a growing willingness of governments to acknowledge the authority of human rights (narrowly conceived as civil and political rights). Such a vision was no longer challenged ideologically by Marxist/Leninist thinking or geopolitically by a bloc of states under the dominion of a nuclear superpower. Indeed, the collapse of the Soviet Union, the embrace of the liberal model by the successor states in Asia, and the incredible rate of capitalist growth achieved by Communist China in the 1990s seemed to confirm the historical weight of a post-Marxist materialist and market-guided approach to global politics.

In retrospect, it is evident that such an outlook was a mixture of wishful thinking and blinkered perception. There were clear indications even before the end of the Cold War that this Western model of the future of states and world society was not universally acceptable, especially in the countries of the South. The Iranian Revolution in 1978–1979 against the Shah's White Revolution prefigured larger trouble. The emergence on the world stage of Ayatollah Khomeini suggested the potency of another way of envisioning governance and human destiny that rested on traditional values, the primacy of religious leaders and institutions in shaping the life of society, and a deep-seated political and cultural hostility to the West and Western values. Beyond this, Khomeini enunciated what amounted to a declaration of war against the United States and its worldview, calling America "the Great Satan" (an Islamic anticipation of "axis of evil"!). What was most significant about this unexpectedly formidable challenge was that it mobilized Iranian society to rise en masse and overthrow a leader who had previously been regarded as strong and secure. It is worth recalling that the government of the Shah of Iran enjoyed the ardent patronage of the United States, and also managed to have positive diplomatic relations with neighboring states including the Soviet Union, Iraq, and Turkey. Khomeini's message also seemed to resonate powerfully beyond Iran with "the Islamic street," the peoples of the Islamic world even as it frightened their secular leaders who had staked their credibility on the Western model of development and modernization. When youthful Islamic radicals seized the American embassy in Tehran in late 1979, the U.S. government was embarrassed and frustrated while the American diplomatic community was held hostage as the TV cameras churned this inflammatory footage day after day for well over a year, intensifying the impression that political Islam conceived of America as its main enemy.

The Iranian Revolution had these two faces: to base domestic governance on Islam, relying on *sharia* law, and to define the historical situation by referring to a postcolonial struggle of Third World countries against American-led globalization, which included secularization. Both of these faces found varying parallel expressions in other civilizational circumstances. The rise of Hindu nationalism in India was directed, at least initially, against an abandonment of tradition so as to achieve the benefits of economic globalization, although it ended up embracing the most salient geopolitics of modernity by crossing the nuclear threshold and seemingly moving toward an alliance with the United States — especially in the aftermath of September 11, when both countries viewed their prime adversaries as associated with Islamic extremism. Even authoritarian China, with its long antimetaphysical cultural traditions, seemed most challenged from within by the religious movement known as the Fulan Gong and by the Muslim separatist Uigur movement in the Xinjiang province seeking to establish an independent East Turkistan — alleged by Beijing to have close relations with Osama bin Laden and al Qaeda. Elsewhere, as in Turkey, Pakistan, Russia, the Philippines, Indonesia, and Malaysia, extremist opposition and separatist movements inspired by Islam pose serious threats to public order that seem impossible to eliminate under current conditions.

In the West, especially the United States, the political leverage of the religious right was more strongly felt than ever before in the central citadels of governance, although this influence has been largely concealed and indirect, and the main global perceptions have involved anxieties about American empire-building and global reach. The fear of American cultural and economic primacy was paramount in Asia, where economic globalization was uncritically pursued by most of the governments, at least until the roadblocks of the Asian Economic Crisis of 1997, leading the most visible resistance to take mainly a cultural form. Moves to stress "Asian values," which thinly masked growing concerns about U.S. dominance, were seen to uphold civilizational identities while reaping the benefit of the world economy. Shortly thereafter, first at the 1999 Seattle meetings of the World Trade Organization (WTO) and later at various meetings associated with the management of globalization, climaxing at the Geneva meeting of the G-8 in the summer of 2001, a grassroots antiglobalization movement took shape that went further, and challenged the American led market-driven view of global policy as unfair in its impacts, especially on the poor in the South, and antidemocratic in its management. (See Chapter 4.)

Against such a background, it is not surprising that the Huntington thesis of "a clash of civilizations" caused a stir when it first appeared in 1992, provoking a strong countertendency in ensuing years that has endured beneath the banner of "a dialogue of civilizations." The clash thesis seemed dangerous and simplistic, drawing ethnic and religious battle lines that anticipated a new epoch of cultural wars based on intercivilizational enmity, culminating in the slogan "the West against the rest." Such an outlook was at odds with the globalization thesis, as well as with the liberal idea that the American model of state and global governance was the only relevant model for the achievement of a human rights culture and global prosperity, and could and should be exported to non-Western countries. By emphasizing civilizational identities, the clash thesis also rejected the economic determinism of the globalization model that seemed to make markets the new driving force of history, thereby perversely adopting the basic Marxist hypothesis of materialism at the very moment when Marxism had lost its historical relevance as an ideological weapon previously wielded against capitalism. It was as if the East/West struggle was a façade disguising a deeper commonality of worldview that could only become manifest with the collapse of one of the antagonists.

Counterposing culture to economics created an opening for religion that had seemed closed by reference to either economistic or highly rationalistic worldviews that were essential features of modernity as shaped by the West. And finally, by asserting "civilizations" as the unit of primary relevance to the future, Huntington encouraged the view that the long period of dominance exercised by territorial sovereign states was in the process of being superseded, which put into question traditional state-centric forms of global governance.[1] But by linking civilizational identities with the intensification of conflict, the clash thesis cast a shadow over the resurgence of non-Western cultural and religious identities, seeming to suggest that a more peaceful world would result from embracing the technological gifts of modernity and the organizational benefits of a networked world, the alleged wave of a humanistic future.[2]

It against this complex background that the events of September 11 and their aftermath must be taken into account. The character of the attack, its inspiration deriving from Osama bin Laden's extremist views of Islamic faith and his genocidal hostility directed against Americans, Jews, and "Crusaders," gave this experience of apocalyptic terrorism religious overtones.[3] These overtones were reinforced by the identity of the hijackers as militant foot soldiers of Islam fully prepared to engage in suicidal missions of megaterrorism. In fashioning a response, the U.S. government has consistently designated the enemy as "terrorism," and not Islam, insisting that Arab Americans and adherents of Islam should not be singled out for discrimination. But the practices of the U.S. government at home and abroad have contradicted these attitudes, seemingly targeting Islam and Arab Americans as inherently suspect, and often the object of humiliation. At the same time, the wider sympathies evoked by the Bin Laden outlook, especially its castigation of the United States for its policies toward Palestinians, its maintenance of sanctions against Iraq a decade after the Gulf War ceasefire, and its general military encroachment on the most sacred Islamic sites, suggest that the risk of provoking a civilizational war cannot be ignored, nor can the relevance of religion to the encounter be overlooked.

It is not surprising that there are contentions in this setting that the September 11 attacks prove that Huntington was, after all, correct in his main thesis, even prophetic.[4] Equally disturbing, with dangerous policy implications, are misleading civilizational readouts that suggest that Osama Bin Laden was emboldened to act because the United States was squeamish about the use of force in response to prior terrorist attacks and instances where its troops experienced resistance that produced casualties, most notably in Somalia during 1993 peacekeeping operations.[5] Bin Laden encouraged these conjectures by his own apparent confusion about the unwillingness of the United States to accept losses where its strategic interests were low or nonexistent, as in Somalia, as contrasted with its robust engagement with the defense of allies and oil, as in the Gulf War.

An unfortunate aspect of the current world setting is the polarization of views about the relevance of religion to humane forms of global governance. There are those who view religion as disposed toward extremism, even terrorism, as soon as it abandons its proper modernist role as a matter of private faith and intrudes upon public space, especially on governance. The most ardent antisecular opponents insist on the opposite view, which contends that without basing governance on the dictates of religious doctrine and values, the inevitable result is decadence, decline, and impotence. This chapter seeks to advance a different view of the relevance of religion. It argues that all great religions have two broad tendencies (and many shades of variation in each) within their traditions: the first is to be universalistic and tolerant toward those who hold other convictions and identities; the second is to be exclusivist and insistent that there exists only one true path to salvation, which, if not taken results in failure and futility, if not evil. From such a standpoint, the first orientation of religion is constructive, useful, and essential if the world is to find its way toward humane global governance in the decades ahead; the second is regressive and carries with it a genuine danger of a new cycle of religious warfare carried out on a civilizational scale. The best hope for the future is to give prominence and support to this universalizing influence of religion and, at the same time, to marginalize and discredit dangerous forms of religious extremism based on a variety of alleged dualisms between good and evil.

It should also be noted that secular views that hold the line most rigidly against their hostile perceptions of religion also may adopt fundamentalist canons of belief and view those who seek to center their identity on religious affiliation as intrinsically evil. Such secular intolerance is as unwelcome with respect to informing patterns of global governance as is its religious counterpart.[6] This regressive secularist trope has resulted in the suppression of religious freedom in a number of countries, including Turkey and China, where the leading representatives of the established order perceives any collective or political expression of religious identity as dangerous and subversive. Both religionists and secularists can only contribute to the emergence of humane forms of global governance if they jointly adhere to an ethos of tolerance, abandon rival metaphysical claims of certitude, and seek from distinct vantage points to address the deep causes of human despair and discontent. It is these claims that generally provide the foundation for intolerance and repression of "the other" and a variety of extremisms enacted in the lifeworld of political engagement.

The issue of governance is central at this historical moment. The transnationalization of social, cultural, political, and economic relations is overwhelming the capacities of territorial states to provide secure patterns of governance for their citizenry. (See Chapter 1.) Whether the issue is crime prevention, the control of immigration, the flows of arms and drugs, the elusiveness of money, business practices, environmental protection, or trade and investment, the limits and frailties of state regulatory authority are apparent. The most effective international institutions, several of which make major (but not necessarily positive) contributions to global governance, especially with respect to economic interactions and in relation to certain regional settings (particularly evidenced by the rise of regionalism in Europe). These institutions are sharply criticized by the antiglobalization movement as exhibiting "a global democratic deficit" and as nonrepresentative of the peoples of the Global South and their religious/cultural perspectives. (See Chapter 5.)

While establishing the present context of religious relevance is necessary, it is also essential to take into account antecedent conditions and long-term trends. At this point, it is difficult to assess the degree to which the revived preoccupation with "security," along with its accompanying recourse to global war by the leading country to address "terrorism," will bend these trends in enduring ways. It is currently impossible to discern the scope and disorienting effects of the war on global terror: partly because its goals have not been clearly defined; partly because the degree and success of terrorist countermoves has not been established; partly because the antiterrorist campaign has been enlarged beyond the al Qaeda threat to encompass self-determination struggles and to validate American empire-building; and partly because it remains uncertain as to whether the current extremist American leadership is durable. The remainder of this chapter proceeds on the assumption that global normalcy will reemerge within the next several years, and with it, a renewed preoccupation with global governance in an era of globalization, almost as if September 11 had not occurred. (See Chapter 5.)

Possibly, the traumatizing impact of this unanticipated war experience on the United States and other societies will even make leaders and social forces more attentive to the reconciliation of markets and human well-being, the greatest challenge of worldwide significance before September 11. In retrospect, there was a great failure of leadership after the collapse of the Berlin Wall in 1989 to devote resources and energies to the construction of a viable world order that had better prospects of being fair and stable. This includes the neglect of such initiatives as eliminating weaponry of mass destruction through negotiated disarmament treaties and establishing volunteer peacekeeping capabilities under United Nations command to deal with ethnic turbulence and micronationalism of the sort that resulted from the collapse of cold war geopolitical discipline and the disintegration of the Soviet Union and Yugoslavia. This collapse certainly is not regrettable, as it facilitated the pursuit of rights of self-determination by many peoples long oppressed; but much more could have been done to achieve an improved prospect for a peaceful world and present and future human well-being by way of peaceful transitions, compromises, and even reconciliation.

Narrating the Interplay of Religion and Politics: The Emergence of Modernity

The religious dimension of human experience has been generally excluded from the serious study and practice of governance for several centuries, especially in the West. The exclusion is a direct consequence of the European Enlightenment and its endorsement of autonomous reason as the only reliable guide for human affairs, as well as its general tendency to ground politics on a secular ethos, a principal feature of which is the separation of church and state. Of course, as with many questionable moves in history, this swing of the cosmological pendulum had important positive aspects and was rooted in a particular set of historical circumstances in Europe at the time of the formation of the modern state system, a process whose origin is difficult to locate with precision but is often, although somewhat arbitrarily, dated to coincide with the Peace of Westphalia in 1648.[7]

Without entering into this complex story in any detail, the justification for the exclusion of religion had to do with the perception that religious institutions and beliefs were inimical to the rise of science and material progress in human affairs and the undeniable reality that the split in Christendom had contributed to a series of terrible religious wars. The exclusion of religion always had certain normative costs, including the realization that religious attachments are so strong in society that religion, disallowed to enter the front door of political life, will find other entrances, including concealed trap doors. The effects of this reassertion of religious relevance may be to obstruct an understanding of how public policies are actually shaped, covertly as well as overtly.

So in an important sense, historically, it is necessary to understand that the exclusion of religion from political life was seen as a vital step in the ongoing struggle to establish humane governance — that is, governance based on reason, religious and ethnic tolerance, gender equality, and the individual and collective dignity of the human species, as well as by encouraging scientific inquiry and technological innovation. In many respects Hugo Grotius, a typical Renaissance figure of Protestant Europe, was generally regarded as the founder of modern international law and an intellectual figure who sensitively embodied the passing of Medieval Europe to the new Europe of independent, sovereign, territorial states. Grotius was a witness to the Thirty Years War that ravaged Europe and represented a struggle fought along the geographical, ideological, and theological fault lines that separated Catholicism from Protestantism. Grotius was, in one sense, seeking to restore the religious possibility for human life by removing it from the violent rivalries of the political realm. In his vivid, often-quoted words, "Throughout the Christian world I observed a lack of restraint in relation to war, such as even barbarous races should be ashamed of; I observed that men rush to arms for slight causes, or no cause at all, and that when arms have once been taken up there is no longer any respect for law, divine or human; it is as if, in accordance with a general decree, frenzy had openly been let loose for the committing of all crimes."[8]

In adopting this critical stance, Grotius combined two of the defining characteristics of modernity, a claim of moral superiority associated with the specific identity of "the Christian world" that should inform political life wherever possible and an implicit deprecation of non-Christian societies as the vast domain of "barbarous races."[9] The first impulse led to the idea that the relations among states are to some extent governed by law, while the second gave a sort of underpinning to the Eurocentric hegemonic conceptions of world order and hierarchical relations between Western and non-Western peoples that came to flourish in the colonial

age. Such liberal rationalizations for the politics and structures of domination were later produced by several of the most admired and influential
Enlightenment figures: among others, Hegel, Kant, and John Stuart Mill.
None of these were fully implemented or led to humane governance for
the peoples of the world: International law was too weak and Eurocentric
to contain the passions of nationalism or dreams of empire, and the validation of colonial rule amounted to little more than a rationalization for
the exploitation and domination of non-Western peoples. In many
instances, it generated deep patterns of ethnic resentment and frustration
based on divide and rule tactics that resurfaced in the form of intense
intrasocietal violence in postcolonial settings, especially Africa.

There have been attempts in the recent past to associate this normative
orientation toward political reality with an emergent and evolving world
order that had within it the potential to achieve humane governance for
the entire world. Hedley Bull, an influential Oxford professor of international law, depicted an international society of states that sustained a balance between sovereign rule within territorial limits and a kind of prudent
geopolitical moderation, safeguarded by the benevolence of leading military powers in the relations among states, a type of world order described
by Bull as an "anarchical society."[10] Myres McDougal, the founder of the
New Haven School of Jurisprudence and International Law, together with
a group of collaborators, depicted the spread of Enlightenment values
through the commitment to democratic types of public order systems as
an evolving foundation for a humane intercivilizational pattern of governance that had the capacity to produce, by stages, peaceful and equitable
governance structures of benefit to the entire world.[11]

Both of these normative approaches to the future were premised on the
persistence of the states system as the basis of world order, the role of
power in managing relations among states, and were in these respects
rooted in the anti-utopian traditions of political realism.[12] Additionally,
building on the heritage of Woodrow Wilson and the experiments in world
organization represented by the League of Nations and the United Nations,
there emerged a more utopian strain of secular thought that fundamentally
believed that the only secure and legitimate form of world order depended
on the establishment of juridical universalism in the form of world government, a body of thought that came to be associated with world federalism
and is probably still best represented by the reform proposals of Grenville
Clark and Louis B. Sohn in *World Peace through World Law*.[13]

Even the World Order Models Project (WOMP), with its explicit undertaking to consider the diverse world order perspectives representative of
the leading regions and ideologies active in the world of the 1980s and
1990s, failed to include in any serious or systematic manner the relevance
of religion, although it did acknowledge that world order values, widely
shared on an intercivilizational basis, provided the normative framing of
any successful project to establish, or even to envisage, humane global gov-

ernance.[14] In this sense, although not explicitly religious or utopian, WOMP is easily reconcilable with inclusivist understandings of religion and secular utopianism.

Although the perspectives arising from the work of Bull and McDougal remain useful as moderating guides with normative foundations for operations within the existing framework of world order, the regulative capabilities and potentialities associated with these perspectives seem far too modest to address the deficiencies of international political life that arise from the persistence of war and militarism, from the pervasiveness of poverty and economic deprivation, from the circumstances of political oppression and religious extremism, from the disregard of environmental decay and danger, from the neglect of the spiritual sides of human nature and aspiration, and from predatory market forces associated with transnational finance and corporate operations. The advocacy of world government as a normative project, in contrast, seems far too drastic, being strangely discordant with the current weakening of support for even the feeble efforts to sustain existing world political organizations.[15] Such weakening is epitomized by the recent travails of the United Nations, and although there is an increasingly frequent framing of political life in relation to the metaphor of a "global village," it is seen primarily as an expression of the potency of economic globalization, intense preoccupations with transnational terrorism, criminality, drug trafficking, patterns of human migration, and expressive of the new borderless cyberworld of the Internet.[16] In effect, the best of secular thinking falls short of providing either a plausible path to travel in pursuit of humane global governance or a sufficiently inspiring vision of its elements that would mobilize a popular grassroots movement for drastic global reform.[17] The paucity of alternatives to capital-driven globalization and American global hegemony exhibits the absence of plausible agency for constructive social change; the nihilistic efforts of Islamic extremists merely reinforce the point both by their dismal image of an alternative civic order (as apparently exemplified by the Iranian experience of the last two decades and the ill-fated Taliban regime in Afghanistan) and by their historical impact of consolidating and intensifying, rather than weakening, the American drive toward global dominance.

This failure of political imagination is partially due to the exclusion of religious and spiritual dimensions of human experience from the shaping of the vision and practices associated with the quest for global humane governance. This chapter presents an overview: first, a section on dominant world order trends and tendencies with respect to global governance; then some consideration of the extent to which these recent world order trends, which are shaping the historical situation at the start of the third millennium, are also creating new, unexpected openings for religious and spiritual energies — a development that also, as with the secularist era of exclusion, has deeply disturbing, as well as encouraging, aspects. This religious resurgence is discussed as part of the double-edged relevance of religion for the kind of global governance most likely to emerge. The final section argues for the inclusion of emancipatory religious and spiritual perspectives in world order thinking and practice, along with an enumeration of their potential contributions.[18]

Current World Order Trends, or Pathways to Inhumane Governance

Without entering into a detailed inquiry, it seems evident that several dominant world order trends are converging in such a way as to generate a more integrated form of governance at the global level, but in a form that undermines several critical world order values to a significant degree, and thus qualifies the emergent world order as a variant of "inhumane governance." Such an indictment is not meant to be a total condemnation.[19] Aspects of these globalizing developments represent normative improvements on prior conditions (for instance, a reduction in the prospect for large-scale nuclear war, a diminishing likelihood of traditional warfare among states in general, and the alleviation of poverty and economic deprivation for hundreds of millions of people, particularly those living in several of the most populous, and previously some of the most severely and hopelessly impoverished, countries of the Pacific Rim). Nevertheless, corporate globalization has overall fractured the peoples of the world, neglected the plight of those who are most deprived and vulnerable, placed nonsustainable burdens on the environment that seem likely to diminish the life quality of future generations, deepened over time the disparities between rich and poor, and engendered an ethos of consumerism that forecloses the most fulfilling forms of individual and social self-realization.[20]

Despite this mixed picture, it seems appropriate to label the current arrangements of global governance as cumulatively contributing to a variant of "global inhumane governance." This assessment is reinforced by the severity and durability of the terrorist backlash, which in turn has produced a renewed phase of global militarism that is taking shape as a continuing war without geographical limits of a discernable end –point, waged by an American-led coalition of states against the nonstate, transnational, and nonterritorial Al Qaeda network with operations in as many as sixty countries. Such a war of territorial versus nonterritorial political actors is creating an unprecedented crisis of sovereign rights, where states become targets of potential military intervention because they are perceived as havens of terrorists. Since the Iraq War, with its now discredited rationalizations about weapons of mass destruction and links to al Qaeda, it seems evident that American global ambitions are not being acknowledged by the current political leadership in Washington that is hiding its true goals in the thick patriotic haze that continues to dominate the political landscape despite the passage of time since the September 11 attacks.

Normative Appraisal from the Perspective of Global Governance, or Why "Inhumane?"

To some extent, the preceding paragraphs explain why economic global-ization, while clearly improving the material and social conditions of life for millions, is still properly viewed as responsible for a dangerous momentum leading in the direction of inhumane global governance. Four adverse normative effects will be stressed here, although there are others:

Polarization and global apartheid: It is undeniable that globalization has fostered widening income and skill gaps, whether these are measured by class, region, gender, or race.[21] A crucial dimension of polarization is what some call the "digital divide," a term used to identify those who acquire the Internet skills needed for gainful access to the information age. This digital divide tends to accentuate the other, more familiar, dimensions of polar-ization. The contrast between the economic conditions, work skills, and political supremacy of Euro-American whites in the Global North and sub-Saharan African blacks in the Global South as situated at the two ends of the poles gives plausibility to the allegation that world order as now constituted bears a significant resemblance to apartheid as it functioned in South Africa during its period of racist governance (although there are also some important differences). This inflammatory contention of global apartheid also pertains to the flows of refugees, migrants, drugs, nuclear and other ultrahazardous wastes, and weapons, with the white Global North acting as ever more vigilant gatekeepers while the darker portions of the Global South are increasingly considered dumping grounds for whatever is unwanted by or dangerous for those who are prospering. It should also be noted that the affluence of the Euro-American North has not succeeded in diminishing either absolute or relative poverty.[22] Given the rates of economic growth experienced on a global level for several decades, it is shocking to realize that more than half of the world popula-tion earns less than $2 per day and lacks access to safe drinking water and basic health care.

Neglect of human suffering: This dynamic of polarization, even if sepa-rated from its racial and civilizational implications, is also destructive of an ethos of human solidarity and community, as it rationalizes the distinc-tion between winners and losers, treating the range of outcomes as justifi-able results of market operations and not occasions for remedial action. To the extent that the state becomes implicated in this outlook, there is a shift in stages from the compassionate to the cruel state, a social circumstance that recalls the earliest phases of the Industrial Revolution, when market logic reigned supreme and worker abuse was rampant These conditions from the early nineteenth century were influentially depicted in Marx's critique of capitalism and in the novels of such writers as Charles Dickens and Emile Zola. By neglecting vulnerable sectors of national, regional, and global society, globalization has the unintended side effect of creating forms of governance that are minimally motivated to act for the relief of human suffering. Of course, this trend should not be exaggerated. Government spending on social services, especially in Western Europe, remains close to historic highs. Actually, it is a change of mood and outlook — that is, of ideas — rather than a shift of resources that best captures the essence of the link between government and social well-being.[23]

Decline of the global public good: Globalization, as accompanied by neoliberal economic outlooks, relies on private sector initiatives to uphold the claims of the public good. Such an orientation operates in various ways, including the social disempowerment of the state, by constraining its capacity to mobilize resources and by undermining public confidence in the willingness of political leaders to engage in disinterested action for the public good of their own citizenry. One expression of this disposition is the current effort to "downsize" the United Nations, while making sure that the organization does not challenge the priorities of global capital or interfere with the global reach of counterterrorism. In this regard, to the extent that portions of the UN system earlier became oriented in favor of an overall ethos of global equalization, the right to development, and overall democratization, the organization was widely perceived in the North as an antagonist of globalization. Such a perception seemed confirmed by the tenor of UN-sponsored conferences on large global issues during the early 1990s, when transnational social forces (women's groups, human rights and environmental NGOs, people's coalitions against Third World debt) challenged the market/statist coalition with ideas about governance premised on human solidarity, empathy with the marginalized, and a commitment to upholding the public good of all peoples in the world. The UN Social Summit of 1995, held in Copenhagen, tried in its way to place the social claims of people on the global agenda, thereby seeming to reject the economistic world picture as the wave of the future.[24]

Such events engendered a series of negative reactions within the United Nations led by its dominant members, giving rise to reforms that would remove or drastically downgrade UN activities regarded as hostile to market forces. "Downsizing" was less about money than about this restructuring of the organization to satisfy the demands of the guardians of globalization and to ensure that the United Nations operates primarily as a vehicle for neoliberal ideas and relies mainly on the market-oriented Bretton Woods institutions (that is, the World Bank and the International Monetary Fund, or IMF) when it comes to the economic matters. Significantly, the World Trade Organization was deliberately located outside the formal organizational network comprising the UN system as a way of underlining the autonomy and primacy of a capitalist world economy. In part, this was a concession to the anti-UN mood prevailing in the U.S. Congress. Beyond this, the United Nations is seen as selectively and potentially useful to implement global security in situations of the sort vividly prefigured in the Gulf War of 1991. Later developments, starting with

Somalia (1993) and culminating in the NATO War over Kosovo (1999), cast doubt on the future of the United Nations even with respect to peace-keeping. This marginalization of the UN is also evident in the current setting of the response to September 11, with the UN role up through 2001 being confined, as foreshadowed by Kosovo, in Afghanistan and Iraq, to postconflict reconstruction efforts. Such an allocation of functions leaves global security firmly in the hands of geopolitical forces with only the most minimal deference to the standards of limitation embedded in international law. The unilateralism of the United States in the course of the Bush presidency has shocked most of America's closest allies, leading even Britain to indicate mild degrees of disapproval. The resistance to American occupation of Iraq has led Washington to enlist the United Nations in its efforts to bring stability to post-Saddam Iraq.

What has been said about the United Nations also extends to the efforts to protect the global commons. Already, at the Earth Summit in Rio (1992), there was an effort to subordinate the environmental movement to the guiding role of the market. The UN director of the conference, Maurice Strong, made a thinly disguised move to give business effective control over the way in which environmental standards were to be implemented. He articulated and even nurtured the grand illusion that business could be trusted to heed market signals in a sufficiently timely fashion to provide adequate environmental protection with only the most minimal reliance on institutional governance.[25] During the late 1990s, UN Secretary General Kofi Annan made a series of well-publicized overtures at Davos to the leaders of corporate globalization. His basic proposal culminating in the Global Compact of 2000 was intended to induce multinational corporations to make a voluntary commitment to uphold international standards in relation to human rights, the environment, and labor practices as an independent responsibility in the spirit of good corporate citizenship — that is, even if the territorial government did not itself impose such standards. These undertakings, dubbed by critics as "blue washing," while not yet fairly tested, did distract attention from this determined shift of emphasis in relation to global problem-solving from reliance on public sector initiatives to an encouragement of private sector solutions.

In effect, the social forces aligned to globalization were acting to ensure that governance structures and policy initiatives responsive to the public good were contained by a combination of cosmetic gestures and baby steps of concession, if not rolled back. This required challenging certain democratizing tendencies that were moving the United Nations in an opposite direction and were giving the United Nations and other governance structures a stronger identity as agents of the global public good. This visionary undertaking was primarily delimited by civil society forces acting on behalf of the peoples of the world.[26] (See Chapter 4.) Such a confrontation can also be schematically simplified as an encounter between globalization from above (transnational corporations, banks, states) and globalization from below (transnational civic initiatives, women, indigenous peoples, human rights, environmental activists).[27]

Looming technological horizons: Another complicating aspect of the current era is the emerging prospect of technologies with radical implications for human existence and the meaning of life. The human genome project, biotechnology, superintelligent machines, and menacing robots are all on the horizon, developed in response to private sector priorities. The capacity to clone or fashion human genotypes, identify "weak" and "strong" genetic traits, and construct "thinking" computers with super-human capabilities and sensitivities seems likely to confer upon technological innovators a role that far exceeds their regulative wisdom, posing great challenges to human survival and civilizational identity. In this sense, the problematic adjustment to nuclear weaponry within the public sector, where profits don't drive behavior to nearly the extent they do in the private sector, is a small foretaste of profoundly destabilizing and divisive challenges likely to face the next few generations.[28] At stake will be the administration of the highly contested and often elusive boundaries applicable to the outer limits of human nature and scientific freedom of inquiry and technological innovation.

These negative developments confront us with the likelihood that the third millennium will witness the fashioning of a durable form of inhumane governance that will pose severe risks of ecological, social, political, and cultural catastrophe. Such an outcome is the latest, purest, and most ambitious phase of the fundamental application of the Enlightenment values (reason and science) to human affairs: The continuous stream of technological innovations adapt to secularized political space in order to achieve the greatest material advantage for the owners of capital goods. To be sure, important contradictory tendencies and progressive varieties of resistance are evident, described by the rubric globalization-from-below. But the political leverage of such forces is likely to remain limited to local battlegrounds, content with the nuisance value of a global gadfly unless such dispositions are decisively strengthened by religious commitments and support from important sectors of the organized religious community. It is this possibility of a religiously grounded transnational movement for a just world order that in the end alone gives hope that humane global governance can become a reality, or at least an alternative future, sometime early in the twenty-first century. This hope is, of course, currently clouded over by the perceived dangers to minimum order and stability associated with religious extremism in all its forms. In the West, this situation encourages efforts to put religion back in the box constructed by secularism over the centuries, thereby confusing religious extremism with religion generally, and failing to recognize that religion generates both intolerance and an ethos of human solidarity.

Why Religion? Openings and Regressions

Among the surprises of the last several decades has been a multifaceted and intense worldwide resurgence of religion as a potent force in the public arenas of human affairs. From the perspectives of humane governance, this religious resurgence has a central, double-coded message. It portends the hopeful possibility and necessity of transcending the constraints of economistic secularism, which has become the signature of a disturbing interface between late modernity and a nihilistic postmodernity. But it also simultaneously discloses regressions from modernity in the form of extreme variants of inhumane governance that arguably, in certain instances, makes the repudiation of secularism a terrifying descent into political extremism as a prelude to cultural repression and political violence.

On the negative side, I have in mind the mainly regressive politics that religion has brought to such countries as Iran, Afghanistan, Algeria, Saudi Arabia, and, to some extent, India and Sudan in recent years; but also the tragic and gruesome behavior of religious cults such as Heaven's Gate and Aum Shinrikyo, which seemingly have been incubating in the midst of secularized contemporary modernity.[29] And most negative of all, of course, is the disturbing potency of the al Qaeda network, apparently constituted and led by Osama Bin Laden; as of September 11, it has emerged, at least temporarily, as the most credible opponent of the American role in the world, although an insignificant political actor if measured by statist criteria. Al Qaeda possesses the will and demonstrated capacity to shake the foundation of the existing structures of world order, and so doing, has altered, perhaps permanently, our understanding of power and influence in world affairs.

Historically, it would appear that the outer limits of secularism are giving rise to transformative possibilities that lead in several diverse directions, and principally toward humane governance and regressive potentialities that mix in various ways the most severe deficiencies of premodernity with the most frightening accentuations of modernity. The dialectical implications of these developments must not be discounted, giving rise to a space-governed imperial control system that is entrusted with facilitating the extension of globalization-from-above in its most predatory attributes, while crushing the hydra-headed Medusa, the megaterrorists.

It is, of course, difficult to give an account of this religious resurgence that adequately situates it within the framework of the present. But this resurgence seems closely related to an exhaustion of the creative capacity of the secular sensibility, especially as it is embodied in the political domain. It is within this domain, of course, that modernity has been so closely associated with the preeminence of the territorial sovereign state and the state system of global governance.[30] Such a preeminence has been virtually unchallenged thus far with respect to the organization of governance in international society, and is powerfully, if imperfectly, reinforced by nationalism, by far the strongest ideology of modern times.[31] Even the innovations associated with establishing the League of Nations and the United Nations were deeply rooted in a statist system of world order as epitomized by their membership rules and participatory procedures.

These institutional experiments mainly represented extensions of statism that perpetuated the allocation of governance capabilities to territorial sovereigns, although idealistic segments of the public have always believed that more was possible, or that the League of Nations, and later the UN, could be morphed in the direction of humane global governance. In actuality, the management of the whole was entrusted to geopolitical arrangements that continued to rely on the special governance role of leading states, what political scientists have called "hegemonic actors." In other words, a statist world order, although claiming to respect sovereign equality as a basic principle, was always operating in accordance with a series of hierarchies, especially strong against weak, center versus periphery, Western or Eurocentric versus non-Western, and, most recently, North versus South.[32] As well, many secondary hierarchies associated with regional and subregional relations, and with spheres of influence in economic, political, and cultural domains, seriously eroded the content of juridical equality. The state system in modern times also presupposed the availability of war as a geopolitical instrument of dominant and dissatisfied sovereign states, despite a certain lip service given to legal and moral restraints on the use of force in this century.

But although this statist world order validated many patterns of abuse, either by way of immunizing domestic political order from scrutiny or through the interventionary and exploitative behavior of dominant states, it also gave rise to important normative ideas that, despite the ebb and flow of world politics, seemed to have gained in stature over the centuries:, human rights, humanitarian intervention, asylum, criminal accountability of leaders, and limitations on the legitimate use of force. These normative ideas often have been subordinated to geopolitical manipulations of various sorts, but they provided some cumulative encouragement for liberal perspectives, which were imbued with the idea of progress in human affairs, and anticipated a gradual evolution of this statist world in the direction of peace and harmony. This approach to humane global governance is also often associated with the "democratic peace" hypothesis, which asserts that the spread of constitutional democracy brings with it a strong assurance of peaceful relations among democratic states; thus, if the whole world could be made to consist of nothing but democracies, it would be a peaceful world. And if it were buttressed by effective international laws of human rights, defined to include economic and social rights (and not just civil and political), it would fulfill the requirements of humane governance for the planet without requiring either disarmament or the centralization of political authority in international institutions.[33]

The difficulty with this approach to humane governance is that it neglects the social impact of economic globalization as enacted in an ideological climate shaped by neoliberalism and reinforced by geopolitical militarism. As discussed earlier, the overall impact of globalization, despite its positive aspects, is to predispose world order toward third millennium forms of inhumane global governance. What is more, the influence of the economistic world picture upon governing political elites and the mainstream media is such as to condition and constrain the social roles of states to an undesirable extent. States, as now oriented, increasingly lack the will and capacity to safeguard their own autonomy, much less to fashion the ingredients of a just and peaceful world order. In this regard, it is notable that it is political elites who are most enthusiastic about institutionalizing the economistic worldview at regional and global levels, as seen, for instance, in the political controversies associated with the World Trade Organization, North American Free Trade Agreement (NAFTA), and European Union, despite the fact that such advocacy means that significant governance responsibilities are transferred from the level of the state to incipient supranational actors.

The European developments are the most dramatic in this respect, especially the European governments' remarkable relinquishment of their national currencies, long a central symbol of social and political identity and distinct statehood. The establishment of a Euro currency zone, together with the suspension of border controls for intra-European travel, does move a long way toward functional and ideational unity, creating a European identity that supplements the identity associated with citizenship in a particular state. Of course, for some repressed and dissatisfied ethnic minorities, the prospect of a regional identity may offer a partial escape route from statist entrapment. Contrariwise, as rightward swings in the electorate have disclosed, populist reactions are mounting in Europe against the dilution of national identities expressed politically via chauvinism and disturbing expressions of racism, disclosing deep pockets of grassroots hostility toward Europeanization in all its forms, institutional and especially cultural.

Expressing this interpretation in the context of my wider argument, then, is a matter of understanding that the secular imagination is dependent upon the problem-solving capacities of the state, and that these have increasingly, if only tacitly, transferred to the main arenas of economistic authority (that is, World Economic Forum, G-8, WTO, etc.). One possible development is the degree of territorial backlash and revived security agenda that might conceivably reverse this political energy and restore the role of the state as an autonomous and creative source of authority, thereby potentially rendering it capable of fashioning a new social equilibrium between human needs/public goods and the logic of the market.[34] In the nineteenth century, a kind of social equilibrium emerged out of societal reactions to market-led industrialization, partly as an effort by elites to co-opt, or at least moderate, working-class discontent and a growing fear of revolutionary challenges. It was essentially a secular reaction that had its most influential expression in the Communist revolutionary movement spearheaded by Marxism/Leninism/Maoism, which was avowedly atheistic and aggressively antireligious, blaming submission of the poor and exploited to an unjust social order and to the otherworldliness of religious teaching and doctrine. Of course, there was an important insight in the assault on the role of religion, as religious institutions were generally aligned with ruling elites. Regardless, theologically radical religious leaders (e.g., Luther, Calvin) were at the same time characteristically socially conservative, if not reactionary, repudiating the claims of the poor and of underclasses generally. But beneath this social line of criticism was the more fundamental spirit of modernity, with its search for truth in the realms of secular knowledge. This is illustrated by Marxists' insistence that their interpretations were based exclusively on social laws, and that the resulting normative outlook was one of "*scientific* socialism," as contrasted with the earlier and later visionary gropings of "utopian socialism," which were scorned by Marxists as lacking political relevance. That is, the acute social tensions of the early industrial revolution were addressed within the frame of modernity and secularism, treating religion as either irrelevant or as a mind-pacifying obstacle to social progress and the improvement of the human condition.

In the present global setting, the revisioning of governance is by way of the market, and, to some extent, this outlook is reinforced by the self-organizing, globalist ethos of the digitized sensibility that shapes the Internet world picture. Such a revisioning is generally skeptical about the social functions of government, public goods, and any deliberate effort to achieve humane governance by way of social engineering. Opposed to these views is the diverse transnational array of networks, coalitions, associations, actors, and initiatives labeled "globalization-from-below," or categorized as "civic globalization."[35] (See Chapter 4). I contend that this early effort to construct a democratic global civil society is already selectively informed by religious and spiritual inspiration, and if it is to move from the margins of political reality to challenge entrenched constellations of power in a more serious way, it will have to acquire some of the characteristics and concerns of a religious movement, including building positive connections with the emancipatory aspects of the great world religions.[36]

Without a religious worldview, prospects for global humane governance appear to lack a credible social or political foundation, and, more importantly, do not possess the spiritual character that can mobilize and motivate on a basis that is potentially more powerful than what the market, secular reason, and varieties of nationalism have to offer. Such a religiously informed worldview need not be an amalgam of existing perspectives associated with the world religions. It can additionally forge a more synthetic ecumenical character that fashions over time a synergistic world religion that embodies the inclusive features of the plural religious universe that now exists. Also, unaffiliated individuals and groups exhibiting a spiritual understanding of the meaning of life can help with over-coming the negative aspects of secularism.

What is meant by "religion" here requires considerable clarification in the course of constructing a global civil society and recasting the meaning of citizenship and democratic practice.[37] (See Chapter 7.) It is evident that religion cannot be reduced to any single religious tradition, although it can draw strength from the collaborative support of the various traditions. Some aspects of certain religious traditions are antithetical, especially claims of being "the chosen people" or the exclusive or superior instru-ments of a divine or sacred design; or of the enactment of some apocalyp-tic scenario for ascending to higher or purer forms of existence, especially as achieved by way of holy war or *jihad* involving a struggle to crush infi-dels and nonbelievers. Such aspects of religious heritage may authentically engage the lives and sensibilities of persons of genuine faith, but they offer nothing constructive in relation to the struggle to create patterns of humane global governance for all the peoples on earth. As the global vio-lence against civilians of al Qaeda exemplifies, such initiatives pose a great threat to all efforts to move history forward, are particularly damaging to the potential contributions of religion, and may induce a regressive statism beneath the banners of national security and counterterrorism. As well, such extremist challenges evoke ultranationalistic responses, allowing political leaders to hide their geopolitical designs within an alleged defen-sive necessity aroused by the menace of such extremism.

Religious Pillars of Humane Global Governance

Having identified forms of religious expression inimical to the quest for humane governance, considering the potentially positive contributions of religion remains.[38] In setting forth these contributions, it is necessary that we allow considerable cultural space for a wide spectrum of interpreta-tions of specific religiously based undertakings. It is also important to acknowledge that humanist and socialist traditions are also capable of reaching parallel points of ethical and political reference, but lack the deep historical foundations and universal roots of religion in the collective memories and revered traditions of peoples of varied backgrounds and identities. Such an appeal without borders seems needed to arouse wide-spread adherence. The relevance of religion cannot be separated from its persistence in human consciousness and its role throughout history in the social construction of human nature. Religion is understood here as encompassing the teachings, beliefs, and practices of organized religion and all spiritual outlooks that interpret the meaning of life by reference to faith in and commitment to that which cannot be explained by empirical science or sensory observation; it is usually associated with an acceptance of the reality of the divine, the sacred, the holy, the transcendent, the mys-terious, or the ultimate. Religion is also the most abiding source of limits on sustainable human discretion, identifying outer and inner boundaries of acceptable behavior for the human species, a deep structure of guidance for humanity that has great current relevance with respect to discovering and imposing limits on scientific inquiry and technological innovation, as in the instance of human cloning. As elsewhere, religion has two faces that point in opposite directions. Religion then must be understood as providing a rationale for the unconditional, for the refusal to accept limits to the extent that the divine is being served. In these respects, religion encompasses the belief in God and gods, but does not depend on affirming a theistic metaphysics such as monotheism, or for that matter, the adoption of any theological dogma whatsoever.

The introduction to the complex matter of *positive* religious relevance offered here is only suggestive, designed mainly to stimulate discussion, reflection, and dialogue on the beneficial roles of religion in the context of a global democratic movement for humane governance. The *negative* relevance of religion is not considered here, although, as earlier sections suggest, these detrimental impacts on the human condition bear upon any comprehensive evaluation of religion and human well-being — past, present, and future. In a heuristic spirit, a series of domains associated with religion and its practice are identified and summarily described, without elaboration at this point, and absent any appraisal of the wide spectrum of intercivilizational and intracivilizational variations that pertain to all aspects of religion.

An appreciation of suffering: The religious path can be strongly associated with a Gandhian acknowledgment of the "last man" (or woman), of the lowliest class, caste, or race, and with a central commitment to lift up those who suffer acutely, a dedication to those most victimized. It was Gandhi's insistence that politics be practiced so as, above all, to lift up persons at the bottom of the social, economic, political, and cultural hierarchy. Jesus and The Buddha were also particularly oriented toward enhancing the life and stature of those who were poor and outcast. In these regards, religion represents a social revolution against worldly injustice, against the societal myths that convey the impression that hierarchy and suffering is intrinsic to the human condition and itself part of the divine plan.

Typically, the religious establishment of the day defends the status quo, and its leadership partakes of and benefits from the oppressive social and political order. Religious institutions find the more radical visions of social reformers — who interpret the religious path as necessitating justice on earth for the poor — as extremely disruptive and threatening, and tend to marginalize their impact or even align religion against such claims of justice.

These issues are important at the present time. To what extent can religion be a force in the struggle against global poverty, social injustice, and the inequities of globalization? If it is an oppositional force, can religion avoid mobilizing movements that challenge injustice from the perspective of rigid, premodern traditionalism (as with the Taliban in Afghanistan or the hardline Islamicists in the unfolding of the Iranian Revolution)? Much of the recent intellectual turmoil in Iran has been between those who seek to interpret the Islamic path of belief as consistent with modernity, democracy, and cosmopolitanism (for example, Abdolkarim Sorush) and those who view the Islamic orientation of the state as entailing ultraliteral religious practice and constraint.

Civilizational resonance: Whereas secular transformative thought tends to appeal mainly to intellectuals not strongly bonded with existing structures of governance, religious revolutionary language and utopian aspirations enjoy a sense of legitimacy in popular culture and possess great mobilizing potential, despite modernity, if activated at certain historical moments by charismatic individuals. What the religious resurgence has demonstrated, against all predictions flowing from Western Enlightenment circles, including its revolutionary Marxist exponents, is the persistence of religious outlooks in the body politic of even most modern states — and, beyond this, the susceptibility of the postcolonial world to a variety of religiously framed alternatives to the adoption of Western secular modernism. Part of this susceptibility needs to be understood in experiential terms, as expressions of disillusionment with a series of deforming encounters with modernity: corruption, selling out of the national economy to global capitalists, serving as geopolitical servants of the West, and betraying the just causes of their own civilizational traditions to achieve a consumerist future.

Iran under Pahlevi rule was a perfect example. The Shah with his "white revolution" was promising the people of Iran the benefits of prosperity via secular modernity, following roughly the path taken more successfully by Ataturk in Turkey two generations earlier. This path involved: major investments in science and education, marginalization of Islam, adoption of Western lifestyles and popular culture by the elites in Teheran, subordination of regional identifications to the foreign policy priorities of the United States (e.g., supplying oil to such regional pariahs as Israel and South Africa during apartheid), an acceptance of major deployments of American military forces in the country, and public displays of corruption and decadence by the royal family and its entourage. The Iranian Revolution, under the inspiration of Ayatollah Khomeini, mobilized mass discontent with the Shah's regime around the symbols and convictions of Islam, revealing to a stunned world the extraordinary mobilizing power of religion in the postcolonial world of the late 1970s and 1980s. It was not significant, in this respect, that Iran was never itself a colony in a formal sense. It became part of the postcolonial world.

An ethos of solidarity: Closely related is the unitive feature of religious consciousness, the oneness of the human family that can give rise to an ethos of human solidarity, the unity of all creation, and, with it, the sense of both the wholeness of human experience and the dignity of the individual. Such solidarity is a sign of religious inclusiveness and a celebration of religious diversity, contrasting with the narrow paths of intolerance traveled by exclusivist religiosity. Such an inclusive view also bonds the human spirit with the stranger and the guest, dissolving the sharp boundaries of political community engendered by nationalism and patriotic fervor, as well in relation to class, gender, race, sexual, and ethnic barriers to acceptance. This inclusivity is particularly important in strengthening civic globalization and countering the Westphalian tradition that overwhelmingly associates the outer edges of solidarity with the citizenry of territorial sovereign states. The religious vision provides a potential political grounding for humane global governance that cannot otherwise be achieved on a massive scale, although some forms of socialism come close. Humanists with a global outlook are viewed as sentimentalists and utopians promoting world governments and the like without any attention to agency or transition, and without any mass appeal.

Even inclusivity that is bounded by culture and religion rather than by world identities could induce positive trends toward regional political arrangements, thereby weakening the regressive sides of a statist world order. Of course, regionalism, as in Europe, rests primarily on functional considerations of competitiveness in the world economy and war prevention in relation to neighbors, but its viability as an approach is undoubtedly based also on the premodern collective heritage of Christendom and a shared experience of geography and climate. And in Asia, Latin America, and Africa, religious identities both facilitate and obstruct efforts to forge regionalism. Part of what has made the postcolonial period so anguishing for Africa is the relative weakness of most transnational, and even national, religious identities, and the comparative strength of ethnic and tribal ties. Such weakness has been accentuated in Africa by the difficulties of postcolonial state-building, as well as by the legacies of resentment, envy, and domination associated with the colonial era that so often deliberately engaged in the upgrading and downgrading of previously equal ethnic communities so as to offset resistance to colonial rule by fashioning internal tensions.

The current concerns about the "clash" and the "dialogue" of civilizations also expresses this realization that identities relevant to the era of globalization are increasingly shaped by religious orientations, suggesting the erosion of nationalism as a dominant and sufficient foundation for human community. As with other aspects of the religious resurgence, the shadow side may seem to be of greater historical relevance. The rise of religious exclusivism has captured the lion's share of the political imagination, especially in the aftermath of the Iranian Revolution, and even more so, in the wake of September 11. To the extent that the central issue of human destiny is posed as resistance to the West (and specifically, to the United States) and to globalization rather than to the wider challenge of global transformation and humane global governance, the greater militancy of exclusivist religious orientations gains the upper hand with respect to defining the political role of religion in our time. As a consequence, the West has been able to mobilize its own nontransformative response against "terrorism," and there is a tendency for its apologists to look upon the struggle as one between the emancipatory modernity championed by the United States and the forces of repressive religious fundamentalism arising out of the Islamic world. Such an interpretation, while responsive to aspects of the religious resurgence, overlooks the wider role of religious pedagogy in preparing political consciousness for humane globalization through the encouragement of an awareness of human solidarity. Thinking dialectically, the greater the salience of exclusivist religious outlooks, the more historically significant will become the opportunities for religious inclusivism.

Normative horizons: A compassionate response to suffering and the affirmation of human solidarity imply a belief in normative horizons that define human potentialities in an affirming and hopeful manner that contradicts and transcends present conditions, including the market ethos, which neglects many forms of acute human suffering. This ethos tends to elevate the claims of the part or the fragment over those of the whole, of winners over that of losers, and is fraught with the sort of consumerist and materialist preoccupations nurtured by mass advertising and franchise capitalism. Religiously oriented normative horizons embody and converge in many respects with the secularly defined priorities of a human rights culture, especially with regard to economic and social needs of the most materially disadvantaged or impoverished individuals and peoples. Such normative horizons also incline toward the replacement of power as the regulative basis of order with law and ethics.

It appears to be the case, especially given the seeming historical irrelevance of socialist modes of political analysis and influence, as well as the strength of market forces, that only religion has the possibility of filling the normative vacuum that exists in settings where extreme versions of capitalism go almost unchallenged. There are other reactions to this reality, including a right wing backlash that blames adverse change on immigration and loss of identity and a religious exclusivist backlash that promises to restore purity by institutionalizing one or another ultraorthodoxy. Only inclusivist religion with a sense of the sacredness of all human beings can provide the political foundation in this global setting for a global humane governance that uses the resources of the world to deal with the fundamental needs of humanity: food, shelter, health, sustainable environment, peace, and meaningful life.

Although some humanists have advanced the idea that "a law of peoples" or "a human rights culture" provides the ethical basis of humane global governance, there has been no convincing way to establish a parallel political basis or to identify the agencies of change and reform that might actualize such philosophizing. References to human rights as "a secular religion" also miss the point that it is the nonsecularity of religion that accounts for most of its continuing mobilizing appeal, consisting of the realization that religion speaks to the widely shared quest for an account of human existence that includes a spiritual dimension, whereby some sort of reconciliation with mortality is achieved for most persons.

Faith and power: A belief in the transformative capacities of an idea that is sustained by spiritual energy lends itself to nonviolent forms of struggle and sacrifice, thereby challenging most secular views of human history as shaped primarily by governing elites, warfare, and a command over innovative military technology. Especially in the disillusioning aftermath of Marxist experiments in governance and in the face of subsequent outbursts of religious fanaticism, the secular imagination is suspicious of and hostile toward any advocacy of utopian solutions, whereas religious consciousness is not so constrained. The religious framing of reality is rooted in the present, but also hopeful about an eventual deliverance from suffering and privation. Indeed, the central founding narratives of the world's great religions are preoccupied with liberation from oppressive social and political arrangements, promising that by adhering to faith, emancipation will be found despite the seeming overwhelming weight of oppressive structures. It is also true that the institutionalization of religions to ensure their persistence often suppresses its emancipatory potential, substituting rigidities of ritual and dogma, and striking bargains with the rich and powerful.

What has been happening around the world in the last several decades suggests a new set of oppressive circumstances for humanity that cannot be addressed by secular authority or the sorts of "progress" achieved by science and technology. In such a global setting, the opportunity for and responsibility of religion becomes evident, to provide hope for emancipation and, in effect, give a spiritual grounding to efforts to move toward global democracy and humane globalization. Religious hope of this nature can be influential on all levels of social interaction, from the very local, to the planetary, and even the cosmic, encouraging a reconstructive postmodernism dedicated to finding the ideas and energies for a sustainable world that affirms the sacredness of life.

Limits: Religion, in its inclusivist modes, is capable of contributing profound humility to human thought and action that is particularly sensitive to human fallibility, if not sin and evil, and appreciates the limited capacity of the inquiring mind to grasp the fullness of reality or to claim the truthfulness and correctness of any particular interpretation of what needs to be done in the world. This allows persons to remain open at all stages to dialogue with strangers and apparent adversaries — which can serve to correct mistakes and insensitivities — and to experience a sense of awe in face of the divine, which can protect humanity from idolatry and from a false sense of human autonomy.

There are grounds for serious concern in the West as a result of the degree to which modernity was premised on the autonomy of the individual, the importance of free inquiry, and the supposed benefits of unrestricted science as the necessary foundation of material abundance and overall social progress. Such prevailing ideas were fought out centuries ago in the struggle against the efforts by the Catholic Church to protect religious dogma and authority against scientific inquiry, most famously in relation to Galileo. The secular victory, especially in Protestant countries, was associated with rapid economic progress and the excitement of education and culture no longer constrained by religious beliefs and interferences that failed to correspond to the sense of empirically based reality in the rising scientific civilization. The whole idea of history and progress that came to define modernity rested on this positive impact of scientific freedom, and the confinement of religion to spheres of private consolation and belief.

Such attitudes were always questioned to some degree by prophetic cultural voices, drawing on ancient myths such as the Prometheus story. Goethe's *Faust* and William Blake's "dark satanic mills" were warnings about the dire consequences of a modern pact with the devil to exchange the spiritual for the worldly promise of knowledge. These attitudes revived and became much more widely considered after the explosions of the atomic bombs at Hiroshima and Nagasaki, raising the question about whether limits had been exceeded in a manner that threatened human survival, and how to find a way to restore such limits in the future. The most valuable cultural resources for striking balances between the competing values of gaining knowledge, extending life, improving economic performance, and respecting limits are mainly situated within religious frameworks. Even the possibilities, first apparent in the 1990s, of wars conducted by the United States that were casualty free (at least on the U.S. side) raises profound issues of limits about which secular civilization has little to say, especially as secularists have endorsed the idea that whatever power a warring state can mobilize in support of its security can be introduced onto the battlefield so long as it satisfies minimal notions of "military necessity" (that is, conforms to the rather modest restraints of international humanitarian law). Again, the absence of a vital political alternative means that such issues go unquestioned unless the religious perspective is brought into play in central respects.

Identity: Identity can emerge from many sources and is existentially being reshaped by overlapping appeals to aspects of human nature, the shifting boundaries of community, and the scientific validation of an enhanced concept of human consciousness and genuine experience. Also, the era of exclusive subjection to the nationalist expectations of loyalty to the sovereign state are being superseded in many settings by various modes of reexperiencing the deepening reality of the whole and by the increasing sense of the yet-unfulfilled future, an emphasis that can be highlighted and explored by replacing the idea of "citizen" with that of "citizen pilgrim." This distinctly religious understanding of essential political identity is gained by reference to a spiritual journey that is unseen and unlikely to be completed within the span of this lifetime but the value of which is an object of intense faith and dedication that extends beyond prescribed and instinctive loyalties to nation and state. Such a pilgrimage embraces temporal loyalties to a future that brings justice and peace to the entire human family and is dedicated to the process of establishing humane global governance for all the peoples of the world. The citizen pilgrim can find a home within either established religious traditions or by a more personalized spirituality, but the essence of such an exemplary identity is to move energies and hopes from structure to process, from present to future, from states to world.

But the challenge of identity is more complex than this image of citizen pilgrim suggests, embracing all forms of participation in collective experience, and responding to the appeals of social movements and regional restructuring, especially for the sake of democratizing the operation of the world economy and finding ways to extend the rule of law beyond the reach of sovereignty. European experience is suggestive of what is possible under certain conditions. The more global efforts to establish a functioning International Criminal Court and to build support for a global parliament are indications of the relevance of identities that can no longer be reduced to state/society relations. Religion fits into this dynamic by providing support for such efforts through its conceptualization of community and authority without being doctrinally and experientially tied to statist definitions.

Reconciliation: Diverse ways of knowing are alternative respected means of coping with the effects of human finitude and the impingement of limits, thereby diminishing the obstacles to a needed and desirable reconciliation of science, reason, and spirituality. Whether this reconciling process occurs within the domain of formal religion or without, or in both, is of secondary significance. The need for reconciliation in the setting of severe conflict is a pressing need and must be associated with mechanisms of accountability that can ground gestures of forgiveness in prior negotiations of acknowledgement and some process of justice. Many of these issues have surfaced in a range of efforts to facilitate a transition from an abusive past to a more democratic future at the level of the state. Truth and reconciliation commissions in Latin America and South Africa have tried to find way to acknowledge past criminality without relying on punitive and vindicative responses, but such efforts involve a delicate balance of competing concerns, especially when past abuse was severe, widespread, and long-lasting. Religious traditions and respected religious leaders have a special capacity to lend legitimacy to such efforts by articulating both sets of objectives in coherent and resonant language.

A further challenge is posed more explicitly by the degree to which rival parties to bloody conflicts are posed wholly or partially in religious terms, as is the case in such prominent instances as Palestine/Israel, Kashmir, and Northern Ireland. The religious community can either fuel the conflictual energies of either or both sides, making reconciliation impossible, or use their influence to seek mutual accommodation. It is not evident that religious leaders will often play such constructive roles, themselves often acting as the voices of polarization, but the opportunity exists to an unprecedented degree because the struggles are defined by reference to religious identity, and secular solutions are not responsive to the goals of the parties.

Finally, religious discourse can bring clarity and charity to debates concerning a range of grievances about historical abuses. Lately, much attention has been given to claims from the World War II era associated with the lost wealth and uncompensated labor of Holocaust victims in Europe and parallel patterns of victimization relating to Japanese militarism in Asia. Also, claims have been made relating to the dispossession of indigenous peoples throughout the Western Hemisphere and the Pacific to obtain reparations for the pain and suffering wrought by the institutions of slavery. (See Chapter 5). Although religion cannot provide a definitive response to such efforts to reconcile the past and present, it can offer a setting where such issues can be addressed in a manner that moves toward reconciliation rather than recrimination and mutual dismissal. These are difficult issues that may require symbolic solutions by way of apologies, memorials such as museums, and trust funds that acknowledge the past without burdening and embittering the present. Religious institutions and modes of rectifying thought can encourage such approaches more readily than can the adversary methods of law, which tend toward either/or outcomes that validate one side while rejecting the other and even intensifying anguish and a sense of injustice.

These positive contributions of inclusive religious outlooks provide an intercivilizational grounding for transnational efforts to improve the normative and institutional governance of human affairs. Patterns of governance are situated at all levels of social interaction from local efforts to challenge the siting of high dams and nuclear power plants to planetary concerns about global warming and human cloning. Religious dialogue can facilitate understanding and the development of the sort of ethically sensitive consensus that engages popular participation in way that cannot be achieved by intergovernmental diplomacy and treatymaking.

Religion and Humane Global Governance: Concluding Observations

The perspective proposed here is that a religious/spiritual orientation needs to inform the energies of civic globalization if such transformative approaches to world order are to have any serious prospect of effectively launching a political project that offers an alternative to that being foreshadowed and actualized by the largely economistic forces and collaborative geopolitical forces associated with corporate globalization and empire-building. It is not a matter of repudiating state or market, but of insisting that these organizing arenas of authority and influence be spiritualized in accordance with the generalized attributes of religion. But it is also not expecting a miraculous rescue from above (deus ex machina), whether in the form of a sudden populist embrace of world government or the emergence of regional institutions and the United Nations as political actors no longer constrained by imperial geopolitics and the reigning neoliberal world picture.

Humane global governance will only occur as the outcome of human struggle, and in this sense is similar to past efforts to overcome slavery, colonialism, apartheid, and other entrenched patterns of injustice. Direct and indirect religious thought as embodied in the lives and works of devout adherents has substantially inspired each of these struggles. Each undertaking seemed impossible to achieve at its inception, given the array of opposed social forces, fixed beliefs, and institutional supports affirmed by the conventional wisdom of the day to validate and uphold prevailing inhumane practices. In the recent past we have witnessed successful struggles against oppression carried on by the peoples of Eastern Europe and the Soviet Union, of many countries in Asia, and of the victims of apartheid in South Africa. They have enjoyed limited or overall success against great historical odds, although following through with humane patterns of reconstruction has not impressively occurred in any of these historical instances.

We do not now know enough to conclude pessimistically that humane global governance is an impossibility given human nature as genetically and socially constructed. We do know enough to understand that such an outcome, if it occurs, will not come about spontaneously or without anguishing struggles. We also know that, given the historical ascendancy of market forces, the widespread acceptance of the economistic world picture, and the pervasiveness of political violence, an alternative orientation can only hope to emerge if nurtured and guided by inclusive religious energies creatively adapted to the specific problems and concerns that exist at all levels of social reality. Religion is crucial if the agency problem is to be solved in the course of seeking justice and sustainability for the peoples of the planet.

The complexity and precariousness of a globalizing world is bringing into being an unprecedented degree of global governance. The forms of this governance cannot be understood by reference to the United Nations, but are related above all to the efforts of market forces to coordinate and stabilize their operations on a regional and global basis, and to some extent by their geopolitical allies, especially the United States, which provides protection via global policing mechanisms. The extension of this type of global governance, especially as abetted by empire-building designs, threatens human well-being and the quality of social and political life at the level of the state. The religious challenge is to infuse the struggles of the peoples of the world for democracy, equity, and sustainability with a vision of human existence that is human-centered yet conscious of the relevance of a surrounding nature, of the sacred, and of mysteries beyond the grasp of reason and machines. In a sense, religion remains the best and primary custodian of premodern wisdom that was almost entirely forgotten throughout the experience of modernity, and is also the best receptor for transition to a fulfilling experience of postmodernity.

The complexity of this undertaking is heightened by September 11, especially its bloody aftermath, both by diverting energies and resources from the policy agenda associated with alternative patterns of globalization and by reviving a paralyzing preoccupation with the dynamics of one-sided war. Such a preoccupation freezes the structural character of global governance and leads to underestimating the threats to stability and justice that fall outside the domain of the war effort, which is simultaneously an expression of imperial globalization. Such observations seem particularly true with respect to the American war against global terror, which lacks a clear definition of goals, whose doctrines of engagement defy the minimal constraints of international law, and whose limits cannot be geographically or conceptually specified. The territorial base of nonstate political extremist activities is fluid, if not nonexistent. The locus of such networked political violence can be situated anywhere. Even the country leading the supposed antiterrorist campaign can discover that it is a "haven" for such extremism. A further difficulty relating to the inquiry of this chapter is the linkage, real and projected, between al Qaeda extremism and religious commitment. Osama bin Laden's mobilization of support and rationale for political extremism and the commission of crimes against humanity is avowedly premised on his interpretation of Islam, which Islamic scholars overwhelmingly reject as wrong and perverse. Despite this, what saves bin Laden's interpretations from being dismissed as the ravings of a demented and death-fixated mind is that his words evoke a wide and potent resonance in the Islamic world, especially with respect to its animating message of anti-Americanism, and have been actualized in schemes that are at once diabolical and startlingly effective, especially given the ratio between capabilities and the actual harm inflicted.

This ambiguous reality provides ammunition for those who would generalize the response to September 11 by taking on the entire Islamic world, especially its Arab sectors, and use this context as an occasion to confront religion as the enemy of modernity and democracy. From such a vantage point Turkey is mindlessly celebrated for its secularism, generally understood as epitomized by its military containment of political Islam, and no inquiry is made as to whether positive or negative dispositions of religion, or both, are opposed in Turkey. It needs to be stressed that to the extent secular energies suppress inclusive religious tendencies, they act to diminish the emancipatory forces at the disposal of society.

In this setting, the most sinister renderings of the implications of September 11 attain a quality of plausibility. A supposedly erudite and extremely influential Middle East specialist has put forward the idea that Osama bin Laden's challenge has been mounted so formidably because he was encouraged by the supposed prior reluctance of the United States to use its military power to crush opposition to its interests. Without a word of criticism of the U.S. role in relation to either the Israel/Palestine conflict or the maintenance of cruel and indiscriminate sanctions against Iraq, Bernard Lewis advocates a maximal approach to the antiterrorist war, his focus is on the Middle East, encouraging Washington to seek regime changes in Iraq and Iran. Bernard Lewis writes, "it is difficult for Middle Easterners to resist the idea that this refusal to implicate Saddam Hussein is due less to a concern for legality than to a fear of confronting him."[39] Such an assertion is made in the spirit of taunting American "squeamishness" with respect to the use of force against its challengers, which, according to Lewis, pushes Islam into the arms of the bin Laden worldview, and thus ends up with a mighty clash of civilizations. Such thinking argues that the two alternatives open to the United States after September 11 are either to wage an expansive war now against hostile forces in the Islamic world or to be faced with a far more massive religious war later on.

This sort of counterapocalyptic reading of September 11 is dangerous and unnecessary. The al Qaeda attack needed to be addressed by an effective response that probably necessitated regime change in Afghanistan and intense law enforcement wherever else the network operates. It also should be extended to determined peacemaking within the wider Islamic world, which will above all depend on a fair resolution of the Palestinian ordeal, the internationalization of Jerusalem, the elimination of all weapons of mass destruction from the military arsenals of all countries, the abandonment of imperial globalization, and a credible effort to make economic globalization operate in a manner that is more equitable and protective of the most vulnerable peoples in the world. Lifting the gaze beyond the battlefield will also enable a recovery of the degree to which Islam, and religion generally, is part of the solution, and not only the problem. Considering these more distant horizons, the challenge of establishing humane global governance takes on the importance it deserves and contributes to our understanding that defeating extremist violence in the world is associated with justice as well as with the weaponry of counterterrorism and war.

Unfortunately, the September 11 attacks appear to have eclipsed the hopeful democratizing tendencies of the 1990s The attacks give rise to a strengthened marriage of economic and state power — taking the unprecedented form of a nonterritorial, counterterrorist crusade that wields its interventionary authority throughout the world and seeks to perpetuate and extend this role to global security through the exercise of monopoly control over the militarization of space and oceans. Only the great world religions have the credibility, legitimacy, and depth of understanding to identify and reject the idolatry that seems to lie at the core of this American project of planetary domination.

Endnotes

1. Others, of course, had also pointed out the emergence of a post-Westphalian world. For an astute appraisal along these lines, see Joseph A. Camilleri and Jim Falk, *The End of Sovereignty? The Politics of a Shrinking and Fragmenting World* (Aldershot, UK: Edward Elgar, 1992); see also Jean-Marie Geuihenro, *The End of the Nation-State* (Minneapolis, Minn.: University of Minnesota Press, 1993).
2. This thesis is stated in a popular form in Thomas Friedman, *The Lexus and the Olive Tree: Understanding Globalization* (New York: Farrar, Straus, Giroux , 2000); for a more academic perspective, see Mehdi Mozaffari, "A Triangle of International Ethics, Law, and Politics: Global Standard of Civilization," pamphlet, September 2000, Department of Political Science, University of Aarhus, Aarhus, Denmark.
3. There is reported a scholarly initiative underway to show that bin Laden's campaign of terrorism violates fundamental Islamic principles regulating the use of force against innocent civilians and the authority to issue fatwas (religious decrees). Alan Cooperman, "Scholars Plan to Show How Attacks Violated Islamic Law," *Washington Post*, Jan. 20, 2002, A15.
4. Robert D. Kaplan, "Looking the World in the Eye," *The Atlantic Monthly*, December 2001, 68–82; see also Andrew Sullivan, "This Is a Religious War," *NY Times Magazine,* October 7, 2001, 44–47, 52–53.
5. Bernard Lewis, "The Revolt of Islam," *The New Yorker*, November 19, 2001, 50—63, esp. 60–63.
6. Comprehensive antifundamentalism is well articulated in relation to the United States and Islam by Tariq Ali, *The Clash of Fundamentalisms: Crusades, Jidhads, and Modernity* (London, UK: Verso, 2002).
7. This interplay of religion, politics, and world order as established within the Westphalian frame is a theme of Scott M. Thomas chapter, this volume.
8. Hugo Grotius, "Prolegomena," in *On the Law of War and Peace* (New York: Bobbs Merrill, 1925), 20.
9. For general assessments of the Grotian impact, especially as facilitator of the transition to modernity by way of the passage from religious to secular authority, see Hedley Bull, Benedict Kingsbury, and Adam Roberts, eds., *Hugo Grotius and International Relations* (Oxford University Press, 1990); see also Yasuaki Onuma, ed., *A Normative Approach to International Relations: Peace, War, and Justice in Hugo Grotius* (Oxford University Press, 1993).
10. Hedley Bull, *The Anarchic Society: A Study of Order in World Politics* (New York: Columbia University Press, 1977).
11. See Myres McDougal and associates, *Studies in World Public Order* (New Haven, Conn.: Yale University Press, 1960); McDougal and Harold D. Lasswell, *Jurisprudence for a Free Society*, 2 vols. (New Haven, Conn.: New Haven Publishers, 1992); see esp. vol. 2.
12. The anti-utopian outlook was, perhaps, best articulated in response to the peace settlement of World War I by E. H. Carr, *The Twenty Years' Crisis, 1919–1939* Reprint of 1946 edition. (New York: Harper & Row, 1964).
13. Grenville Clark and Louis B. Sohn, *World Peace through World Law*. 3rd ed. (Cambridge, Mass.: Harvard University Press, 1966).
14. For representative works from WOMP over the period of its existence, see Saul H. Mendlovitz, ed., *On the Creation of a Just World Order* (New York: Free Press, 1975); R. B. J. Walker, *One World/Many Worlds: Struggles for a Just World Peace* (Boulder, Colo.: Lynne Rienner, 1988); Richard Falk, *On Humane Governance: Toward a New Global Politics* (University Park, PA.: Penn State University Press, 1995); and Ali Mazrui, *A World Federation of Cultures* (New York: Free Press, 1976).
15. For one assessment of this UN weakness, especially relative to the strength of international financial institutions and European regionalism, see Richard Falk, "Meeting the Challenge of Multilateralism," in Thomas H. Hendriksen, ed., *Foreign Policy for America in the Twenty-first Century: Alternative Perspectives* (Stanford, Calif.: Hoover Institution Press, 2001), 33–48.
16. But see articulate argument in favor of world government in David Ray Griffin, "Global Government: Objections Considered," in *Toward Genuine Global Governance: Critical Reactions to Our Global Neighborhood*, edited by Errol E. Harris and James A. Yunker (Westport, Conn.: Praeger, 1999), 57–68.

17. A more obscure secular theme focuses on the European regional experience as a prelude to a "world of regions." Such an image, while more promising than world government, remains a dim and remote prospect at present.

18. The emphasis on "emancipatory religious and spiritual perspectives" is premised on a distinction between "inclusive" and "exclusive" interpretations of the meaning of human existence. Inclusive interpretations are nondogmatic, allowing moral and political space for alternative interpretations and worldviews. Exclusive interpretations insist that there is only one true path and that the embrace of alternatives is inherently false, immoral, and worthy of destruction. This endeavor is similar to Fred Dallmayr, "A Global Spiritual Resurgence: On Christian and Islamic Spiritualities," in Fabio Pelito and Pavlos Hatzopordos, eds., *Religion in International Relations* (New York: Polgrave, 2003), 209–236. Dallmayr anchors his concern less in extremist interpretation than in the possibilities that religion becomes commodified by the cultural hegemony exerted through the capitalist market-place.

19. In this respect, I share the view of Michael Hardt and Antonio Negri in *Empire* (Cambridge, UK: Harvard University Press, 2000) that globalizing tendencies have greater emancipatory potential than did a Westphalian world, and that the way forward for progressive thinking is not to grasp as the straws of a revived statism. The militarization of American state power after September 11 illustrates the dangers of looking backward rather than forward in search of global justice. Is it purely sentimental to dream of the emergence of more compassionate states in the future, and to build a politics in global civil society with this end in view?

20. For negative assessments of globalization, see John Gray, *False Dawn: The Delusions of Global Capitalism* (New York: New Press, 1998); Richard Falk, *Predatory Globalization: A Critique* (Cambridge, UK: Polity, 1999); also George Soros, *On Globalization* (New York: Public Affairs, 2002).

21. For documentation, see United Nations Development Program, *Human Development Reports* (New York: Oxford University Press, 1990–1999).

22. See John Williams, "Look, Child Poverty in the Wealthy Countries Isn't Necessary," *International Herald Tribune*, 12 July 2000, 8.

23. See Vito Tanzi and Ludger Schuknecht, *Public Spending in the Twentieth Century* (Cambridge, UK: Cambridge University Press, 2000); see also interpretation of findings in Martin Wolfe, "The Golden Age of Government," *Financial Times*, 12 July 2000, 17.

24. For a valuable review of the ideals and undertakings of the Copenhagen Social Summit, see the volume reporting on the "Copenhagen Seminars for Social Progress." *Building a World Community: Globalisation and the Common Good* (Copenhagen, Denmark: Royal Danish Ministry of Foreign Affairs, 2000).

25. Stephan Schmidheiny and the Business Council for Sustainable Development, *Changing Course: A Global Business Perspective on Development and the Environment* (Cambridge, Mass.: MIT Press, 1992); also Richard Falk, "Environmental Protection in an Era of Globalization," *Yearbook of International Environmental Law* (Oxford: Oxford University Press, 1996), 3–25.

26. See Daniel Archibugi and David Held, eds., *Cosmopolitan Democracy* (Cambridge, UK: Polity, 1995); David Held, *Democracy and Global Governance* (Stanford, Calif.: Stanford University Press, 1995).

27. This encounter is a major theme of Falk, *Predatory Globalization*, n. 9, 127–36.

28. For eye-opening discussions, see P. Kurzweil, *The Age of Spiritual Machines* (New York: Viking, 1999); also see an essay by a founder of Sun Microsystems, Bill Joy, "Why the Future Doesn't Need Us," *Wired* 8, 4 (April 2000): 238–47.

29. Robert Jay Lifton, *Destroying the World to Save It: Aum Shinrikyo, Apocalyptic Violence, and the New Global Terrorism* (New York: Metropolitan Books, 1999); Mark Juergensmeyer, *Terror in the Mind of God: The Global Rise of Religious Violence* (Berkeley, Calif.: University of California Press, 2000).

30. See Stephen Toulmin, *Cosmopolis: The Hidden Agenda of Modernity* (New York: Free Press, 1990); R. B. J. Walker, *Inside/Outside: International Relations as Political Theory* (Cambridge, UK: Cambridge University Press, 1993); Hendrick Spruyt, *The Sovereign State and Its Competitors* (Princeton, N.J.: Princeton University Press, 1994).

31. "Imperfectly" to the extent that national identities do not necessarily correspond with state boundaries.

32. See Immanuel Wallerstein, *The Modern World-System*, 3 vols. (New York: Academic Press, 1974–1989); Samir Amin, *Eurocentrism* (New York: Monthly Review, 1989); Samir Amin, *Rereading the Postwar Period: An Intellectual Itinerary* (New York: Monthly Review, 1994).

33. For example, see Bruce Russett, *Controlling the Sword: The Democratic Governance of National Security* (Cambridge, Mass.: Harvard University Press, 1990), esp. 119–45; Bruce Russett, *Grasping the Democratic Peace for a Post–Cold War World* (Princeton, N.J.: Princeton University Press, 1993); for a critical view, see Joanne S. Gowa, *Ballots and Bullets: The Elusive Democratic Peace* (Princeton, N.J.: Princeton University Press, 1999).

34. This argument is developed in Richard Falk, "Siege of State: Will Globalization Win Out?" *International Affairs* 73, 1 (January 1997): 123–36.

35. For further clarification, see Paul Wapner, *Environmental Activism and World Civic Politics* (Albany, N.Y.: SUNY Press, 1996); Ronnie D. Lipschutz, *Global Civil Society and Global Environmental Governance* (Albany, N.Y.: SUNY Press, 1996); Richard Falk, *Explorations at the Edge of Time: The Prospects for World Order* (Philadelphia, Pa.: Temple University Press, 1992).

36. The work of Hans Küng has moved in this direction in recent years. See Hans Küng, *Global Responsibility: In Search of a New World Ethic* (New York: Crossroads, 1991), and Chapter 6 of this book.

37. For a closely comparable revisioning of religious consciousness, see the important book by Charlene Spretnak, *The Resurgence of the Real: Body, Nature, and Place in a Hypermodern World* (Reading, Pa.: Addison-Wesley, 1997).

38. In many respects, the approach adopted in this section is complementary to and parallel with what Scott M. Thomas is proposing under the rubric of "virtue-ethics" as embodied in the great world religions. It is also seeking to turn the energies of the religious resurgence in the direction of what I have been calling humane global governance. See Thomas, "Taking Religious and Cultural Pluralism Seriously: The Global Resurgence of Religion and the Transformation of International Society," Note 18, 21–53. It is also similar in intention to the chapter of Fred Dallmayr who vividly depicts the ways in which religion in practice and concept can shape behavior and outlook in humanly positive directions. Note 18, 209–236.

39. Lewis, note 5, at 63; see also Lewis, "A War of Resolve: American Kowtowing to 'Moderate' Arabs May Embolden bin Laden," *Wall Street Journal*, April 26, 2002.

Chapter 7
Challenging Citizenship

Overview

The essential argument of this chapter is that the rise of transnational economic forces during the 1990s exerted a major influence on the understanding and practice of citizenship that marks itself off from the preceding period of statism, as well as the emergent subsequent period of global warfare directed at overcoming the challenges of megaterrorism. In the pre-1990s, the Westphalian model of world order based on a society of states prevailed to such an extent as to associate citizenship, as a meaningful dimension of political participation, unconditionally with full membership by persons in a particular sovereign state.[1] The state, with the reinforcing support of international law, deliberately appropriated the idea and practice of nationality by denying claims of "nationality" on the part of ethnic and religious minorities, attaching the status of citizen only to nationality understood juridically as applicable to all persons who qualify, regardless of identity.

As a result, the state ignores the divergent nationalist identities and loyalties of its minority inhabitants. This effort was not consistently successful. Periodic attempts were made by dissatisfied minorities to reconfigure the boundaries of states or to establish zones of autonomy within existing boundaries, if not to break away entirely to form a state of their own. The rise of "nationalism" as the basis for community was itself a major dimension of the secularizing process that accompanied the rise of statism from the seventeenth century onward, and was complementary to the determined effort to exclude religious and ethnic influences from the public sphere of governance. But this statist approach to citizenship often reached ambiguous results in practice. The insistence on conflating juridical ideas of membership and affiliation with a more spontaneous politics associated with identity and desire gave rise to resistance that assumed varying forms.

The main sources of popular resistance to this dominant statist trend arose among groups that perceived themselves as marginalized and dissatisfied with political identity's prevailing legal arrangements. This often reflected intense ethnic attachments or arose from strong antisecular refusals to supersede religious solidarity and accept a rigid separation of church from state. Such captive "nations" remained trapped within state boundaries generating autonomy and secessionist movements designed to achieve a maximal overlap of personal and group solidarity, nations, and states in fully legitimate political units, what were claimed to be "natural political communities." Also, especially during the colonial period, citizens of colonial powers were given varying degrees of extraterritorial exemption from and protection of their special status when physically present in various non-Western countries, an invidious departure from territorial law that inculcated relations of superiority and inferiority, leading the latter over time to resist and revolt. Despite these qualifications, the core reality of citizenship in the modern era could be accurately related to the territorial domain of the sovereign state. To be sure, there were all along idiosyncratic and visionary claims of "global citizenship," particularly in the aftermath of the two twentieth century world wars; but these claims were usually animated by antiwar fervor and associated with isolated yearnings of individuals for world government, world peace, and affirmations of human solidarity. These globalizing perspectives never acquired grassroots backing, remaining so marginal in their political relevance as to be treated as sentimental anomalies of an overwhelmingly statist reality and of no conceptual or political importance. Exemplary individuals seemingly dedicating their lives and energies to humanity, such as Albert Schweitzer and Dag Hammarskjöld, were often identified as "citizens of the world" or "world citizens," giving a certain weight to this idealist image of an essentially unified human species.[2]

The secularization of politics was also generally descriptive of an evolving reality in the West, although from time to time a resurgence of religious identity intruded on the affairs of state in ways that contested the mainstream orientation of modernity. This religious undercurrent that persisted in the face of ascendant secularism was in many respects a tension that could be contrasted with that of ethnic and nationalist resistance. Those who were advantaged under the established order often resented the self-restraints implied by the commitment to the body politic as a whole to keep the state free from any specific religious engagement. This bargain or implicit contract relating to citizenship meant that in exchange for subordinating particular identities and accepting the state as internally sovereign, the society as a whole would benefit from law and order, from larger markets, and from protection against external enemies.

What the 1990s brought to the fore was the erosion of the modern prevalence of statism, the rise of regionalism and globalism as a restructuring of the reigning political imagination, the prominence of such non-state actors as global corporations and banks, and an array of transnational civic associations. At work was a cumulative process that was gradually giving shape to a post-Westphalian world most commonly labeled "globalization." (See Chapters 1 and 4).[3] Two principal tendencies began to reshape our understanding of citizenship in this period: first, a multilayered and flexible sense of secondary membership and participation in nonstate political and economic communities of varying scope; second, a vague but significant association of citizenship and loyalty with entities lacking territorial boundaries and not qualifying for membership in standard international institutions, most notably the United Nations.[4] An important part of this reconfiguring of identity and participation can be associated, especially in retrospect, with the declining prospect of *international* warfare following the collapse of the Soviet Union and the accompanying disappearance of socialism as a challenge to capitalism. The security functions of the state, earlier so linked to its military capabilities to defend borders against intruders, were beginning to wither away, increasingly seen as either unnecessary or useless. One result was to weaken the formal sort of nationalism juridically managed by the state and the rise of a variety of ethnic and religious nationalisms that challenged the modern secular state from within, intensifying state-shattering claims of self-determination in many parts of the world. Of course, in the main, the state maintained its centrality in political life for most peoples in the world, including a military role seen as necessary for the security of territorial inhabitants.

Until the 1990s the state succeeded in defining the right of self-determination so that it could only be legally implemented in ways that did *not* result in the dismemberment of existing states.[5] After the Cold War, the breakup of the Soviet Union, but more so, the fragmentation of Yugoslavia into its constituent republics with the backing of much of the international community, introduced a measure of uncertainty as to the scope of the right of self-determination, thereby shifting some of the legal and moral ground from under the sovereign state as a stable political unit.[6] Along these lines, as well, was the rise in the 1990s of the idea that international society had some responsibility for intervening to prevent severe abuses of human rights, and that under such conditions normal deference to territorial sovereignty would be suspended. The Kosovo War of 1999, operating under the controversial regional auspices of NATO, became an exceedingly controversial test case for so-called humanitarian intervention. In essence, the rise of human rights and the growth of external procedures for accountability and enforcement further challenged the logic and praxis of territorial supremacy. This idea of territoriality had been the crucial feature in the formulation of the sovereignty-oriented conception of citizenship that had dominated the doctrines and practices of citizenship during the modern era.

This cumulative subversion of the foundations of statism also gave rise to a renewed interest in civilizational identities, reflected in the global resonance accorded "the clash of civilizations."[7] Beyond the hype surrounding the clash thesis, what was at stake was the realization that the state was being displaced from above by market forces and technological innovation, from below by a resurgence of traditional religious and cultural identities, and from without by a more aggressive approach to the implementation of international human rights standards. Even the computer played a role in this process, creating "virtual communities" exhibiting a contemptuous disregard of international boundaries and governmental institutions. Some Internet addicts referred to themselves as "netizens" and professed their confidence in "self-organizing systems" and a libertarian ethos that had little need for and little sympathy with governmental institutions. These ideas so prevalent in the dot.com world of the 1990s meshed perfectly with the neoliberal sentiments that were dominating global economic policy, emphasizing confidence in the market to allocate resources in a far more socially beneficial manner than could be achieved by activist governments with a social engineering mandate.

It was in this atmosphere of the 1990s that the state, struggling to retain its authority and legitimacy, generated increasing support for ambitious normative (law and morality) projects that did not call for increased spending on the discredited welfare sector. The state was seeking to recast itself, especially in light of criticisms of its top-heavy bureaucracy and heartless passivity in the face of market priorities, as a different kind of ethical actor, less preoccupied with the well-being of its own citizens and more concerned with its international role and reputation. Expanding political space existed for humanitarian diplomacy of various sorts that responded to the sufferings of vulnerable peoples; support was given for strengthening the human rights regime of the UN and in relation to foreign policy; past and current political leaders were formally charged with crimes against humanity and severe abuses of their own citizens and were held individually accountable; and suddenly, historical grievances of long ago associated with the Holocaust, slavery, the dispossession of indigenous peoples, and other suppressed causes were gaining a hearing and were assuaged by a variety of symbolic and substantive gestures of accommodation. (See Chapter 5.)

These moves were a consequence of unprecedented degrees of cooperation between moderate governments and a coalition of civil society actors, culminating in the treaty establishing an International Criminal Court (ICC) that came into being in July 2002, giving a certain rudimentary institutional reality to the still visionary idea that the rule of law did not stop at the borders of sovereign states. Such an evolution was difficult to assess in relation to citizenship, although it clearly contributed to an enlarged sense that meaningful participation in political life, whether measured by rights, claims, entitlements, or responsibilities, was undergoing a profound set of changes that were building the foundations, at least, for constructing an eventual global polity. These changes related particularly to the loosening of state/society bonds and an increasingly plural sense of political community.

September 11 dramatized the grim underside of globalization, including the moral/legal pretensions of this dominant strand of a post-Westphalian world order. By exposing the acute vulnerability of the most powerful and complex modern state to the extremist hostility of its Islamic opponents, a dynamic of action and reaction was unleashed with a wide range of divergent consequences, the outcome of which remains to be determined at this point. In an important respect, the attacks reveal a continuity with the 1990s, exhibiting in a shocking set of acts the potency of nonterritorial, multistate networking, and the functional necessity of global reach as the precondition for societal security.[8] Indeed, the al Qaeda network was also a post-Westphalian phenomenon in the primary sense that its struggle and Osama bin Laden's vision did not center on seizing or reforming state power or a territorial base of operations, but seemed instead resolved to launch an intercivilizational war. The stated political goal was to reconstitute the historic caliphate, abolished with the fall of the Ottoman Empire after World War I, so that it could again over time unify the Islamic world in a single, nonstate religious community; it would thereby overcome the political and cultural fragmentation associated with the imposed Westphalian order, which was deeply criticized as a European invention and incompatible imposition. The modernist ideas of nationalism, patriotism, and secular political life were all treated as decadent from the perspective of bin Laden, and were blamed for decades of Islamic humiliation, especially by Arabic peoples, at the hand of Western domination.

The American response to al Qaeda was the mirror image in some respects, the exact opposite in others. In waging war against terrorism in general, the United States seemed to embark on a war without any clear lines of spatial or temporal demarcation: the battlefield could be anywhere, a global reach was claimed, the scope of the adversary was greatly expanded by identifying the enemy as "terrorism" in general, and there was no prospect that an ending to such a war could be confidently established.[9] Such a campaign was launched with a White House invitation issued to all foreign governments to participate in the antiterrorist coalition, with a warning that failure to do so would identify a government as part of the terrorist threat, and hence an enemy. This ultimatum was then superimposed on the American-led struggle against "rogue states," which were relabeled "the axis of evil." The relevant point being that the U.S. response was of a scale and intensity that ignored the sovereign rights of other states and refused to be bound by the contemporary restraints of international law governing recourse to force or the antiwar framework and procedures of the United Nations Charter. Given the exigencies of the situation in the immediate aftermath of the al Qaeda attacks, including the prospect of further attacks and the inability to be secure in a defensive mode against such suicidal extremism, there was a strong case for altering the Westphalian template to meet the distinctive challenge of megaterrorism.[10] (See Chapters 9 and 10.)

Simultaneously, and with opposite effects, September 11 revived the security role and territoriality of the sovereign state in a dramatic form, at least for the United States, the current uncontested hegemon as far as global security politics is concerned — and with it, an American revival of statist patriotism and nationalism in a variant more intense than anything previously experienced within this country. (See Chapter 11.) For this most powerful of states, citizenship suddenly reverted to waving the American flag and entrusting the government with dangerously expanded police powers and implicit authority to undertake warfare anywhere on the planet in secret and without the meaningful participation of the U.S. Congress. These dramatic developments had the effect of suddenly reversing the precepts of economic globalization by endowing the state with an activist and predominant *global* regulatory role that abruptly subordinated market considerations. Of course, a Westphalian society of states was not reconstituted in this setting, but an inchoate American informal empire that created a spectrum of responses from political actors around the world and from global civil society, ranging from willing subjugation to worried defiance.[11]

What seems evident is that the patterns of citizenship in such a world beset by disruptive and confusing tensions are in the process of undergoing fundamental change, which will lead to a dynamic of growing differentiation as to the quality of citizenship for at least the next several decades. The regionalization of political community around normative ideas in Europe contrasts with the reinscription of imperial nationalism as the basis of political community and identity in the United States.[12] Trends in other regions exhibit other features combining statist ideas with those of a less territorially specific character. There is also an important Asian anti-interventionist trend that emphasizes the inalienability of sovereign rights in a postcolonial setting and strict adherence to a Westphalian ethos with implications for the nature of citizenship.

It leads overall to posing two questions that underlie the discussion that follows: How does the switch from economic globalization to military empire-building by the United States government bear on these diverse citizenship trends? What types of resistance to such a prospect are likely to take hold around the world, with what impacts on traditional and postmodern forms of citizenship?

Tensions of the Times

John Walker Lindh, the so-called American Taliban, exemplifies the deeper tensions of identity and obligation in a globalizing world. To the extent the world is borderless, an altered sense of citizenship would be coming into being in such a manner as to take account of the complex multiple layering that individuals experience with increasing intensity. But to the extent that the security imperatives of September 11 achieve priority, the flattening of identity and obligation results from the imposition of nationalist criteria. Lindh was caught in the middle of this firestorm, apparently following his religious conscience where it would lead without regard to conventional boundaries, including nationalist affiliations, yet made criminally accountable by the application of territorially based criminal law, an instance of vindictive patriotism with an undoubted intention of citizen indoctrination. The fact that Lindh eventually accepted a plea bargain, pleading guilty to some of the charges brought against him so as to avoid the likelihood of a life sentence in a trial, does not change the realization that he found himself trapped between conflicting conceptions of his own identity priorities and the statist conception of membership that illustrate a far more general cosmodrama, pitting territorial affiliations against those of a nonterritorial or transterritorial character.

From another perspective, Osama bin Laden's worldview involves an uncompromising rejection of a world order based on sovereign states and a demonic capability to pose a formidable threat to the life and liberty of statist enemies — despite the absence of statist military capabilities. Osama bin Laden believes that Mohammed intended a unified Islamic *umma*, that the fragmentation of this community in the form of distinct sovereign states is itself a Western invention and intervention that by its very nature produces corruption and decadence. This negativity is decisively revealed by the fact that Arab governments allowed the non-Islamic West to gain footholds close to the most sacred of Islamic sites on the Arabian Peninsula. It was the deployment of American troops in Saudi Arabia near Mecca and Medina in the setting of the Gulf War in the early 1990s that evidently represented the breaking point for bin Laden. So conceived, such an Islamicized individual remains deeply obligated to Islam, but is freed from duties of obedience to the state of residence or citizenship. This rejection of a nationalist approach to membership in a community, and indirectly to citizenship, also represents a flattening of identity and obligation, but in the direction of religious and civilizational identity, and away from territorially based identity.

Such generalizations seem to pertain with particular force to the circumstances and ambitions of the United States, the target of the September 11 attacks and the epicenter of both economic and imperial globalization, and in an opposite manner to the followers of its hidden adversary. There is an irony manifest here that would be comic if its impact did not seem so tragic: the state most associated with dominating the policy agenda of globalization retreats to an apparent posture of ultranationalism, while its ultratraditionalist enemy carries into the lifeworld a virulent vision of the clash of civilizations. Much of the rest of the world is caught in the middle, which has itself become a zone of increasing danger, concern, and seeming impotence.

But there are further complicating factors. Even before September 11, the Bush administration was doing its best to move away from the internationalizing side effects of economic globalization. The Bush White House seemed intent on repudiating several multilateral treaties that were important pillars of international cooperation, making the antiglobalization point that it did not need or want many of the binding ties of multilateralism. (See Chapter 3). Particularly significant, it was going ahead with the militarization of space (defensively and offensively) in defiance of the views of its closest allies. These attitudes have persisted, even intensified, in the aftermath of September 11. The overall situation has become confused by the seemingly inconsistent American demand that others cooperate in the global war against terrorism, and indirectly by the Enron scandal that makes a mockery of neoliberal claims that economic globalization is best guided by the self-regulating forces of market capitalism.

There is increasing reason to believe that the undisclosed priority of the Bush presidency is to establish the first truly global empire in history, and that it is to be unabashedly governed from Washington.[13] (See Chapter 8.) Arguably, prior to Bush there existed a strong imperial element in the American global role associated with presiding over a capital-driven dynamic of globalization.[14] This imperial alternative to a deterritorialized economic globalization raised two linked concerns relating to the future of globally conceived citizenship: How does the switch from economic to military empire-building by the United States bear on global citizenship trends? What types of resistance to such a prospect are likely to take hold around the world, and with what impact on traditional forms of citizenship?

On the one side, there is the revival of American nationalism associated with the anger and sense of continuing vulnerability associated with September 11. (See Chapter 11.) On the other side, there is the latent concern elsewhere about neutralizing some of the unilateralist and empire-building tendencies of this new American world crusade directed against terrorist networks. It is important to take account of the degree to which this "new war" pits the most globalized state against a nonterritorial network allegedly "present" in more than sixty states, including quite likely the United States itself. In this latter sense, there is a hostile convergence of globalizations: the global empire versus the global network.[15] The American turn toward unilateralism and empire may thus be paradoxically interpreted as the state fighting for its life — the last stand of modernity so to speak, with the state fighting to save its soul (that is, the struggle to retain the primary allegiance of its citizenry). If this line of analysis has any purchase on reality, then the disposition of the Lindh case is of major symbolic importance, a collective reaffirmation of nationalist patriotism achieved by ritual sacrifice of a secular apostate, as performed by a compliant criminal justice system that is itself currently led by an evangelical patriot.

There is one further observation relating to the modalities of resistance as bearing on the nature of citizenship. The most disturbing metaphor is that of the most severe cycle of violence unleashed against the Palestinians during Sharon's tenure as leader of Israel. Along this axis of speculation, if America persists on its present course, it will be confronted by the equivalent of "suicide bombers" around the world, resisting by the only effective means available to them as a preferred alternative to surrender and subjugation. The more hopeful alternative is the strengthening of regional tendencies as defensive shields, bypassing the state as the custodian of security, building up a post-Westphalian hierarchy of overlapping political identities and relying to the extent possible on nonviolent approaches to conflict resolution. An intermediate prospect is a retreat from economic globalization in favor of a new phase of "old geopolitics," the American imperial quest generating defensive alliances that seek to reestablish some sort of balance of power, which in the nuclear age would imply efforts to impose deterrence on the United States. The peculiar feature of the period since 1990 is that the United States is essentially undeterred, even with respect to nuclear weaponry, a condition that has not existed since the closing days of World War II when atomic bombs were used in a context where no threat of retaliation existed (what I have elsewhere termed "the Hiroshima temptation").[16]

What this new global setting suggests is a highly dialectical dynamic bearing on citizenship — the leader of corporate and imperial globalization insisting on chauvinistic patriotism, while much of the rest of the world is struggling either with the ordeals of statelessness (consider the entrapped nations: Kurds, Tibetans, Chechens, indigenous peoples, and many, many others), seeking to find regional or civilizational alternatives to statism, or relying on defensive statism to uphold its political and cultural autonomy as resistance against economic globalization and empire-building. The contradictory pulls exerted by complex interdependence and multidimensional globalization are tending to simultaneously strengthen and undermine traditional forms of Westphalian citizenship.

Constructing Global Citizenship: Reviving the 1990s

With the end of the Cold War and the collapse of the Soviet Union, several international developments ensued, and others that had been previously backgrounded by war/peace preoccupations suddenly emerged into the sunlight of global consciousness. (See Chapter 5.) The most prominent of these adjustments was the shift in policy priorities of leading governments from security concerns to the challenges posed by the world economy. The controversial labeling of this dynamic as "globalization" gave rise to a new phase of public debate, which pitted the dominant ideas of neoliberalism (globalization-from-above) against the perspectives of a range of critics (globalization-from-below). (See Chapter 4.)[17] It was against this background that a renewed interest in citizenship emerged, especially to take account of the diminishing adequacy of relying on a purely Westphalian conception of political identity in the face of the growing role of nonstate actors, the diminishing capacity of the territorial state to safeguard and promote human well-being, and an upsurge of identity politics through-out the world.

Such a reconfiguring of citizenship had several distinct features reflect-ing new patterns of thought, action, values, and sentiment that were achieving prominence. "Global citizenship" could be conceived as either the sum of these parts, or as those post-Westphalian identities that were global in scope or that rested on an ethical or anthropological premise of human solidarity.

If the first approach to global citizenship is adopted, then two strands of reconfiguration need to be taken into consideration: the regional conferral of European citizenship as contained in the Maastricht Treaty establishing the European Union, and the more informal patterns of regional identifi-cation that achieve a certain kind of de facto "citizenship" for sub-Saharan Africa, Asia, the Arab World, and Latin America. Closely related to this emerging regional citizenship, itself diverse in character, are overlapping patterns of religious and civilization identity that both reinforce regional-ism and extend it geographically and conceptually. (See Chapter 2). The formation by Osama bin Laden of an Arab Brigade to join the Afghan resistance against the Soviet intervention during the 1980s is emblematic, linking this religious/civilization sense of transnational engagement to the sort of security crisis that has been generated by September 11.

The second approach is what is more conventionally understood by the rubric of "global citizenship." It has several distinct orientations that need to be analyzed separately to assess their wider implications. There are the "one world" postulates of world federalists. These seek to achieve, by steps or through a leap in political consciousness, a centralized form of world order capped by "world government." Such attitudes derive essentially from the belief that war is intolerable, and that the most promising global path to peace is likely to resemble the state path — that is, by a reliance on constitutionalism and the buildup of governmental authority backed by police capabilities. Such views have no political base, derive from a detached Enlightenment consciousness that privileges the rational mind, are formulated almost exclusively in the West, and are viewed with suspi-cion in non-Western countries as largely pretexts for empire-building.

A second dimension of global citizenship is associated with the opera-tives of the world economy who view the world as essentially a borderless market.[18] The role of states is to serve this market, to take their instruc-tions from financial markets and to accord deference to any consensus that derives from the World Economic Forum (Davos) and like bodies that speak for upper-end private sector interests. There is a cultural rootless-ness that accompanies such "global citizenship," expressed by the empty and sterile commonality of international hotels, popular culture, consumerism, franchise capitalism, airports, lifestyle, and the universalizing of the English language. It is not surprising that critics of globalization regard such tendencies as extensions of American global ambitions rather than as expressions of the existence of an authentic global community. The corporate embrace of globalism should perhaps not even be associated with citizenship as it posits and acknowledges no accompanying global community, and hence contains no bonds of solidarity with those who are weak and disadvantaged, or with people generally. At the same time, those who operate in such settings see themselves as mobile "global citizens," at home everywhere, but lacking any definitive address. These global citizens of privilege advocate lowering most obstacles to boundary-crossing by goods, ideas, and money, combined with raising such obstacles for ordinary people and especially for economic migrants.

Closely related are the inhabitants of cyberspace who view the Internet as the basis for a reconstituted world that relies on self-organizing systems, disavowing regulative roles for governmental institutions on the ground of both values and efficiency. Their citizenship is often articulated as "netizenship" to set it off from the bonds of commitment associated with a world of sovereign states. Netizens have constructed their libertarian community within cyberspace, possessing its own protocols of freedom and technological optimism.

Fortunately, there are more positive forms of global citizenship visible on the horizons of change. The human rights and environmental movements gave rise to a variety of social and activist orientations that associated identity with normative commitments — without territorial content more than with traditional approaches to reform on a state/society basis.[19] In the first half of the 1990s, these more global identities were often impressively networked, especially in the arenas provided by a series of UN conferences on global issues (such as the environment, human rights, population, social welfare, women), which also served to incubate a nascent aspiration and demand for global democracy. In reaction, there was a statist backlash that strongly opposed allowing these forces of global civil society to be provided with such potent arenas in the future, replete with opportunities for media exposure and the ability to expose vividly the refusal of leading governments to respond to normative (moral and legal) challenges of global scale. Such a backlash was both exemplified and intensified by the U.S. walkout from the 2001 UN Conference on Racism held in Durban.

From the perspective of citizenship, these initiatives situated the activists in various zones related to global civil society. The sense of participation and affiliation or membership is quite complex, varying from issue to issue, and evolving over time, especially in relation to the changing global setting. For the purposes of this chapter, these activists complement or supersede their Westphalian citizenship with a new connectedness to global civil society.[20] It is a politically engaged modality of global citizenship that is oppositional in part, reformist in part, and visionary in part. In the latter part of the 1990s, these transnational energies were most effectively expressed in collaboration with a coalition of governments dedicated to shared treaty making undertakings.

This orientation toward global citizenship was also exhibited in the one-time Millennium Assembly of representatives of nongovernmental organizations (NGOs) held in 2000 within the halls of the United Nations. (See Chapter 4.) UN Secretary General Kofi Annan vigorously pushed for this initiative despite considerable foot-dragging by Washington. As might be expected, the participants were eager to extend their beachhead in the UN system by institutionalizing their access in the spirit of global democracy. While corporate actors have enjoyed some success in their efforts to gain a legitimizing presence within the United Nations, civil society actors have been rebuffed. Offsetting this exclusion, the antiglobalization movement has enjoyed increasing success in establishing its own arenas, the most notable of which so far has been the annual sessions of the World Social Forum meeting in Porto Allegre, Brazil, dialectically modeled to imitate the structure and counter the influence of the World Economic Forum. In further reaction, there is considerable advocacy around the world in support of the creation of a Global Peoples Assembly, chosen by some sort of electoral process.[21] (See Chapter 5.) The general idea is to promote global or cosmopolitan democracy, building on the European experience, especially the European Court of Human Rights and the European Parliament.[22] In this regard, the recent resolve of the African Union to definitively commit to establishing an African parliamentary institution is encouraging.

Visionary approaches to global citizenship that draw on utopian and religious traditions is another recent trend. In the past, I have tried to suggest such a perspective on participation and membership by the expression "citizen pilgrim."[23] (See Chapter 6, 161–162.) In this trope, "citizen pilgrim" is a global citizen with a predominantly temporal identity that contrasts with the world federalist, who is a captive of spatial identity. The citizen pilgrim embarks on a long journey, the fulfillment of which is to be achieved at some undesignated point in the future. The consciousness of a citizen pilgrim is more closely aligned with that of the transnational activist who identifies global citizenship with an engagement in a values-driven process — promoting specific goals, but necessarily rooted in present urgencies, and typically to some degree anti-utopian in relation to adopting any grand overarching solution, although not inherently or permanently so. If the present world order crises lead to an eruption of major warfare, especially if nuclear or other weapons of mass destruction are used, it would not be surprising to witness the emergence of a movement dedicated to a one world polity organized along normative democratic lines, coupled with a strong commitment to the demilitarization of global security.

I think this matrix of global citizenship was facilitated by the decade of the 1990s (see Chapter 5). There was a sense that globalizing trade, investment, and labor policy were redefining political space in such a way as to diminish the significance of the sovereign state. Indeed, those who had earlier seen states as obstacles to humane global governance reversed course and came to regard a strong, people-oriented social democratic state as the most feasible means to promote the goals of civic globalization. Dramatic breakthroughs in European regionalism also had the effect of weakening the Westphalian grip on citizenship and loyalty, as did the absence of credible strategic conflict among major states.

September 11 has reasserted the primacy of the security state, at least in the United States, and made economic, but not imperial, globalization seem a secondary phenomenon, by no means repudiated or irrelevant, but definitely subordinated to both the war against al Qaeda and empire-building. More damaging in relation to the theme of global citizenship, the military focus and nationalistic climate that September 11 generated has disrupted the promise of the 1990s normative revolution, at least for now. The debate on the shape and future of global governance has been reduced to a single-minded preoccupation with wars and the construction of a unified structure of global security administered from Washington. Of course, if this attention were to be extended to address the root causes of nonstate and anti-Western violence, it could rapidly revive the normative revolution. By and large, American leadership has been unwilling to engage in the sort of self-criticism that might open such a path to global governance, but there are glimmers of hope. The Bush administration surprisingly, given its overall hostility to governmental approaches to social issues, upped the U.S. direct contributions to foreign economic assistance by about $5 billion in 2002, seemingly in recognition of the connections between poverty and political extremism in the countries of the South. But such a gesture pales beside the huge increase of resources devoted to military purposes, including the resources for developing and deploying an expensive defense shield against incoming nuclear weapons and a new generation of nuclear weaponry. It pales even more in relation to a new American doctrine relating to the use of nuclear weapons, which basically seems to make these instruments of war available for use in situations whenever important battlefield advantages would ensue. Most damaging so far has been the coupling of security with nationalistic forms of patriotism that views criticism of government policy as tantamount to disloyalty. (See Chapter 11.)

As suggested by the earlier discussion of the Lindh case, a surge of anti-globalist political feeling has dominated the American scene since September 11. Given the leading role of the United States, this means a retreat from global citizenship by some constituencies and a tighter embrace by others, including offering the peoples of the world an alternative future to that of an American empire imposed by force. In this sense, September 11 could actually strengthen global (and regional) citizenship to achieve countervailing power and influence to that wielded by the United States, but it may also lead to a revival of nineteenth and twentieth century alliance politics and rivalries shaped by Westphalian actors. In essence, the impact of September 11 is substantial, yet inconclusive, and certainly not unidirectional. The most probable pattern of influence is enhancing statism in some settings, both offensively (imperial and apocalyptic globalization) and defensively (avoiding hegemonic encroachments and civic globalization), and weakening it in others (economic globalization and interventionary and hegemonic statecraft).

In sum, citizenship as a dimension of world order is no longer, if it ever really was, a simple matter. The Westphalian framework, although still crucial, cannot by itself provide an adequate purchase on political reality, and never could account for patterns of loyalty as distinct from the formalities of citizenship as a legal status. A more complex, nuanced, and differentiated model of citizenship is sorely needed — one that includes different styles and trends relating to traditional citizenship, but also is open to regional, transnational, and global identities that give rise to a variety of nonstate citizenship claims.

Endnotes

1. This traditional world order was most successfully specified by Hedley Bull, *The Anarchical Society* (New York: Columbia University, 1977); see also Robert Jackson, *The Global Covenant* (Oxford, UK: Oxford University Press, 2000).
2. See the prologue in Marie-Noëlle Little, ed., *The Poet and the Diplomat: The Correspondence of Dag Hammarskjöld and Alexis Leger* (Syracuse, N.Y.: Syracuse University Press, 2001), 3–38, esp. 7–8.
3. See Falk, *The Role of Law in an Emerging Global Village: A Post-Westphalian Perspective* (Ardsley, N.Y.: Transnational, 1999) and Falk, *Predatory Globalization: A Critique* (Cambridge, UK: Polity, 2000).
4. For varying perspectives, see Will Klymlicka, *Multicultural Citizenship: A Liberal Theory of Minority* Rights (Oxford, UK: Oxford University Press, 1995; Aihwa Ong, *Flexible Citizenship: The Cultural Logic of Transnationality* (Durham, N.C.: Duke University Press, 1999).
5. See important consensus formulation at the UN in General Assembly resolution on Friendly Relations among States, GA Res. 2625.
6. These state-shattering tendencies are discussed in Falk, "The Right of Self-Determination under International Law: The Coherence of Doctrine versus the Incoherence of Experience," in Wolgang Danspreckgruber with Arthur Watts, eds., *Self-Determination and Self-Administration: A Sourcebook*, (Boulder, Colo.: Lynne Rienner, 1997), 47–63.
7. See the more careful statement of Huntington's position in book version, as contrasted with the inflammatory impact of the original article in *Foreign Affairs*. Samuel P. Huntington, *The Clash of Civilizations and the Remaking of World Order* (New York, N.Y.: Simon & Schuster, 1996).
8. A phenomenon chronicled in other respects by Manuel Castels, *The Information Age: Economy, Society, and Culture*, 3 vols. (Malden, Mass.: Blackwells, 1996–1998), especially vol. 1, *The Rise of the Network Society.*
9. Gore Vidal, *Perpetual War for Perpetual Peace: How We Got To Be So Hated* (New York, N.Y.: Thunder's Mouth Press/Nation Books, 2002); Tariq Ali, *The Clash of Fundamentalisms: Crusades, Jihads, and Modernity* (London, UK: Verso, 2002).
10. Falk, *The Great Terror War* (Northhampton, Mass.: Interlink, 2003).

11. The apologists and rationalizers of this new order are receiving mainstream approval at this point, but the consensus is fraying around the issue of waging war against Iraq. Among the more interesting presentations, see Philip Bobbit, *The Shield of Achilles: War, Peace, and the Course of History* (New York: Knopf, 2002); Stephen G. Brooks and William C. Wohlforth, "American Primacy in Perspective," *Foreign Affairs* 81, 4: 20–33 (July/August 2002); Robert Kaplan, *Warrior Politics: Why Leadership Demands a Pagan Ethos* (New York, N.Y.: Random House, 2002); Niall Ferguson, "Clashing Civilizations or Mad Mullahs: The United States between Informal and Formal Empire," in Strobe Talbott and Nayan Chanda, eds., *The Age of Terror: America and the World After September 11* (New York, N.Y.: Basic Books, 113–41); and also a new breed of "humanitarian imperialists" most articulately depicted in the writings of Michael Ignatieff. Ignatieff is an interesting instance, as he was a forceful advocate of humanitarian intervention in the 1990s, and has now recast the argument to take account of post–September 11 realities, but with an equivalent justification for interventionary diplomacy under an American aegis. See, for instance, Ignatieff, "How to Keep Afghanistan from Falling Apart: The Case for a Committed American Imperialism," *New York Times Magazine*, July 28, 2002, 26–31, 54.

12. See a geopolitical assessment of this civilizational comparison by Robert Kagan, "Power and Weakness: Why the United States and Europe See the World Differently," *Policy Review* 113 (June/July 2002): 3–28.

13. Nicholas Lemann, "The Next World Order," *The New Yorker*, April 1, 2002, 42–48.

14. See Michael Hardt and Antonio Negri, *Empire* (Cambridge, Mass.: Harvard University Press, 2000).

15. The structural importance of networking as subversive of territoriality is the major theme of Castels, *The Information Age: Economy, Society and Culture* (Mauldin, MA: Blackwells, 3 vol., 1996–1998).

16. For analysis along these lines, see Richard Falk and David Krieger, "Taming the Nuclear Monster," *Asahi Shimbum*, May 13, 2002.

17. For elaboration, see Richard Falk, *Predatory Globalization. A Critique* (Cambridge, UK: Polity, 1999).

18. For more on this theme, see the writings of Kenichi Ohmae.

19. Among the large literature suggestive on these issues, see R. B. J. Walker, *One World, Many Worlds* (Boulder, CO: Lynne Rienner, 1988); and Margaret Keck and Kathryn Sikkuk, *Activists beyond Borders: Advocacy Networks in International Politics* (Ithaca, NY: Cornell University Press, 1998).

20. For background, see Alejandro Colas, *International Civil Society* (Cambridge, UK: Polity, 2002; R. D. Lipschutz, "Reconstructing World Politics: The Emergence of Global Civil Society," *Millennium: Journal of International Studies* 21, 3 (1992): 389–420; *Global Civil Society 2002* (Oxford, UK: Oxford University Press, 2002).

21. To consider various alternatives, see Falk and Andrew Strauss, "On the Creation of a Global Peoples Assembly: Legitimacy and the Power of Popular Sovereignty, *Standford Journal of International Law* 36(No. 2): 191–219, 2000.

22. See contributions to Daniele Archibugi and David Held, eds., *Cosmopolitan Democracy: An Agenda for a New World Order* (Cambridge, UK: Polity, 1995).

23. The idea of "citizen pilgrim" was earlier introduced in Richard Falk, *On Humane Global Governance: Toward a New Global Politcs* (New York: Polity, 1995).

Part Three
Regression

Chapter 8
Grasping George W. Bush's Postmodern Geopolitics

President George W. Bush's June 2002 graduation address to the cadets at West Point deservedly attracted worldwide attention, mainly because it was the fullest articulation, at that point, of a strategic doctrine of preemption that was critically interpreted to be the most open embrace yet made of imperial globalization.[1] A few months later, the Bush White House issued its more comprehensive prescriptions along the same lines for a secure America in the National Security Strategy of the United States of America, but the essential points were all made in the West Point speech. The radical doctrine touted by the White House and the Pentagon is that the United States claims the right to militarily attack any state that American leaders view as either harboring "terrorists" or allegedly acquiring weaponry of mass destruction, whether nuclear, biological, or chemical. The obvious initial test case for preemption was Iraq, which for years was continuously threatened with an American interventionary diplomacy overtly seeking regime change, either on the model of the displacement of the Taliban in Afghanistan, or by promoting an anti-Saddam indigenous uprising.

Washington's plans for preemptive war went forward, despite the numerous objections voiced by governments in the Middle East, European allies, and a worldwide groundswell of opposition to initiating a preemptive war against Iraq. This forward momentum was slowed to the extent of inducing the Bush White House to seek an endorsement from the UN Security Council so as to build a stronger political consensus and blunt criticism. In evaluating these developments, it should be realized that it is less the doctrine of preemption that provoked such intense concern around the world and more its application to Iraq in the absence of any credible threat directed at American security.

This new approach to the use of international force was proclaimed by the United States beneath the banner of counterterrorism and in the domestic climate of fervent nationalism that has prevailed in America since the September 11 attacks. (See Chapter 11.) It was disturbing that this approach was adopted without even mentioning the relevance of the core idea of the United Nations Charter (reinforced by decisions of the World Court in The Hague), which consists of a prohibition of any use of international force that is not undertaken in self-defense *after* the occurrence of an armed attack across an international boundary or pursuant to a decision by the UN Security Council. The president could have at least advanced the case for preemptive war as a reinterpretation of the right of self-defense given the distinctive security challenge posed by the al Qaeda threat.

International lawyers have been arguing about the proper scope of the right of self-defense under the Charter ever since 1945 when the UN was established, but always with an agreement that it is necessary to provide a reasoned and principled explanation for why a particular state is putting forward an expanded claim at any given time. The specificity of the claim is essentially an appeal to a rule of reason as the basis for interpretation, suggesting that it is not reasonable to expect a country to risk their fundamental security if confronted by a threat that does not allow for defensive force by an overly literal reading of the legal prohibitions contained in the Charter. At the same time, there had been a tacit understanding among diplomats and jurists that such departures should be related to concrete circumstances, joining facts to generalities in a manner that builds a persuasive justification for the claimed use of force. Breaking this understanding in a context in which the perceptions of governments and grassroots public opinion failed to buy the American argument in relation to Iraq led to a firestorm of criticism around the world directed at American war mongering.

When Iraq conquered and annexed Kuwait in 1990, international law supported reliance on a claim of self-defense either by Kuwait alone or in coalition with other states. Even without awaiting any specific UN authorization, Kuwait was legally entitled to act in self-defense to recover its territorial sovereignty, although Article 51 imposes a duty on such a claimant to report its actions to the Security Council in a timely manner. In such circumstances, the United States and others were able to join Kuwait in bolstering the prospects for successful defense, thereby acting in what international lawyers call collective self-defense. Back in 1956, when the American commitment to this Charter effort to place legal limits upon the discretion of states to use international force was at its height, the U.S. government surprised its allies and adversaries by opposing the Suez Operation of Britain, France, and Israel, in large part because it was a non-defensive use of force against Egypt that was inconsistent with the UN

Charter and modern international law. Such a law-oriented stand was particularly impressive, given Washington's intense dislike of Nasser's anti-Israeli, anti-West militancy.

This legal commitment by states to renounce their discretion to use force in conflict situations evolved by stages in the period after World War I. The general idea was dramatized when the surviving leaders of Germany and Japan after World War II were prosecuted for their alleged war crimes and crimes against peace. The Nuremberg and Tokyo trials focused on demonstrating that those accused were responsible for initiating wars of aggression. Such behavior was declared worse even than the atrocities committed in the course of the war in the historic judgments reached. The related task of the Charter was to give this fundamental limit on the sovereignty of states and the discretion of leaders as clear a definition as possible, which explains why international force is unconditionally prohibited in general as a security option of states (Article 2(4)), with the single exception, already mentioned, taking the form of a somewhat artificially delimited right of self-defense (Article 51). In the mid-1980s, for instance, when the United States argued vehemently that Sandinista efforts in Nicaragua to help a revolutionary movement overthrow the government in neighboring El Salvador by armed struggle legally allowed the existing Salvadorean government to act in collective self-defense, a strong majority of the World Court refused to accept the argument; this, in the mid 1980s, angered the Reagan White House to the extent that it withdrew its acceptance of the compulsory jurisdiction from the judicial arm of the United Nations system. In this sense, the American refusal to conduct its foreign policy in conformity to the UN Charter and international law is not new. What is new is extending its claims to initiate a *major* war without any pretense of responding in the spirit of self-defense, and doing so, in defiance of world public opinion as well as international law as generally understood. Even more disturbing is the application of this unilateralism to Iraq, where a sovereign state seemed falsely accused of mounting a threat to the United States and the region, coupled with an American insistence that it alone would determine when its security interests vindicated recourse to war.

Preemption, in contrast to the delimitation of the self-defense in the Charter, is based on striking first, and this time not in a crisis, as was done by Israel with plausible justification in the 1967 War when enemy Arab troops were massing on its borders after dismissing the UN war-preventing presence. The U.S. argument for war alleged shadowy intentions of Baghdad, pointed to supposed links with terrorist groups, emphasized Iraqi possession of weaponry of mass destruction, and stressed the future dangers of inaction in the face of these realities. But were these realities real? Increasingly, in the aftermath of the Iraq War, the facts relied on by Washington appear to be factoids. But even if the White House, Pentagon, and State Department did present the situation realistically, it did not add up to a reasonable case for recourse to war. It failed to persuade the members of the Security Council, although the Iraq debate in the UN accepted the main premises of the American argument. (See Chapter 10.)

Preemption, if unilaterally applied, is a doctrine without limits, without accountability to the UN or international law, without any dependence on a collective judgment of responsible governments, and, what is worse, without requiring any convincing demonstration of practical necessity. Preemption itself was stretched beyond its own limits in the Iraq context, as the key element of an imminent and serious threat arising out of inaction was not demonstrated, and does not appear to have existed. Some contended that because of this absence, the American action should be viewed as one of "preventive war," and not preemption. Preventive war, which is a step further away from Charter constraints because it drops the requirement of imminence, rests on a vague claim of removing from the international scene an actor that might pose a threat at some later time. Some have been arguing recently behind closed doors for such a strategic option in relation to China, provoking a preventive war while China was relatively weak as an adversary rather than allowing it to become a rival challenging American geopolitical preeminence. Recourse to preventive war makes no pretense of resting on international law. It is pure geopolitics with a Machiavellian twist.

But even a preventive war rationale did not seem to fit the Iraqi case. It was almost impossible to project a plausible scenario in which Iraq would pose a serious threat to the security of the United States at any point in the future. It is for these reasons that the war against Iraq seems so clearly to qualify as a war of aggression — that is, even stretching international law and invoking geopolitical reasoning does not provide adequate justification for it. It would thus seem to be the case that either the Bush administration badly misconstrued the facts or possessed undisclosed motives for initiating the Iraq War. In any event, its action has been generally understood as an expression of irresponsible and radical geopolitics that arises from its main, underlying resolve to base global security upon American global dominance, and that demonstrated control over the Middle East is a vital step in achieving this goal. From this line of thinking, the Iraq War was a key American move designed mainly to achieve regional dominance.

Before jumping altogether in this critical direction, it may be useful to consider the argument that, regardless of the motivations, the war qualified as a successful instance of "humanitarian intervention" as it liberated the Iraqi people from the oppressive rule of Saddam Hussein. Certainly, such an outcome is a beneficial side effect of the Iraq War, but should it be allowed to provide a justification either in law or from the perspective of the geopolitical management of world order? In passing, it should be noted that the specific American goals of the war may produce a prolonged occupation that deprives the Iraqi people of their right of self-determination, and ends up substituting one form of oppression for another. But beyond this, war is too serious a matter to allow it to be declared on one basis and justified after the fact on another. Even the American public and Congress would not have accepted the risks and costs of the Iraq War if it had been presented as a humanitarian undertaking. To hide the true rationale for war is to violate the basic trust between citizen and state pertaining to the most basic of all public issues. But again, the facts did not support a claim of humanitarian intervention. There was no humanitarian emergency, the worst excesses of the regime had been committed years ago, the suffering of the civilian society was more a function of UN sanctions than of Saddam Hussein's brutalities, and, above all, there was no requisite humanitarian emergency in Iraq that might justify an exception to the normal reliance on internal politics to achieve change and reform. In this respect, the situation before the Iraq War could be contrasted with that existing in Kosovo before the war in 1999 or presently in African countries such as Ethiopia and Liberia.

It is true that the reality of the megaterrorist challenge requires some rethinking of the relevance of rules and restraints based on armed conflict in a world of territorial states. The most radical aspect of the al Qaeda challenge is a result of its nonterritorial, concealed organizational structure as a multistate network. Modern geopolitics was framed to cope with conflict and relations among sovereign states; the capacity of a network with modest traditional financial and military resources to mount a major attack and wage a devastating type of war on a global scale against the largest state does require an acknowledgement of a different structure of security that will need to be constructed by a *postmodern geopolitics*, reinforced by responsive adjustments in legal doctrines pertaining to the use of force and self-defense. Postmodernity refers here to its world order implications associated with the realization that security preoccupations can no longer be reduced to the interaction of state actors in relation to conflicts that can be understood by reference to their territorial dimensions. This contrasts with "modernity" born geopolitically in 1648 at the Peace of Westphalia with the ascent of the secular sovereign state, and a world politics that could be expressed, without gross distortion, by reference to territorial ambitions and protection. Postmodern geopolitics did not begin on September 11 — far from it. The process of undermining world order conceived along Westphalian lines has deep and diverse roots. (See Chapter 1.)

In recent years, economic and civic globalization crossed the threshold dividing the modern from the postmodern, especially by the double shift in the locus of authority from state to market and from state to civil society, including its transnational dynamics. The spread and rapid evolution of nonterritorial and nonspatial information technologies to coordinate behavior on a global scale truly subverted an ordering framework based on territorially bounded political units. What Osama bin Laden and George W. Bush did on and after September 11 was grant postmodern geopolitics a turn back toward war and conflict, back to issues of conquest, and away from markets and the logic of capital. For bin Laden, the focus was on nonterritorial empowerment via megaterrorism, a culminating imaginary of establishing the Islamic *umma* to replace the modern, Western-inspired structure of distinct sovereign states currently administering life in the Muslim world. For Bush, the emphasis was on carrying the retaliatory war to the networked enemy concealed in some sixty countries, and declaring war on all those nonstate forces around the world that were engaged in armed struggle — that is, a war without a territorial enemy and waged in disregard of international law, which is from this perspective an outmoded *modernist* creation. And in the process of resisting al Qaeda an unprecedented American-led global empire is being established. There is nothing new about political actors pursuing imperial ambitions. Achieving empire — in the sense of control and dominance, without territorial expansion, and without an outer limit — is new and innovative. The project to establish a global empire will not show up on maps in the future, but it will override, for many purposes, the independence of countries set off by boundaries highlighted by different colors.

Responding to the threat of megaterrorism does require some stretching of international law to accommodate the reasonable security needs of those sovereign states under attack, and possibly, the state system as a whole. Prior cross-border military reactions to transnational terrorism over the years by the United States, India, Israel, and others were generally tolerated by the UN and international public opinion because they seem proportionate and necessary in relation to the threats posed, and the use of force was in its essence *reactive*, not anticipatory, and seemed consistent with the rule of reason and the discipline of prudence relating to the uses of international force. International law was consistently bent to serve these practical imperatives of security — but reasonably in the spirit of adaptation, and not broken with respect to fundamentals.

But the Bush doctrine of preemption goes much further, encroaching on the highly dangerous terrain of unreason and imprudence. It claims an abstract right to abandon both the rules of restraint and the guidelines embodied in international law patiently developed over the course of centuries to govern the use of force in relation to territorial states, not networks. To propose abandoning the core legal restraint on international force in relations among states is to badly misread the challenge of September 11. This abandonment permits states to use force nondefensively against their enemies, thereby creating a terrible precedent for possible future use by other political actors. There is every reason to think that "containment" and "deterrence" remain effective ways to approach almost any state that threatens unwarranted expansion. There is no evidence to suggest that Iraq could not have been deterred from undertaking further aggressive behavior. After all, the whole pattern of Iraqi behavior in relation to its war against Iran in the 1980s, as well as its conquest and annexation of Kuwait in 1990, was based on a rational calculation of gains by Baghdad. When these proved woefully incorrect, it led to a reversal of policy and a grudging acceptance of the failure of expansionist geopolitics.

Brutal and oppressive as was regime in Iraq, it was accepted by the West until 1990 as a geopolitical ally of sorts, especially in relation to the spread of radical Islam in the aftermath of the Iranian Revolution. As a state, Iraq acted and behaved normally — that is, by weighing benefits and costs, although not very intelligently given its failures to accurately assess its prospects of military victory in either Iran or Kuwait. In recent years, it was surrounded and threatened by the greatly superior force of the United States, as well as by Israel, which had demonstrated by its attack on the Iraqi nuclear reactor at Osirak that it was prepared to use force preemptively in the face of a concrete security threat. After the Gulf War of 1991, any Iraqi attempt to lash out at neighbors or others, even in the form of threats, would almost certainly have resulted in an annihilating response leading to the immediate and total destruction of Iraq. There is no reason whatsoever to think that deterrence and containment would not have succeeded in relation to Iraq, even if Baghdad had managed to acquire or retain some significant amount of biological, chemical, or nuclear weaponry. Deterrence and containment succeeded in relation to the Soviet Union for more than four decades under far more demanding circumstances, and only disregarded extremists advocated in the inner circles of power that the United States act preemptively or preventively. Again, the Iraq debate was colored by the dogs that didn't bark: oil, geopolitical goals in the region and beyond, and the security of Israel.

What is at stake with preemption, especially as tied to the axis of evil imagery, is more hidden and sinister than some questionable expansions of the right of self-defense under international law. Washington fears, I think, not aggressive moves by these countries, but *their* acquisition of sufficient weaponry of mass destruction that might give them a deterrent capability with respect to the geopolitical ambitions in the region of United States and Israel. Since the end of the Cold War, the United States has enjoyed the luxury of being undeterred in world politics except by considerations of self-restraint. This degree of "unilateralism" is particularly disturbing to other countries and needs to be understood in relation to the moves of the Pentagon, contained in a report leaked in December of 2000 to increase U.S. reliance on nuclear weaponry in a variety of strategic circumstances, and later confirmed in congressional hearings.

At West Point, Bush declared with self-righteous moral fervor that "our enemies … have been caught seeking these terrible weapons." It never occurs to our leaders that these weapons are no less terrible as seen by others when acquired by the United States, especially when American advisors have explicitly and repeatedly contemplated their use. Nothing better illustrates the double standards that are part of the existing world order than the idea that nuclear weapons are legitimate security instruments for a few states and a criminal option for the rest. There is every reason for others to fear that as long as the United States remains undeterred, it will again become subject to "the Hiroshima temptation," that is, a willingness to threaten other states with the use such weapons in the absence of any prospect of retaliation should the battlefield and strategic arguments favoring use seem persuasive. It is not only displays of unilateralism in relation to global policy issues and recourse to war against Iraq in a legally dubious context, it is even more the degree of geopolitical imprudence exhibited by American leaders with respect to the fiscal and political project of empire-building, which makes the policy so disturbing.

And Bush goes further, combining empire with utopia. At West Point, he reminded his audience that "the twentieth century ended with a single surviving model of human progress based on non-negotiable demands of human dignity, the rule of law, limits on the power of the state, respect for women and private property and free speech and equal justice and religious tolerance." The clear intention is to suggest that America is already the embodiment of this sole model of political legitimacy. And while Bush concedes that "America cannot impose this vision," he does insist that the U.S. government "can support and reward governments that make the right choices for their own people," and presumably punish those that don't. Not only does the United States claim a right of global dominance, including setting the rules of the game with respect to the crucial matter of weaponry of mass destruction, but it also professes to have the final answers for the pursuit of societal well-being, seeming to forget its own homeless citizens, its crowded and expanding prisons, its urban blight, and countless other domestic reminders that the United States may not represent the best of all possible worlds, and especially not for other peoples adhering to quite different traditions and priorities. Bush's worldview, among other flaws, denies the validity of diversity and experimentation, and seems in deep, dark denial when it comes to acknowledging any legitimate grievances that others may have with respect to the American role in the world. Such an absence of self-doubt brands this postmodern stance promoted by the United States as a dangerous variant of fundamentalist geopolitics.

This vision of postmodern geopolitics causes further alarms as it is underwritten by a strong dosage of evangelical moralism (gives added influence due to collaboration with secular right wing extremism that has taken due form of a heavy neocon presence in the inner circle of government advisors and notables). Bush unabashedly confronted the issue of grounding America's approach to the world on the basis of religious and moral convictions: "Some worry that it is somehow undiplomatic or impolite to speak the language of right and wrong. I disagree," adding, "[m]oral truth is the same in every culture, in every time, in every place." Such absolutism is then applied to the current global realities. Bush insisted that "we are in a conflict between good and evil, and America will call evil by its name. By confronting evil and lawless regimes, we do not create a problem, we reveal a problem. And we will lead the world in opposing it." Aside from assuming the moral high ground, which exempts America from even the hint of self-criticism or from addressing the grievances others have with respect to U.S. policies, such sentiments imply a repudiation of dialogue and negotiation about the shaping of world order. As there can be no acceptable compromise with the forces of evil, there can be no reasonable restraint on the forces of good. We may lament fundamentalism in the Islamic world and decry the fulminations of Osama bin Laden, but what about that fashioned in the inner circles of Washington power wielders?

In contemplating this grandiose geopolitical vision for the American future, it is natural to wonder about what might happen to the starkly different rhetoric Bush used when he was a presidential candidate, reminding the country aptly about the virtue of "humility" in depicting America's role in the world. At the time, Bush was then trying to discredit the humanitarian diplomacy attributed (mostly wrongly) to Bill Clinton and Al Gore, but the contrast in tone and substance is still striking, between Bush on the campaign trail and Bush in the White House. One wonders whether the heady atmosphere of the Oval Office has fed these geopolitical dreams, or whether this president, so known for his lack of foreign policy knowledge, has been manipulated into this crusading mode by bureaucratic hawks who seized the opportunity to take command that was so tragically provided by September 11.

In fairness, many influential Americans share this dream of a borderless global empire, but adopt less forthright language. For instance, Eliot Cohen, the respected conservative military commentator, wrote the following in *Foreign Affairs*: "In the twenty-first century, characterized like the European Middle Ages by a universal (if problematic) high culture with a universal language, the U.S. military plays an extraordinary and inimitable role. It has become, whether Americans or others like it or not, the ultimate guarantor of international order."[2] To make such an assertion without apology or justification is to say, in effect, that the imperial role of the United States is no longer in doubt, or even subject to useful debate, and that no relevant consultative process is available to exercise the authority that flows from such a preponderance of power. To acknowledge that it makes no difference whether Americans or others support this destiny is to reveal the fallen condition of democracy and the irrelevance of international public opinion. Along similar lines of presupposition, in the same issue of *Foreign Affairs* Stephen Biddle observes, in relation to the problems of the Balkans and, specifically, Kosovo, that "Americans do well in crusades," but "they are not suited … to the dirty work of imperial policing to secure second- or third-tier interests."[3] Such an outlook treats the reality of an American global empire as a foregone conclusion.

But preemption, double standards, and evangelical moralism were not the only troubling features of this postmodern geopolitical outlook outlined in the West Point speech. There is, above all, the pursuit of global dominance, a project to transform world order from its current assemblage of sovereign states in the direction of a postmodern (that is, nonterritorial) global empire — effectively, if informally, administered from Washington. Bush misleadingly assured the graduating cadets that "America has no empire to extend or utopia to establish" before he proceeded to describe precisely such undertakings. The president mentions that past rivalries among states have arisen because of their diverse ambitions and competitive security policies, but insists that the future will be different because of American military superiority: "America has, and intends to keep, military strengths beyond challenge, thereby making the destabilizing arms races of other eras pointless, and limiting rivalries to trade and other pursuits of peace." The ambition expressed by Bush, if reflected on, is truly breathtaking and imperial — nothing less than a proclamation informing *all* other states that the era of self-help security is essentially over, that America will henceforth act as the global gendarme. If acting rationally, other states should accept this reality by devoting their energies and resources to advantageous economic and peaceful pursuits, leaving both national and global security in Washington's safe hands.

One can only wonder about the reaction of foreign ministries around the world, say in Paris or Beijing, when confronted by this language that encourages, and even instructs, states to dramatically abandon their traditional sovereign rights associated with security functions. This emphasis on the American global \role is reinforced by moves to scrap the Anti-Ballistic Missile Treaty, to build a missile defense shield, to plan for the militarization of space, and to work hard on futuristic techniques of warfare based on robotics and electronic guidance. As the neocon intellectual community was arguing in the 1990s, America's imperial opportunities and ambitions can only be realized by a heavy reliance on military superiority, combined with the will and capacity to project overwhelming force anywhere on the planet. In this respect, the Iraq War, much more than the Afghanistan War or the Balkan Wars of the 1990s, represented a powerful first expression of imperial globalization.

Whether it is Bush at West Point or the more sedate writings of the foreign policy elite writing for each other in *Foreign Affairs*, or for that matter intelligent and progressive criticism, there is a need to anchor any such analysis in a postmodern realization that the core security issue of the day is addressing the dangers posed by a menacing nonstate adversary — one concealed in a shadowy network that is simultaneously everywhere and nowhere, and may or may not constitute an organization in the normal sense of administrative coherence. These new circumstances definitely call for fresh thinking that adapts international law and global security to these challenges in an effective and constructive manner. But the adjustments proposed by Bush are blunt instruments that do not meet the specific challenges of megaterrorism, and unleash a variety of dangerous forces that could have the ironic effect of intensifying the threat.

What is needed is new thinking about security for the peoples of the world that sees the United States as part of a global community seeking to appropriate ways to restore security and confidence, building on existing frameworks of cooperative law enforcement and legal restraints to work toward constructing a more robust United Nations. Such an American leadership does not insist on an imperial role whereby it has the sole authority to make up and enforce the rules of world politics as it goes along. Given the bipartisan gridlock that has gripped the country since September 11, positive forms of new thinking will almost certainly come, if they come at all, from pressures exerted by the citizenry far from Washington — in this country and around the world. All of us, as citizens, wherever we are, have never faced a more urgent duty to make this happen. It can begin with presidential politics, providing the United States with a different leadership that is not so closely identified with the radical right. But as desirable as this would be, it is far from enough. We need to move toward accommodating civic and economic globalization, possibly under the banners of a postmodern world order built on the premises of human rights and global democracy.

Endnotes

1. Text of President Bush's West Point speech of June 2, 2002 can be found at the White House website. <www.WhiteHouse.gov>
2. Eliot A. Cohen, "A Tale of Two Secretaries," *Foreign Affairs* 81(No. 3): 33–46, at 46 (2002).
3. Stephen Biddle, "The New Way of War? Debating the Kosovo Model," *Foreign Affairs* 81(No. 3): 138–144, at 139 (2002).

Chapter 9
The United Nations after the Iraq War

The impact of the Iraq War on the future role of the United Nations is a highly speculative matter at this stage. Even the combat phases of the war are far from over, despite President George W. Bush's ill-conceived proclamation of victory on May 1, 2003. The war is now assuming the form of resistance to unwanted foreign occupation, and its unclear whether, as Washington officially contends, its main perpetrators are remnants of Saddam Hussein's regime. Earlier, American leadership was inclined to minimize UN participation in the restoration of normalcy in Iraq, but as of July 2003, the U.S. government is beginning to suggest a much expanded set of UN responsibilities, and is calling on a wide range of countries to supply troops and share the peacekeeping burdens and risks. Despite this fluidity, it does not seem too soon to consider the bearing of the Iraq War upon the future of the United Nations in the area of peace and security.

Framing an Inquiry

President Bush historically challenged the United Nations Security Council (UNSC) when he uttered some memorable words in the course of his September 12, 2002, speech to the General Assembly: "Will the UN serve the purpose of its founding, or will it be irrelevant?"[1] In the aftermath of the Iraq War, there are at least two answers to this question. The answer of the U.S. government would be to suggest that the UN turned out to be irrelevant due to its failure to endorse recourse to war against the Iraq of Saddam Hussein. The answer of those who opposed the war is that the UNSC served the purpose of its founding by its refusal to endorse recourse to a war that could not be persuasively reconciled with the UN Charter and international law. This difference of assessment is not just factual;

whether Iraq was a threat and whether the inspection process was succeeding at a reasonable pace, was also conceptual, even jurisprudential. The resolution of this latter debate is likely to shape the future role of the United Nations and influence the attitude of the most powerful sovereign state as to the relationship between international law generally and the use of force as an instrument of foreign policy.

These underlying concerns antedate the recent preoccupation, and were vigorously debated during the cold war era, especially during the latter stages of the Vietnam War.[2] But the present context of the debate as to the interplay between sovereign discretion and the use of force and UN authority was framed in the late 1990s around the topic of humanitarian intervention, especially in relation to the Kosovo War. The burning issue in the Kosovo setting was whether "a coalition of the willing" acting under the umbrella of NATO was legally entitled to act as a residual option given the perceived UNSC unwillingness to mandate a use of force despite the urgent humanitarian dangers facing the Albanian Kosovars. In that instance, a formal mandate was sought and provided by NATO, but without what was textually required by Article 53(1) of the UN Charter — that is, lacking some expression of explicit authorization by the UNSC. Legal apologists for the initiative insisted that such authorization could be derived from prior UNSC resolutions, as well as from the willingness of the UN to manage the postconflict civil reconstruction of Kosovo that amounted to a tacit assent, providing the undertaking with a retroactive certification of legality. To similar effect were arguments suggesting that the defeat in the Security Council of a resolution of censure introduced by those members opposed to the Kosovo War amounted to an implied acknowledgement of legality, or at the very least a refusal to categorize the war as "illegal" or in violation of the Charter.

But the tension with the Charter rules on the use of force was so clear that these efforts at legalization seemed lame, and what seems a far preferable approach was adopted by the Independent International Commission on Kosovo, which concluded that the intervention in Kosovo was "illegal, but legitimate."[3] The troublesome elasticity of this doctrine was qualified in two ways: by suggesting the need for the intervening side to bear a heavy burden of persuasion as to the necessity of intervention to avoid an impending or ongoing humanitarian catastrophe; and by a checklist of duties that need to be fulfilled by the intervenors to achieve legitimacy, emphasizing the protection of the civilian population, adherence to the international laws of war, and a convincing focus on humanitarian goals as distinct from economic and strategic aims of benefit to the intervenors.

In Kosovo, the moral and political case for intervention seemed strong: a vulnerable and long abused majority population facing an imminent prospect of ethnic cleansing by Serb rulers, a scenario for effective intervention with minimal risks of unforeseen negative effects or extensive collateral damage; and the absence of significant nonhumanitarian motivations on the intervening side. As such, the foundation for a principled departure under exceptional circumstances from a strict rendering of Charter rules on the use of force seemed present. The legality/legitimacy gap, however, was recognized as unhealthy, eroding the authority of international law over time, and the Commission strongly recommended that it be closed at the earliest possible time by UN initiative. Its report urged, for example, that the permanent members of the Security Council consider informally agreeing to refrain from casting adverse votes in the setting of impending humanitarian catastrophes, and thus suspend the operation of the veto despite disagreeing with the initiative under consideration.[4] The adoption of such a practice would have enabled the Kosovo intervention to be approved by the Security Council even in the face of Russian and Chinese opposition, which would have registered in the debate by way of veto-avoiding abstentions in the vote.

More ambitiously, the Commission proposed a three-step process designed to acknowledge within the United Nations Charter System the enforcement role of the Organization in contexts of severe human rights violations. The first step consists of a framework of principles designed to limit claims of humanitarian intervention to a narrow set of circumstances and to assure that the dynamics of implementation adhere to international humanitarian law and promote the well-being of the people being protected. The second step is to draft a resolution for adoption by the General Assembly in the form of a Declaration on the Right and Responsibility of Humanitarian Intervention that seeks to reconcile respect for sovereign rights, the duty to implement human rights, and the responsibility to prevent humanitarian catastrophes. The third step would be to amend the Charter to incorporate these changes as they pertain to the role and responsibility of the UNSC and other multilateral frameworks and coalitions that undertake humanitarian interventions.[5] It should be noted that no progress toward closing this legitimacy/legality gap by formal or informal action within the United Nations could be anticipated in the near future. There exists substantial opposition on issues of principle as well as policy, especially among Asian countries, to any expansion of the interventionary mandate of the United Nations and other political actors in the setting of human rights. This opposition has deepened since Kosovo because of the controversial use of force claimed by the United States in its antiterrorism campaign that have combined security and human rights arguments in settings where widespread suspicion existed with respect to the geopolitical motives of Washington.

Iraq tested the UN Charter system in a way complementary to that associated with the Kosovo controversy, but more fundamentally. The Iraq test was associated with the overall impact of the September 11 attacks and the challenge of megaterrorism on the viability of the Charter framework governing the use of international force.[6] The initial American military response to the al Qaeda attack and continuing threat was directed at

Afghanistan, a convenient territorial target because it both seemed to be the nerve center of the terrorist organization and a country ruled by the Taliban, a regime enjoying the most minimal diplomatic stature and complicit in the attacks by allowing al Qaeda to operate extensive terrorist training bases within its territory. As such, Afghanistan, as represented by the Taliban, lacked some crucial attributes needed for full membership in international society, including the failure to obtain widespread diplomatic recognition. The reasonableness of waging war to supplant the Taliban regime and destroy the al Qaeda base of operations in Afghanistan was widely accepted by the entire spectrum of countries active in world politics, although there was only the most minimal effort by the U.S. government to demonstrate that it was acting within the UN framework. The al Qaeda responsibility for September 11 was amply demonstrated, although controversy and skepticism persists as to whether the attacks could and should have been prevented. Beyond this assurance about responsibility for September 11, the prospect of future attacks seemed great and possibly imminent, and the American capability to win a war in Afghanistan at a proportional cost seemed convincing. For these reasons, there was no significant international opposition to the American initiation and conduct of the Afghanistan War and varying levels of support from all of America's traditional allies. International law was successfully stretched in these novel circumstances to provide a major state with the practical option of responding with force to one important territorial source of megaterrorist warfare, thereby upholding the White House claim that a government that knowingly harbors such transnational terrorists shares responsibility for the political violence that ensues.

But when American leaders began to discuss the Iraq phase of the September 11 response, most reactions around the world were deeply opposed, generating a worldwide peace movement dedicated to avoiding the war and a variety of efforts by governments normally allied with the United States to urge an alternative to war. The main American justification for proceeding immediately against Iraq was articulated in the form of a claimed right of preemptive warfare, abstractly explained as necessary conduct in view of the alleged interface between weaponry of mass destruction and the extremist tactics of the megaterrorists.[7] It was argued that it was unacceptable in these circumstances for the United States to wait to be attacked, and that rights of preemptive warfare were essential to uphold the security of the "civilized" portion of the world. In his talk at the United Nations, Bush said, "We cannot stand by and do nothing while dangers gather."[8] It was this claim that was essentially rejected by the UN Security Council refusal to go along with U.S./UK demands for a direct endorsement of an enforcement mandate. The precise American contention was more narrowly and multiply framed in relation to the failures of Iraq to cooperate fully with the UN inspectors, the years of non-implementation of earlier Security Council resolutions imposing disarmament obligations on Iraq after the Gulf War, and, above all, by the supposedly heightened threat posed by Iraq's alleged arsenal of weapons of mass destruction.[9]

The Iraq War was initiated and ended militarily with rapid American battlefield victories. President Bush so declared, "In the battle of Iraq, the United States and our allies have prevailed. And now our coalition is engaged in securing and reconstructing that country."[10] The president carefully described the military operations as "a battle" rather than as "a war," subsuming the attack on Iraq within the wider, ongoing war against global terrorism, and implying that the undertaking should be seen as one element in the antiterrorism campaign launched in response to the September 11 attacks. Again, as in relation to Kosovo, the UNSC refrained from censuring the United States and its allies, and the UN has seemed fully willing, even eager, to play whatever part is assigned to it during the current period of military occupation and political, economic, and social reconstruction, so far under exclusive U.S./UK control. Such acquiescence is particularly impressive given the failure of the victorious coalition in the Iraq War to find any evidence of weapons of mass destruction, or to be attacked by such weaponry despite launching a war designed to destroy precisely these capabilities of the regime of Saddam Hussein. It seems reasonable to conclude that either such weaponry does not exist, or if it does exist, it is of no operational relevance and a strategy of deterrence would be fully able to protect against its future use. That is, if such weapons were not used by Iraq to defend the survival of the regime in extremis, then it is highly unlikely that they would ever have been used in circumstances where an annihilating retaliation could be anticipated. If Iraq refrained when it had nothing to lose, why would it use such weaponry in other situations where the response would be the assured destruction of country and regime? There has never existed any basis for supposing the Baghdad regime to be suicidal, and what evidence exists suggest the opposite, a strong willingness to subordinate other goals to survival. Even in this current occupation phase of the war, the impulse to survive as an independent political entity seems to be the primary foundation of fierce Iraqi resistance.

How should such a pattern of circumventing Charter rules combined with the reluctance of the UNSC to seek censure for such violations be construed from the perspective of the future of international law? There are several overlapping modes of interpretation, each of which illuminates the issue to some extent, but none seems to provide a satisfactory account from the perspective of international law:

1. The United States as the dominant state in a unipolar world order enjoys an exemption from legal accountability with respect to use of force irreconcilable with the UN Charter System; other states, in contrast, would be generally held accountable unless directly protected by the U.S. exemption.

2. The pattern of behavior confirms a skeptical trend that suggests the Charter System no longer corresponds, or never did correspond, with the realities of world politics, and is not authoritative in relation to the behavior of states.[11]

3. The American pattern of behavior is in some tension with the Charter System, but it is a creative tension that suggests respect for the underlying values of the world community, viewing legality as a matter of degree (not either/or) and as requiring continuing adjustment to changing circumstances; as such, the claims of preemption in relation to megaterrorism provide a reasonable doctrinal explanation for an expanded right of self-defense.

4. Acknowledging the behavioral pressures of the world on the Charter guidelines with respect to force, the possibility exists that contested uses of force under the Charter are "illegal, yet legitimate" either by reference to the rationale for initiating action without UNSC approval or on the basis of the beneficial impact of the intervention.[12] From this perspective, the failure to find weapons of mass destruction does not definitively undermine the claim that the intervention is "legitimate." It still could be judged as legitimate due to a series of effects: the emancipation of the Iraqi people from an oppressive regime, reinforced by the overwhelming evidence that the Baghdad rulers were guilty of systematic, widespread, and massive crimes against humanity, and an occupation that prepares the Iraqi people for political democracy and economic success.[13]

At this stage, it is impossible to predict how the Iraq War will impact the Charter system with respect to the international regulation of force. It will depend on how principal states treat the issue, especially the United States. International law, in this crucial sense, is neither more nor less than what the powerful actors in the system, and to a lesser extent the global community of international jurists and the global jury of public opinion, say it is. International law in the area of the use of force cannot by itself induce consistent compliance because of sovereignty-oriented political attitudes combined with the gross disparities in power that prevent the logic of reciprocity and the benefits of mutuality operating with respect to the security agenda of states. The "realist" school has dominated the foreign policy process of major countries throughout the existence of the modern state system, being only marginally challenged by a Wilsonian approach that is more reliant on legalism and moralism.[14] To the extent that realists advocate restraint regarding the use of force, it is based on cost-benefit assessments, including the diplomatic virtue of prudence and the avoidance of over-extension that has been blamed throughout history for the decline of major states.[15]

There are grounds for supposing that the approach of the Bush administration may not fit within the realist paradigm, but rather represents a militant and reactionary version of Wilsonian idealism.[16] President Bush has consistently described the war against terrorism in terms of good and evil, which works against even constraints based on calculations of self-interest and prudence.[17] To the extent that such an orientation shapes the near future of American conduct the UN Charter system will be disregarded except possibly in those circumstances where the Security Council would support an American claim to use force.[18]

The Iraq War and the Future of the Charter System

Against the jurisprudential background depicted in the previous section, an interpretation of the Iraq precedent is necessarily tentative. It depends, in the first analysis, on whether the American battlefield victory in the Iraq War can be converted by reasonable means in a short time period into what is generally interpreted to be a political victory. Such an outcome is best measured in Iraq by such factors as stability, democratization, recovery of Iraqi sovereignty, economic development, and public perception. If the American occupation is viewed as successful, then the intervention is likely to be treated as "legitimate," despite being generally regarded as "illegal." Such a perception will be viewed by some as adding a needed measure of flexibility in the application of the Charter system in a world where the possible interplay of megaterrorist tactics and weaponry of mass destruction validates recourse to anticipatory self-defense; it will be dismissed by others as an opportunistic and retroactively rationalized repudiation of legal restraints by the world's sole superpower.

There are two main conceptual explanations of this likely divergence of opinion. The first relates to issues of *factual plausibility*. The doctrine of preemption, as such, is less troublesome than its unilateral application in circumstances where the burden of persuasion as to the imminence and severity of the threat is not sustained. The diplomatic repudiation of the United States in the Security Council resulted mainly from the factual unpersuasiveness of the U.S. arguments about the threats associated with Iraqi retention of weaponry of mass destruction and the claims of a purported linkage between the Baghdad regime and the al Qaeda network, arguably making reliance on deterrence and containment unacceptable. There were no doubts about the brutality of Saddam Hussein's rule, but there was little support for recourse to an international war on such grounds. This skepticism has been heightened by the failure so far to uncover weaponry of mass destruction in the aftermath of the war, despite unimpeded access to suspicious sites, the cooperation of Iraqi scientists and weapons personnel, and a huge intelligence effort.

The second ground of divergence relates to arguments of *retroactive justification*. Here the focus is on whether a war opposed because its side effects seemed potentially dangerous and its advance rationale was not convincing enough to justify stretching the Charter System of restraint after the fact. The justifications offered by Washington combine the quick military victory on the battlefield with relatively low casualty figures, as reinforced by the documentation of Saddam Hussein's criminality as an Iraqi leader. Such an argument would seem more convincing if the American-led coalition forces had been more clearly welcomed as "liberators" rather than viewed as "occupiers," and if the postcombat American presence in Iraq was less marred by continuous and even escalating violent incidents of resistance and further American casualties. It remains too early to reach any sort of judgment as to the political effects of the war and its wider ramifications regionally and globally. If the American occupation turns out to be relatively short, and is generally perceived to benefit the Iraqi people and not the American occupiers, arguments based on retroactive justification are likely to gain support; also, the Iraqi precedent would not be viewed so much as destructive of the Charter System, but as an extension of it based on the emerging enlargement of the role of the international community to protect societies vulnerable to abusive governments.[19]

Of course, the issue of process and the substantive outcome are important. The Iraq War represented a circumvention of the collective procedures of the Charter System with respect to uses of force in contexts not covered by the Article 51 conception of self-defense. To some extent, a favorable view of the effects of such a use of force weakens objections to unilateralism. Adopting a constructivist view of international law, much depends on the future conduct and attitude of the United States government. Constructivism is an assessment of political and legal reality that places decisive emphasis on dominant mental perceptions as to a given set of conditions, whether or not such perceptions are accurate as evaluated from other standpoints.[20] Will the U.S. government in the future generally exhibit respect for the role of the Security Council, or will it feel vindicated by its decision to act unilaterally in conjunction with cooperative allies and continue to rely on such a model for conflict resolution? If the latter interpretation shapes future American foreign policy, then the Charter System is marginalized, at least with respect to the United States, and because the United States sets the rules of the game, the overall acceptance of the prohibition on recourse to nondefensive force is likely to be seriously weakened.

Can the Charter System work without the dominant state in the world adhering to its procedures and restraining rules? The constructivist answer is clarifying to a degree. To the extent that other states continue to take the Charter System as authoritative, it will certainly heavily influence international responses to challenged uses of force by states other than the United States, and will affect global attitudes toward American leadership. There will be complaints about the degree to which geopolitical realities trump international law restraints and about double standards, but these complaints have been made since the United Nations came into being, and arguably were embedded in the Charter by granting a veto to the permanent members.

The approach taken after the collapse of the Baghdad regime by the Security Council in its Resolution 1483 is indicative of a tension between acquiescence and opposition to the United States/United Kingdom recourse to war against Iraq.[21] The resolution divides responsibility and authority between the occupying powers and the United Nations, granting the U.S./UK predominant control over the most vital concerns of security, economic and political reconstruction, and governance. At the same time, the resolution stops far short of retroactively endorsing recourse to force by the U.S./UK under the factual circumstances that existed. It dodges the issue of legality/legitimacy by avoiding any formal pronouncement, while accepting as a legitimate given the realities of the apparent outcome of the war. As a result, a high degree of ambiguity surrounds the Iraq War as precedent. Undoubtedly, this ambiguity will be reduced, and possibly eliminated, by a clearer sense of the political outcome of the war and by patterns of subsequent UNSC practice in future peace and security contexts.

The Charter System, Megaterrorism, and Humanitarian Intervention

In the 1990s there was a definite trend toward accepting a more interventionary role for the United Nations with respect to the prevention of ethnic cleansing and genocide.[22] The Security Council, as supported by the last three secretaries general, reflecting a greater prominence for the international protection of human rights and less anxiety about risks of escalation that were operative during the Cold War, narrowed the degree of deference owed to the territorial supremacy of sovereign governments. As such, the domestic jurisdiction exclusion of UN intervention expressed in Article 2(7) was definitely under challenge from the widespread grassroots and governmental advocacy of humanitarian intervention in the years following the Cold War. Although the pattern of claims and practice remained contested, being resisted especially by China and other Asian countries, there was considerable intergovernmental and grassroots support for humanitarian intervention. The UN was more often and more sharply attacked for doing too little to mitigate human suffering, as in Bosnia and Rwanda, than criticized for doing too much.

A variant on this debate is connected with the instances of uses of force under American leadership in the post–September 11 world. In both Afghanistan and Iraq, recourse to force rested on defensive claims against the new threats of megaterrorism, but the effect in both instances was to liberate captive populations from extremely oppressive regimes, establishing patterns of governance and potential self-determination that seemed virtually impossible for the oppressed citizenry to challenge by normal modes of resistance. Even though the humanitarian *motivations* of the United States are suspect in both instances (due to a past record of collaboration with these regimes while their abusive conduct was at its worst), the effect of the interventions was emancipatory, and the declared intention of the occupation to support human rights and democratization, if implemented, would strengthen the humanitarian argument. Undoubtedly, such forcible liberations would not have taken place without the pressures mounted and the climate created by the September 11 attacks. Nevertheless, to the extent that megaterrorism is associated with criminal forms of governmental authority, would it not be reasonable to construe uses of force that accomplished "regime change" as part of an enlarged doctrine of humanitarian intervention?

I think not for some obvious reasons. Recourse to war is too serious a matter to allow decisions about it to proceed on the basis of retroactive rationales that are not fully articulated and debated in advance. For this reason also, prudential considerations alone would rule out humanitarian intervention in all but the most extreme cases, and even in most of these due to the magnitude of the undertaking and the uncertainty of the consequences. Who would be so crazy as to advocate humanitarian intervention by military means on behalf of the Chechens, Tibetans, or Kashmiris? Of course, there are many options open to the international community and its member states that do not involved the use of force that could range from expressions of disapproval to the imposition of comprehensive sanctions. The case for humanitarian intervention relying on force must be treated as a principled, and even then, a rare exception to the generalized prohibition of the Charter with respect to the use of force embodied in Article 2(4).[23] If the Security Council does not mandate the intervention and a coalition of the willing proceeds, the undertaking could still be substantially vindicated, as in Kosovo, if some sort of collective process was involved and the facts confirmed the imminence of a humanitarian emergency. The Kosovo Commission tackled this issue of principled humanitarian intervention, as have scholars, seeking to provide guidance that preserves the balance between the prohibition on uses of force contained in international law and the moral/political imperatives to mitigate impending or ongoing humanitarian catastrophes by stretching the legal restraints.[24]

A pro-intervention argument should not be treated as acceptable in circumstances where the use of force is associated with alleged security threats posed by the menace of megaterrorism, but the justification tendered after the fact emphasizes the case for humanitarian intervention. In Afghanistan, the security argument was sufficiently convincing as to make the humanitarian benefits of the war a political and moral bonus, but without bearing on the legal case for recourse to force, which was sufficiently convincing on the defensive grounds claimed to satisfy most international law experts. In Iraq, by contrast, the security and related anti–al Qaeda arguments were unconvincing, and the claimed humanitarian benefits resulting from the war were emphasized by American officials as a way to circumvent the illegality of the American-led recourse to force. Such post hoc efforts at legalization should not be accorded much respect, especially in the context of a major war where prior efforts to obtain a mandate for the use of force were not endorsed by the Security Council — even in the face of major diplomatic pressures mounted by Washington in the several months prior to the Iraq War, and where disclosure suggests that the supposed threat associated with weapons of mass destruction was deliberately exaggerated.[25]

A Constructivist Future for the UN Charter System

The position favored here is that the United States would be best served by adhering to the UN Charter System and to international law generally.[26] This system is flexible enough to accommodate new and genuine security imperatives as well as changing values, including a shifting balance between sovereign rights and world community responsibilities.[27] In settings of humanitarian intervention and responses against megaterrorism, the Charter System can be *legally* vindicated *in appropriate factual circumstances.*

From this perspective, recourse to war against Iraq should not have been undertaken without a *prior* mandate from the Security Council, and rather than "a failure" of the United Nations, it represented a responsible exercise of its institutional responsibility to administer a system of constitutional restraints.[28] The facts did not support the case for preemption, as there was neither *imminence* nor *necessity.* As a result, the Iraq War seemed, at best, to qualify as an instance of *preventive war,* but there are strong legal, moral, and political reasons to deny both legality and legitimacy to such a use of force, and even the more remote threat countered by "prevention" was not factually sustained. It is not an acceptable exception to the Charter System, and no effort was made by the U.S. government to claim a right of preventive war, although the highly abstract and vague phrasing of the preemptive war doctrine in the U.S. National Security Strategy would be more accurately formulated and explained as "a preventive war doctrine." But even within this highly dubious doctrinal setting, to be at all convincing the evidence would at least have to demonstrate a credible future Iraqi threat that could not be reliably deterred. This was never done, nor even attempted.

My legal constructivist position is that the United States (and the world) would benefit from a self-imposed discipline of adherence to the UN Charter System governing the use of force. Such a voluntary discipline would overcome the absence of geopolitical limits associated with countervailing power in a unipolar world.[29] It would also work against tendencies by the United States and others to rely too much on military superiority, which encourages the formation of defensive alliances and possibly arms races. International law is flexible enough to allow the United States and other countries to meet novel security needs. Beyond this, neither American values nor strategic goals should be construed to validate uses of force that cannot win support in the UN Security Council. If one considers the course of American foreign policy over the course of the last half-century, adherence to the Charter System with respect to the use of force would have avoided the worst policy failures, including that of Vietnam. Deviations from the Charter system of prohibitions on the use of force can be credited with no clear successes.

It is not the Charter System that is in disarray, providing sensible grounds for declaring the project of regulating recourse to war by states a failed experiment that should now be abandoned. It is rather the leading states, and above all the United States, that need to be persuaded that their interests are served and their values realized by a more diligent pursuit of a law-oriented foreign policy. The Charter System is not a legal prison that presents states with the dilemma of adherence (and defeat) and violation or disregard (and victory). Rather, adherence is the best policy, if understood against a jurisprudential background that is neither slavishly legalistic nor cynically nihilistic. The law can be stretched as new necessities arise, but the stretching must to the extent possible be in accordance with procedures and norms contained in the Charter System, with a factually and doctrinally persuasive explanation of why a particular instance of stretching is justified.

Such positive constructivist attitudes will renew confidence in the Charter System. It is also true that constructivism can work negatively, and so if the types of disregard of the legal framework, public opposition, and governmental resistance present in the Iraq case are repeated in the future, then indeed the Charter System will be in shambles before much longer.

There is little doubt that the Iraq War and the American occupation that has ensued represents a serious setback for advocates of a law-governed approach to world order, as well as to the procedural effort to give the United Nations Security Council primary authority to mandate exceptions to the Charter prohibition on the nondefensive use of force to resolve international conflicts. But history can be cunning. There exists some possibility that the burdens of occupation in Iraq, as well as the discrediting of the rationale advanced to justify the American recourse to war, will cause a political swing in the United States and elsewhere in the direction of greater respect for the cardinal rules and principles of international law, for the United Nations, and for a peace-oriented public opinion at home and abroad.

Endnotes

1. "President's Remarks at the United Nations General Assembly," Sept. 12, 2003, White House Text.
2. For representative contributions, see Richard Falk, ed., *The Vietnam War and International Law*, 4 vols. (Princeton, NJ: Princeton University Press, 4 vols., 1968, 1969, 1972, 1976).
3. *The Kosovo Report: Conflict, International Response, Lessons Learned* (Oxford, UK: Oxford University Press, 2002) 185–98; it should be mentioned that I was a member of the commission.
4. Such a practice could be regarded an an informal and substantive extension of the established practice of treating abstentions by permanent members as not blocking decisions by the Security Council despite the wording of Article 27(3) requiring "the concurring votes of the permanent members." Such a practice shows the degree to which the Security Council was able to contrive ways to overcome a paralysis that would have resulted from an interpretative approach based on textual fidelity, and it is impressive that this approach was established in the midst of the Cold War.
5. These three steps outlined in *The Kosovo Report*, note 3, 187.
6. A discussion of this challenge and the U.S. response is the theme of my book, Richard Falk, *The Great Terror War* (Northhampton, MA: Olive Branch Press, 2003).
7. Initially fully depicted in "Remarks by the President at 2002 Graduation Exercise of the United States Military Academy," June 1, 2002; given a more enduring and authoritative status by their emphasis in the official White House document, *The National Security Strategy of the United States of America*, Sept. 2002, esp. Chapter 5, 13–16.
8. See *The Kosovo Report*, note 3.
9. The most important Security Council resolutions were 678 (1990), 687 (1991), and, of course, 1441 (2002).
10. "President Bush's Prepared Remarks Declaring End to Major Combat in Iraq," text printed in *NY Times*, May 2, 2003, A14.
11. This position is most clearly articulated by Michael J. Glennon, "Why the Security Council Failed," *Foreign Affairs* 82, 3 (2003): 16–35; the overall argument is more fully developed in Glennon's book *Limits of Law, Prerogatives of Power: Interventionism after Kosovo* (New York: Palgrove, 2001); also relevant, Anthony C. Arend and Robert J. Beck, *International Law and the Use of Force: Beyond the UN Charter Paradigm* (New York: Routledge, 1993); A. Mark Weisbrud, *Use of Force: The Practice of States since World War II* (Philadelphia: University of Pennsylvania Press, 1997).
12. See Anne-Marie Slaughter, "Good Reasons for Going around the U.N.," *NY Times*, March 15, 2003.
13. See Charles Krauthammer, "U.S. Cleaning up Hussein's Mess in Iraq," *LA Times*, May 16, 2003; Thomas I. Friedman, "Bored with Baghdad—Already," *NY Times*, May 18, 2003.
14. For the view that American moralism and legalism has had a detrimental impact on U.S. foreign policy during the first half of the twentieth century, see George F. Kennan, *American Diplomacy* 1900–1950 (1951); also Henry Kissinger, *Diplomacy* (1994), esp. 218–45, 762–835. For a more general interpretation of the Wilsonian component as a more widely conceived aspect of the overall American foreign policy tradition, see Walter Russell Mead, *Special Providence: American Foreign Policy and How It Changed the World* (New York: Knopf, 2001), 132–73.
15. Paul Kennedy, *The Rise and Fall of Great Power: Economic Change and Military Conflict 1500–2000* (New York: Random House, 1987).
16. For an argument along these lines, see Max Boot, "George Woodrow Bush: The President Is Becoming a Wilsonian Interventionist," *Wall Street Journal*, July 1, 2002.
17. Aside from identifying specific states as "the axis of evil" in the global setting of the war against terrorism, in his West Point speech the president includes some strongly moralistic rhetoric of a visionary quality, quite inimical to the realist tradition. The following excerpt is indicative of the tone and message: "We are in a conflict between good and evil, and America will call evil by its name. By confronting evil and lawless regimes, we do not create a problem, we reveal a problem. And we will lead the world in opposing it." See *The Kosovo Report*, note 3.

18. See Richard Perle, "Thank God for the Death of the UN: Its Abject Failure Gave Us Only Anarchy, The World Needs Order," *The Guardian*, March 20, 2003.

19. For influential comprehensive presentation along these lines, see *The Responsibility to Protect: Report of the International Commission on Intervention and State Sovereignty* (Ottawa: International Development Research Centre, 2001).

20. Constructivism as an academic approach to the study of international relations is best explained by Alexander Wendt in *Social Theory of International Politics* (Cambridge, UK: Cambridge University Press, 1999).

21. For text see UN Security Council Res. 1483.

22. For useful overviews of this trend, see Sean D. Murphy, *Humanitarian Intervention: The United Nations in an Evolving World* (Philadelphia: University of Pennsylvania Press, 1996); Nicholas J. Wheeler, *Saving Strangers: Humanitarian Intervention in International Society* (Oxford, UK: Oxford University Press, 2000).

23. For a well-crafted narrow doctrine of humanitarian intervention, see Jack Donnelly, *Universal Human Rights in Theory and Practice* 2d ed, (Ithaca, NY: Cornell University Press, 2003), 242–60. For a generally skeptical set of reflections about claims of humanitarian intervention, see Aleksandar Jokic, ed., *Humanitarian Intervention: Moral And Philosophical Issues* (Toronto: Broadview Press, 2003); for a somewhat more optimistic set of accounts, see J. L. Holzgrefe and Robert O. Keohane, eds., *Humanitarian Intervention: Ethical, Legal, and Political Dilemmas* (Cambridge, UK: Cambridge University Press, 2003).

24. For important efforts, see Kosovo Report, note 3; *The Responsibility to Protect*, Report of the International Commission on Intervention and State Sovereignty (2001) 53–57; Lori Fisler Damrosch, ed., "Concluding Remarks," in *Enforcing Restraint: Collective Intervention in Internal Conflicts* (New York: Council of Relations Press, 1993), 348–67; and esp., Damrosch, "The Inevitability of Selective Response? Principles to Guide Urgent International Action," in Albrecht Schnabel and Ramesh Thakur, eds., *Kosovo and the Challenge of Humanitarian Intervention* (Tokyo: United Nations University Press, 2001), 405–19.

25. It may be worth recalling the vigorous objections of the U.S. government to the Vietnamese intervention in Cambodia and subsequent occupation that disrupted the Khmer Rouge genocide during the late 1970s. The American position repudiated the humanitarian considerations, emphasizing the Vietnamese violation of Cambodian sovereignty, urging immediate withdrawal despite the risk of regenerating a genocidal regime.

26. A more generalized view of the benefits arising from a law-oreinted approach are well explained in Nicole Deller, Arjun Makhijani, and John Burroughs, eds., *Rule of Power or Rule of Law?* (New York: Apex Press, 2003).

27. See Oscar Schachter, "In Defense of International Rules on the Use of Force," 53 U. Chi. L. Rev 113 (1986).

28. The reference to failure is to challenge the central conclusion of Glennon's analysis, "Why the Security Council Failed," note 11.

29. My assertion is in direct opposition to the inferences drawn by Robert Kagen in his influential book. See Kagen, *Of Paradise and Power: America and Europe in the New World Order* (New York: Knopf, 2003).

Chapter 10
Patriotism

Patriotism, love of country, can be appreciated both as a political virtue of the highest order and a dangerous political vice that invites governments to take dire risks and make ill-considered commitments. Patriotism in the modern era was linked, of course, to the Westphalian framing of political community by reference to territorial sovereign states, given cohesion by fashioning of a myth of national unity. As with nationalism, so with patriotism, the state seeks to appropriate the loyalty of its citizenry, punishing socially and even legally those who are deemed unpatriotic. Such pressures rise to their height at times of crisis, particularly when the national society perceives itself to be in danger from enemies without and within. The result of these pressures is often conferring on the state vast authority to protect society, including the means to curtail drastically the freedoms of those believed to be aligned in some way with the enemy, perhaps only ethnically. In turn, the state may manipulate such fears and stimulate patriotic sentiments so as to mobilize enthusiasm, support, and sacrifice from its citizenry. Not only are freedoms subordinated, but so is truth. The intensity of patriotic feelings is exhibited by preferring partisanship to objectivity and rationality in assessing the pros and cons of bitter international conflicts. The patriot as nationalist does not question the rightness of the cause pursued by his or her government, nor the legality and morality of the means used to achieve national objectives in times of war. The patriot seeks victory, and is sustained by the one-sidedness of her or his understanding of a conflict.

Westphalian patriotism strives to be statist in scope, although the existence of minorities and pockets of dissatisfaction creates potential tensions in times of crisis. With the rise of international law and growing concerns about the morality and rationality of war, as well as identities shaped by the various facets of globalization, the nature of patriotism, as well as its twin, citizenship, has been subjected to growing critical scrutiny. Granting that love of country is desirable, what should the country represent? Shouldn't the true patriot seek a country principled in dealing with other states, a world of cooperation and mutual respect? With the rise of globalization and postmodernity, the nature of political community becomes far more complicated and multilayered. The state can no longer claim to exhaust the sense of belonging even with respect to political identity. And yet, despite erosion of the foundations of patriotism as conventionally conceived, it remains a potent force in human affairs, perhaps accentuated in some ways by the emergence of many new states around the world in the last half century, and the prevalence of nationalism as still the most powerful political creed active in world, moving people to support wars and the sacrifice of the lives of their youngest, mostly male, citizens.

The attacks of September 11 reawakened and refocused American patriotic impulses in a climate of opinion that was ultranationalist in tone and substance. There was a refusal to explore the sources of resentment around the world, and especially in the Islamic world, that seemed to give rise to such deadly political extremism aimed principally at the United States and its citizens. There was a willingness, even an eagerness, by America to become mobilized for war even though no clear connections could be drawn between the wars undertaken and the threats being posed. And there was an insistence on treating the persons responsible for the attacks as evil enemies who deserved to be exterminated. The treatment of al Qaeda suspects held in the Guantanamo prison is emblematic of both a refusal by the American government to grant rights to detained combatants demanded by international humanitarian law and the acceptance by the country and its governmental representatives of such vengeful practices that cannot be convincingly explained by reference to security considerations.

Westphalian patriotism gives an often dysfunctional blank check to the state when the citizenry is successfully mobilized in reaction to a perceived enemy, and the intensity of the mobilization is often in direct proportion to the magnitude and traumatizing impact of the threat posed. It is dysfunctional because it induces overreactions that can be self-defeating and harmful for everyone. It was Thucydides who first depicted this vulnerability of democracies to demagogic appeals in his classic account of the fall of Athens in the aftermath of the Peloponnesian Wars. As the ultranationalism of Nazi Germany demonstrated, even fascist states can invoke patriotic sentiments to build popular enthusiasm for irrationally grandiose schemes of conquest and expansion. Of course, this mobilization of the public for militarist adventures has taken various forms over the centuries, with each instance exhibiting its own particularity. This concern about the link between patriotism and aggressive war making remains a potentially fatal flaw in existing political arrangements at the interface of modernity and postmodernity. American patriotism in the aftermath of September 11 is the latest manifestation of this phenomenon, allowing the U.S. government to proceed with an ill-advised empire-building project without confronting domestic opposition and an accompanying public debate.

Two separate concerns are explored in this chapter: mobilizing patriotism as a means to pursue an ultranationalist and militarist approach to the specific challenge posed by the al Qaeda network; and reimagining patriotism in light of the advent of postmodernity.

The Impact of September 11

I think it is not an exaggeration to say that the period since the attacks of September 11 poses the greatest threat since at least early in the Cold War to the traditional liberties of the American people, and it may turn out to be worse and more enduring. The U.S. government initially obtained a virtually unconditional mandate from Congress and the public to claim sweeping authority in the exercise of its role to restore and protect what the Bush administration has called the "homeland security" of the American people. With the passage of time and the abrasiveness of Attorney General John Ashcroft, coupled with some horror stories about governmental abuses of Americans and others, a rising tide of critical reaction is visible in the United States, but remains subordinate to the basic mood of submissiveness induced by September 11.

It requires, depending on your point of view, either an extraordinary innocence or an unwarranted level of trust to feel that this new kind of authority being conferred on the United States government will be used in a manner that reconciles the security needs of the citizenry with the values of a free society, and the evidence to date confirms this skepticism. Those of us who care about being members of a free society must not allow anxious attitudes of grief, fear, and anger resulting from the grim reality of the September 11 experience to prevent our realization that there are other threats to our well-being arising from "the security syndrome" that prevail and provide justification for the most fearsome claims by government over our freedoms as a people that have ever been made during the history of the country. For the first time, America has a homeland security czar with vast resources and the authority to consolidate the overall effort to sustain internal security. What this has already meant in practice is a greatly expanded congressional mandate for unregulated law enforcement, wide discretion to maintain secrecy, lengthy detention of suspects without due process, racial profiling as permissible police action, and for a frightening suspension of legal protection for those in our midst who are not citizens, especially if they should come from Islamic countries, and particularly those who are males and from the Arab world.

An American citizen at this time is doubly challenged to worry quite naturally about the terrorist threats that continue to be directed against our society, but also to recognize that under the guise of meeting those threats, basic liberties are sacrificed in ways that are not required to carry on the proper work of government. It is true that the frightening nature of the September 11 attacks leads to what can be accurately described as a popular demand that the government take all necessary steps, regardless of their infringements on rights, to restore as quickly as possible a street feeling of security in relation to terrorism. The events of September 11 combined with the disturbing failure of thousands of FBI agents to identify the source of the anthrax disseminated by mail a few months later left an overall sense that America had become a terribly vulnerable society in a manner that can be exploited by vicious enemies within and without. The deeper significance of September 11 is to instruct enemies of America about this vulnerability and to scare Americans into a sudden awareness of how many soft targets there are within the country that could produce mass tragedies more devastating than the attacks on the World Trade Center.

Such a background does create strong public demands that the state restore the confidence of the citizenry, and that these security requirements do alter expectations about what is reasonable for law enforcement authorities to do under these circumstances of urgency and emergency. Part of this demand is that the government do better than react to terrorism but move quickly to develop the capacity to prevent it. In this atmosphere, the question posed is how to balance the threats to liberty with these new imperatives of security. We must ask ourselves whether we have the kind of leadership in the White House and Justice Department that is capable of striking such a balance in an acceptable form.

The Patriotic Moment

It doesn't take a sophisticated sociologist to conclude that there has been a dramatic surge in patriotism since September 11. I have never seen so many American flags on display or heard so often "God Bless America," especially in the first several months after the attacks. It seemed hardly possible to operate inside the beltway in Washington without the display of an American flag on your clothes. This emotional assertion of American pride associated with these manifestations of patriotism needs to be interpreted from several directions. On the one side, it is, of course, a healthy emotion to express solidarity with those in your own country who have suffered in the manner that those victims suffered, and to show a willingness to stand firm, without fear, and seek retaliation and an effective response. Such a display also expresses a national resolve to do whatever is necessary to restore security. What makes this outpouring of patriotism so ambiguous is that it also acts as a way of celebrating ourselves as we are rather than as we should be, and it results in a suspension of criticism about the approach taken by the elected leaders of the country. This latter aspect of the patriotic problem was especially serious given the uncertainties surrounding Bush's "election" as president, and even more so given the political extremism of the Bush inner circle of advisors.

The encoded meaning of this patriotic message, as it has evolved out of the September 11 experience, inhibits dissent and criticism, especially within government circles and the media, where it is most needed. The mainstream media in the United States voluntarily adopted a rather rigid form of self-censorship, and more than this, acted mainly to fan the flames of the national disposition toward war and war making, especially in the course of the long buildup to the Iraq War. The main TV channels have given much viewing time to an array of previously obscure retired generals, Special Forces veterans, and pro-war think tank specialists night after night up to and including the Iraq occupation. Doubting voices that questioned the direction of the internal or international response, either on grounds of law or morality — or for that matter, on the basis of prudence and effectiveness — were no where to be heard in the mainstream. At the very moment when the novelty of the al Qaeda threat and its persistence challenged the political imagination of the country in a way that it has never been challenged before, we have not had the kind of debate and discussion that should occur in a democracy in times of crisis. Such a failure greatly inhibits the prospects for a creative, effective, and legitimate response that would have required a willingness to engage in self-criticism rather than rely on self-righteous protestations of innocence. A constructive response to al Qaeda was precluded because of this univocal and self-serving insistence that the patriotic imperative is best exhibited by the silence and submission of the citizenry in the face of governmental policy. The absence of skeptical voices in the national discussion also seriously erodes the vital distinction between citizen and subject, seemingly making passivity a political virtue instead of a dangerous liability for a society that supposedly values its freedom, and needs debate and candid discussion to reach desirable decisions.

It is my strong belief that a citizen expresses his or her love of country through the expression of conscience, through taking so seriously the well-being of the country and its potentiality for change so as to be willing to voice unpopular opinions. Those who are good citizens in this sense are always seeking to realize the potentiality implicit in the promise of America. Those who are good subjects are content with the posture of obedience, of deference to the governing authorities and believe, particularly in times of crisis and war, that the way in which one is a good American is to wave the flag vigorously, otherwise shut up, viewing with suspicion those who raise doubt about the actions proposed or undertaken. I am ambivalent about flying the flag, but unconditionally opposed to shutting up, especially under current conditions of crisis and with American warmongers in and out of government pressing for empire-building strategies under the guise of an antiterrorism campaign. The Iraq War dramatized the public willingness in the United States to follow its leadership down a self-destructive path that was deceptively presented to the American people and to the world. Reinforcing this troublesome decline in the quality of the democratic discourse is the relative indifference displayed by the American people and the media when presented with strong indications that the highest levels of government manipulated the evidence relating to the Iraq threat (especially with regard to weapons of mass destruction) so as to build the case for preemptive war. (See Chapter 9.)

Putting this critical perspective in its strongest form, the originality of the September 11 challenge required a lively debate and intelligent criticism based on a far wider understanding of what more is at stake than merely dealing militarily with the perpetrators of the attack. Having expanded the war without adequate justification has meant that the extremist threats directed at America and Americans are likely to increase, perhaps exponentially. It is this element that distinguishes this war, if we agree to call it a war, from all other wars. This is a war without a military solution. It is a war that is essentially between the most militarily powerful state in all of history and a nonterritorial network of political extremists whose location and identity cannot be firmly fixed. It seems certainly correct that the Afghan dimensions of this threat needed to be addressed by relying on force, but the post-Afghanistan approach should have remained sharply focused on the residual al Qaeda capabilities, and thus called for an essentially nonmilitary, law enforcement approach. Instead, expanding reliance on war making by attacking Iraq was unwarranted by September 11, at odds with international law and morality, destructive of the authority of the United Nations, and even imprudent from a geopolitical perspective.

In past wars just at their point of origin, what counted above all else was military effectiveness. If military effectiveness was sustained in such a way as to prevail in a just war, the methods used to fight the war were more or less forgotten or forgiven, or the victorious side engaged in denial that insulated the victors from any remorse or responsibility regarding objectionable methods of combat. World War II provides the best example for Americans, a just war that represented a necessary response to the criminality and militarism of fascism and Nazism, as well as a response to the wars of aggressions waged by Japan and Germany. For the United States, the war commenced with the surprise Japanese attack on Pearl Harbor in 1941, and over the course of the next four bloody years yielded an outcome that rescued the many surviving victims from further abuse at the hands of these totalitarian rulers, and saved the world as a whole from the degenerate menace of fascism.

The conduct of the war, however, involved the indiscriminate area bombing of cities, the deliberate and massive use of military instruments against civilian society in order to weaken the morale of the adversary, and, at the end of the war, a most dubious attack on two Japanese cities with the first and only atomic bombs ever exploded as weapons of war. Americans to this day cannot acknowledge the suffering inflicted on Japanese civilian society by these savage attacks on Hiroshima and Nagasaki.

Several years ago when the Smithsonian Institution in Washington, D.C. tried to arrange an exhibition of the human suffering experienced by the Japanese residents of those cities on the fiftieth anniversary of the attacks, a furor occurred, the curator of the exhibition was dismissed, and the show cancelled and reconstituted in a very anodyne way. It has been politically unacceptable to most Americans to look back on those aspects of their past that cast any doubts on their claims of innocence and virtue, and associated pretensions of moral exceptionalism (and thereby spoiling the conforting illusion of being a Lockean nation in a Hobbesian world).

Let us confront the fact that America is now at war, engaged in a struggle against a threat that does not fall within the traditional statist definitions of international conflict. We do not really know how to describe the enemy or the adversary. We speak in terms not of the enemy state, but of the al Qaeda network. It is not clear what it is, where it is, or how it operates. President Bush initially seemed preoccupied with the demonic role of Osama bin Laden and his support for a visionary extremism that identified America as a hated enemy of Islam. Later on, the White House shifted its emphasis from this extraordinary individual to a supposed "axis of evil" linking Iran, Iraq, and North Korea in an infernal triangle the leaders that were solemnly warned in Bush's 2002 State of the Union Address of impending American pressure. At that moment, these states were singled out openly as potential targets of military intervention and invasion in the follow-up to the Afghanistan phase of the Great Terror War. Such an expansion of the scope of the war effort was only linked to September 11 in a tenuous fashion, and the linkage received scant international support aside from Blair's Britain.

This expansion of the identity of the enemy ignores the degree to which the persisting al Qaeda threat remains real and distinct, but can and should be addressed by primary reliance on cooperative law enforcement, intelligence activities, and possibly, occasional recourse to covert operations. The internationalization of the war by defining states as enemies is a policy almost certain to a backfire on a variety of levels, and mistakenly insists on treating a postmodern challenge as if it represented mainly an instance of modernist international conflict. Of course, it may be a subtle stratagem to pursue a postmodern goal by indirection, namely, to use the pretext of the terrorist threat to remove statist obstacles to an American global empire.

The Great Terror War, narrowly conceived without the imperial overlay, is much more a political struggle than it is a military struggle. It is a political struggle that can only be successfully waged if the great majority of the peoples living in the Islamic World and the Arab parts of the Islamic World do not end up with the conclusion that their suffering and their grievances are a result of the abusive ways in which America uses its power and wealth in the world. If in the pursuit of the al Qaeda enemy, the U.S. government unleashes its military power in the manner of Afghanistan and Iraq, we can be fairly certain that such military assaults will produce many converts to al Qaeda, or at least intensify anti-Americanism around the world. In both instances, the occupation of the countries after the battlefield victories has proved difficult and bloody, casting doubt on whether the earlier military victory would lead to a desired political outcome.

It is strategically wrong to conduct this war as the Gulf War or Kosovo War were fought. The dangerous luxury of casualty-free wars — where American weaponry is used in a one-sided way and the victims are to some extent those who are opposed to what the United States represents, but also include completely innocent civilians on a large scale, and in which the American side does not take any substantial risks — has widened and deepened the rampant anti-Americanism that already exists in most parts of the Muslim world. The noted British historian, Michael Howard, who is a quite conservative observer of international politics, described the American military tactics in Afghanistan as equivalent to using a blowtorch to remove a small cancer. Such criticism of the Afghanistan War disappeared for some months because the Taliban so quickly and unexpectedly collapsed, and this outcome seemed initially to please the great majority of the Afghan people. But with the passage of time the situation has clouded over, the Karzai government has not extended its rule beyond the city limits of Kabul, warlordism is rampant, the drug trade has revived, and armed anti-American militancy is on the rise, including apparent regroupings of Taliban and al Qaeda cadres. The situation in Iraq after the battlefield phase ended exhibits even more questionable political results. The American occupation seems to have produced a deep-seated resistance that is inflicting a steady stream of casualties on a daily basis, the costs of occupation have risen far above anticipated levels, the duration of the occupation has been extended, and the political outcome of these American efforts in Iraq is uncertain, with such dire possibilities such as civil war and the triumph of an anti-American religious nationalism far from excluded.

Revamping Patriotism

The preceding discussion intended to highlight the significance of patriotism in the present war atmosphere, but also to call attention to some troubling aspects of the kind of patriotic mood that has risen from the ashes of September 11. It suggests that we should not take the content and outlook of patriotism for granted, but should rethink its relevance in the altered global setting of the early twenty-first century. The form of patriotism that surfaced in the United States was shaped by the trauma associated with September 11, giving rise to a tribal patriotism that has strong chauvinistic overtones and, as earlier mentioned, devalues an active citizenry and stresses unity as a cardinal virtue. Such patriotism refuses as a matter of principle to see the world from the perspective of the other. Now that the period of mourning those lost in the attacks has faded, it is important to resist the facile temptations of tribal patriotism. As loyal Americans, we need to understand how others perceive and experience the American role in the world, and why this role produces such intense resentment, particularly among Arabs in the Middle East. Tribal patriotism may yet hamper an effective response to these more subtle challenges of September 11.

The outcome in Afghanistan to a large degree superficially and temporarily vindicated the first stage of the American response, despite the apparent inability to destroy the leadership of al Qaeda, especially Osama bin Laden. The logic of this response together with the military success of the campaign seemed at first to bring a new and welcome future to Afghanistan, although the conduct of the war produced an excessive number of Afghan civilian casualties that might have been considerably reduced had the U.S. government been prepared to put its own personnel on the ground earlier and rely less on intensive aerial bombardment. Such a victory given the popularity of the American president and the influence of tribal patriotism made it very difficult to have a critical discussion of post-Afghanistan American responses in a manner that served the global public good, maintained values here at home associated with constitutionalism, adhered to the international rule of law, and displayed respect for the United Nations and the views of foreign governments. Instead of such a responsible process of policymaking, there was the insistence on moving on to achieve regime change in Iraq by means of waging an unprovoked war that was exceedingly unpopular with most of America's allies in the world and with a much agitated public opinion.

At this point in its history, America badly needs another kind of patriotism, what I will call "cosmopolitan" or "worldly" patriotism — a sense of country that blurs the boundaries between the self and others and that is aware that, in an era of globalization, all of us have multiple identities based on nationality, race, religion, gender, age, professional and vocational activities, and civilizational region. The physical boundaries of the state never were and are less and less the principal source of meaning for our collective selves. To adapt to a world of the Internet and the global market and media, we need to soften the exclusivity of our tribal attachments to a single self-serving national narrative. We need to adjust to an increasingly postsovereign world that is richly diverse and grossly uneven in wealth and influence, and we need to address the injustices that this unevenness of wealth and power has produced over the centuries and recognize the dangers of these widening disparities between rich and poor. We cannot dispense with patriotism in such an emergent world, but what is needed are collective attachments that are not tightly tied to an outmoded and myopic nationalist ethos, nor reliant for security on the fierce gods of war.

If we are serious about becoming cosmopolitan patriots, it is helpful to recognize that there were two distinct challenges posed on September 11. The first challenge is preoccupied with security — both international and internal — and how to use the capabilities of the government to meet the al Qaeda challenge in a way that is responsive to the threat that has been posed, including its novel elements, without abandoning the values and practices of a free and decent society.

The second challenge is, of course, that of justice, to render justice unto others in a way that acknowledges our power and past mistakes, as well as the suffering attributable to American policies and influence. Underneath the political fanaticism and pathology of al Qaeda were widely shared attitudes of anger and distress among Arabs about America's role in the Islamic world and generally. This political challenge cannot be understood if Osama bin Laden and al Qaeda are treated merely as a strange cult that represents some sort of crazed politics of suicidal fanaticism, a kind of political cancer that can be removed from the Islamic body politics, thereby restoring political normalcy and health. Although the attacking mentality of al Qaeda is pathological, the threat posed cannot be reduced to political pathology without losing a sense of its overall political significance. The extremism of bin Laden needs to be interpreted as an outgrowth of widely shared grievances that are deep and often well founded. True, some portion of the anti-Americanism arises from the rage that is associated with the mere existence of a state as powerful and rich and pervasive as is the United States, and this hostility has been manipulated in Arab circles to divert attention from their own humiliating failures to deal with national and regional issues, especially their inability to overcome the Palestinian ordeal. These attacks on September 11, although deplored, evoked a sympathetic resonance, in other words, that was in evidenced even in Europe. Such attitudes were an indirect endorsement of the view that the harm inflicted was some kind of payback as the United States so consistently misused its power in ways that have dismayed many people, and particularly people in the Islamic World. So long as Americans are captives of tribal patriotism, they cannot appraise this dimension of the threat and will be unable to take the action needed to overcome or reduce it.

It is also relevant to point out that the only serious resistance to American dominance in the Middle East and elsewhere has been mounted by militant Islam. The Arab governments of secular persuasion have either bought entirely into the American game plan of subordination or have been mired in their own corruption. The secular power of the Arab governments has been a consistent source of humiliation for the peoples of the region, turning out to be ineffectual or worse with respect to the highly charged symbolic issues of Palestinian self-determination and the status of Jerusalem. The only Arab political successes have been associated with the non-Arab Iranian revolution leg by Ayatollah Khomeini, by the Hezbollah in southern Lebanon, and by the early bin Laden effectiveness during the 1980s in resisting the invasion of Afghanistan by the Soviet Union. Americans forget, of course, that bin Laden was Washington's hero during the struggle to defend Afghanistan against Soviet domination.

The reason why the political challenge of September 11 is so bewildering is that it touches on these very severe and persisting grievances and exposes the contradictions of the past American approach to Islamic political extremism. In the background of the al Qaeda challenge is the widespread sense that the United States is responsible directly and indirectly for much Arab suffering and injustice of recent decades. To respond means not only addressing in some fair way the Palestinian–Israeli relationship and creating for the Palestinian people self-determination of the sort that almost all people in the Third World achieved long ago during the period of decolonization. The Palestinians remain forsaken — they are excluded from the benefits of decolonization and they endure a form of occupation far harsher than what the region experienced throughout the colonial era.

Also, in the background is the awareness that the United States was behind the sanctions that produced such large-scale civilian casualties in Iraq throughout the 1990s during the punitive aftermath of the Gulf War, which stopped short of obtaining the removal of Saddam Hussein as oppressive leader. To achieve this removal in 2003 by recourse to an illegal war has compounded the sense of American arbitrariness in the reckless use of its military superiority.

There are other issues that concern the cosmopolitan patriot. How can the United States mount a credible campaign against the development of chemical and biological weapons and against proliferation of nuclear weapons, while retaining and continuing to develop the world's largest and most widely deployed nuclear weapons arsenal of its own? How can the United States expect the weaker countries of the world to give up their weapons of mass destruction while retaining and further developing its own weapons of mass destruction, as well as moving rapidly to control the earth from space?

The cosmopolitan patriot also works for an equitable form of economic globalization — as contrasted with the current form of globalization that has been continually heightening the disparities between rich and poor throughout the world.

To make this policy agenda more than a pipe dream, cosmopolitan patriotism has to become a civic force in American society, and integral to what was earlier called "civic globalization." A new approach to patriotism cannot hope to change the approach in Washington if it espoused by isolated and disorganized individuals. There are glimmers of hope. Universities have sponsored many events to raise the level of critical discussion on questions of security. There are signs that some alternative thinking is gaining a following and that an unusual process of legitimizing dissent in the midst of this period of crisis is gaining support. Such developments indirectly challenge the power that tribal patriotism has over the political and moral imagination of a country and open some space for a future-oriented, hope-centered, cosmopolitan patriotism to take shape and take hold.

From the perspective of tribal patriotism, the rise of cosmopolitan patriotism is certain to be regarded as unwelcome, and as a posture that flirts with disloyalty. From the perspective of cosmopolitan patriotism, the citizen of conscience who voices criticism that offers guidance can alone help the country respond to the deeper challenges of September 11, which have been ignored by tribal patriotism's fixation on winning wars — measured by an almost exclusively military calculus that overlooks the extent to which wars are not really over until the political objectives that were being pursued are achieved. In this respect, both the Afghanistan War and the Iraq War are far from over!

Chapter 11
Human Rights and Civil Liberties

The great German playwright and poet Bertolt Brecht asked: "In the dark times, will there also be singing?" He answered, "Yes, there will be singing about the dark times." What I seek to express as best I can is how we find the strength of character, the faith in the mysteries of history and of our own destiny, to show what another great poet, W.H. Auden, called "an affirming flame" — despite the warmongering clouds darkening the skies of our country and world these days.

Unprecedented Assault on Our Liberties

It is no longer controversial to assert that there has been an unprecedented assault on our liberties as a free people since September 11. There is no question that these events, the attacks of that day, administered a terrible shock to the American sense of itself as secure and safe, as well as caused severe human carnage and untold grief to family, friends, and to all those exposed to this most violent assault on civilian innocence. The attacks were inscribed deeply in our political and moral consciousness by the power of TV imagery that may have done more lasting injury to our sensibility than the devastation itself, putting aside the incalculable damage associated with the human suffering. From the outset it seemed clear that, as terrible as the attacks were, one had to worry that an overreaction by the U.S. government would prove more enduringly dangerous to ourselves and to the rest of the world than the visionary terrorism of the al Qaeda network. There are several reasons for this. We need to take these considerations into account in trying to understand what it is that is so dangerous about the way in which the United States government and our political leaders in and out of government have responded to September 11.

The first element that is important to grasp is the degree to which the world is dealing with a new kind of conflict, a struggle of global scope that has never existed in history. There is a determined terrorist network that has no specific location. Al Qaeda could be everywhere and nowhere. Such an adversary cannot be defeated in the manner relied on in the past by countries under attack, seeking to defend their territory and remove or neutralize the source of threat, either on the battlefield or through diplomacy. There is little that can be done to disable the al Qaeda threat through the use of our extraordinary military machine, which is designed for a different type of combat. Here we were, afraid and angry, as well as frustrated, having invested so heavily for decades in developing a superior military capability that was designed to prevail in wars against other states, or better, to deter provocations and make actual war unnecessary.

To find ourselves a helpless giant under attack by an elusive terrorist network that was spread out and concealed around the world, possibly lurking in sleeper cells even within our own country, was a reality impossible for our leaders to cope with, or even to acknowledge. In this fundamental sense, it is important to recognize that there was a genuine security challenge posed on September 11, and that it is yet to be addressed in an appropriate and effective manner. To meet the al Qaeda threat will indeed justify some changes in the way national security is conceived and upheld. It is not reasonable to expect a government to wait for an attack by a megaterrorist network before seeking to nullify or minimize such a threat to the extent possible. It is not reasonable to wait for a repetition of September 11. It is equally unacceptable to engage in irrelevant or unjustifiable war making because a more effective response cannot be fashioned at this time, or to engage in state terrorism to offset al Qaeda nonstate terrorism, or to launch an unacknowledged empire-building project.

It is necessary to determine what measures are helpful and necessary to diminish the threat, but what seems so disturbing is that what might have been helpful has mainly not been undertaken, and what is definitely harmful to our security and to the peace of the world has been pursued with what one can only call a fundamentalist zeal. In trying to understand this unfamiliar challenge posed to us as a free society, it is instructive to realize that America has tended to curtail the liberties of its citizens while responding to threats that come from outside, and neither has it done well with supposed threats emanating from inside its own borders. We need only to recall bits of our past — the scandalous burning of witches at Salem, the fearful worries about the spread to America of the French Revolution that produced the Alien and Sedition Act in 1798, the infamous Palmer raids after the Russian Revolution that mindlessly rounded up the supposedly dangerous yet truly innocuous American radicals just after World War I.

More recently, we need to recall and reflect on the shameful internment of more than a hundred thousand Japanese Americans held in detention centers during World War II. This denial of the rights of citizens, stigmatized ethnically, was actually upheld as legal by our Supreme Court in the famous *Korematsu* decision. We have to remember the days of blacklisting, loyalty tests, and the discrediting of many decent and gifted people during the Cold War; the excesses of the McCarthy Era in the 1950s; and the degree to which our congressional institutions were used as a means not to uphold the constitutional system, but to challenge the integrity and the well-being of those Americans who were suspected and accused of having disloyal sentiments and affiliations conceived to be subversive in the context of the Cold War. The views and activities of Americans that were attacked in this period often arose out of idealistic concerns on behalf of the victims of economic deprivations that were believed to have been brought about by the capitalist system, which had itself fallen to its knees during the economic depression of the 1930s. This American turn toward socialism represented a humane reaction to economic failure that led a small minority of persons of good will to recommend the Soviet approach as a model, or to look with favor upon Communism and the Soviet socialist experiment. Such people were punished unjustly for these views that later became unpopular during the years of "the Red scare."

This record leads to the unhappy conclusion that ours is a political culture that doesn't handle stress very well. It has set some dreadful precedents involving groups and ideas viewed as hostile to the contemporary beliefs and interests of the American mainstream, beliefs that later were happily disowned, but while ascendant imposed unfair penalties on citizens of good will. A distinguished American intellectual historian, Richard Hofstadter, studied this dynamic and famously referred to it as "the paranoid style of American politics." The American nativist approach reminds one of the Green Berets' ethics of kill or die, an extremist way of thinking about "the other." Hofstadter discussed this tendency as based on a religiously fueled understanding of reality that above all conceives of conflict as an ultimate struggle between absolute good and absolute evil. In the face of such attitudes, it is necessary to avoid compromise, and even more so, to reject any offers of reconciliation. What is counted as political virtue in America is the display of an unflagging will to fight things out to the finish, regardless of consequences. There is little doubt in my mind that we find ourselves in a country currently in the grips of a mood and leadership that fully embodies this paranoid style, indeed represents an extreme version that endangers the world as well as ourselves. President Bush's rhetoric in relation to the Iraq War is emblematic.

Political Extremists Shaping Policy

This situation is made even more serious when we comprehend the extent to which American foreign and domestic policy, at the highest levels of our government, is now shaped by some of the most extreme political figures that have ever been this close to the control of our governmental machinery. In other words, if you look back at these earlier distressing events that were mentioned, they put a troublesome pressure on the political leadership of the time, but the hard core of extremism was always located at a certain distance from the center of power. American values associated with civil liberties eventually generated reactions to repressive moves, displaying a reassuring resilience that enabled the American political culture to correct these unfortunate historic abuses before they tainted the system as a whole. What is here so troubling is that this present national climate of fear and anger evoked by the events of September 11 is tied secretly to an American grand strategy for world domination that had been lurking in the wings of the White House well before the attacks. The attacks allowed this grandiose vision of how the United States should reorganize the world after the Cold War, based on taking advantage of its leverage as the sole surviving superpower, to come out into the open as the official policy of the United States, presented as an acceptable policy by waving furiously the banner of antiterrorism in one hand and the American flag of patriotism in the other. Antiterrorism provided the cover, in effect, for pursuing a geopolitically ambitious design of how the world should be organized in the future on the basis of American dominion.

President Bush has forcefully articulated these ideas — especially in his West Point address delivered in June of 2002, but also in the very important White House document — the National Security Strategy of the United States of America that was issued in September of 2002. (See Chapter 8.) It is significant that these maximalist conceptions of the American global role had been set forth rather clearly in a document released by the New American Century Project in 2000 prior to Bush's election as president. This report was signed by many individuals who are now working in the upper echelons of government and have emerged as the most influential advisors of the Bush leadership, being especially prominent in the Pentagon and the White House. What I think we have to realize, with alarm, is that a group of evangelical geopoliticians has seized control of the government, sensing their historic opportunity to shape the future of the world, and that this reactionary cabal is supported and reinforced by the religious right in America that is also now, for the first time, exerting a direct influence on our political destiny, challenging the secular heritage of the country. Born-again Christianity seems to mesh very well with the geopolitics of world domination. Such a partnership is potent and particularly menacing.

It is important that we understand, as the background of these circumstances that exist today, that this global vision is intimately connected with the suppression of our rights at home and only incidentally and opportunistically connected with the threats posed by terrorism. In introducing the National Security Strategy document, President Bush includes a cover letter in which he makes a rather startling claim. On first reading, it would make us think that the president was unexpectedly endorsing a radical conception of world peace by his seeming enthusiasm on behalf of an idealistic and hopeful view of humanity's future, despite the weight of everyday evidence to the contrary. Bush writes, "Today the international community has the best chance since the rise of the nation state in the 17th Century, to build a world where great powers compete in peace instead of continually prepare for war. The U.S. will build on these common interests to promote global security."[3] This seems, on an initial reading, to be an astonishing statement coming from the Bush White House, but such an impression of amazement vanishes as soon as you read the fine print. The fine print informs the reader that the reason there will be global security for the rest of the world is because the United States possesses the exclusive capacity and necessary will to provide it, that it will continue to spend at least as much as the next fifteen countries on its military budget, that it will weaponize space, that it will maintain a network of military bases around the world, and that it will, in Pentagon jargon, ensure for itself "full spectrum dominance," that is, the capacity to defeat decisively any adversary at any level of political violence and in any theater of operations around the world.[4]

U.S. Military Domination

The message sent around the world is that it has become obsolete for other countries to think of challenging American military domination; instead of engaging in traditional geopolitical rivalries based on a balance of power, these other countries should go about their national business peacefully, concentrating their energies on trade and doing things that are in their national interest, leaving the running of the world to the United States. It is a virtual certainty that the French leadership read this small print and recoiled in "shock and awe." If you put yourself in the position of another sovereign state, watching the U.S. government, despite its advice to others, devoting huge resources to ensuring its own military means to sustain its global dominance while essentially instructing other countries that it is no longer necessary to invest in their own military capabilities, then we can assume a reaction of discomfort by leading foreign governments, and their readiness to consider a range of offsetting moves to constrain American power. What is likely to result in reaction is hard to predict with any precision as to time and character, but it is likely to produce over time an expensive and risky rivalry.

Of course, this is not the first time President Bush's concept of peace is a silent testimony to his apparently unwitting sense of the absurd. Bush has made a practice of associating peace with the espousal of the most aggressive policies, as, for instance, in explaining his dedication to a peaceful solution for the Iraq crisis while taking every possible opportunity to make certain that war ensues. It was hard to believe that Bush would choose the midst of some of the most brutal Israeli operations on the West Bank and in Gaza during early 2003 to identify Ariel Sharon as a man of peace. If President Bush really thinks that Sharon is a man of peace, then I can understand why his West Point vision of peace seems so evidently merged with the policies of military domination.

Two considerations need to be understood. The first of these is this American drive to gain control over the way in which security is maintained in the world. The second element is important to Bush's militarist policy-makers, what is called "asymmetric warfare" by defense strategists. This preoccupation with asymmetric warfare preceded September 11. Asymmetric warfare represents the recognition by American military planners that very weak countries and nonstate political actors have the potential to overcome their inferior capabilities by using unconventional tactics to inflict heavy damage on strong countries. In other words, military superiority as traditionally measured is no longer capable of assuring the control and defeat of hostile forces in the world. From this perspective, the September 11 attacks were themselves an extreme and telling example of asymmetric warfare. Pentagon officials had long been arguing that although the United States had overwhelming military advantages with respect to other states, it was at the same time more vulnerable to devastating attack than ever before. Until September 11, the Pentagon was crying in the wilderness; its warnings about dangers from extremist movements or hostile governments armed with weapons of mass destruction went unheeded. Suddenly the warning was received with an unquestioning sense of the greatest urgency.

This stress on asymmetric warfare identified two kinds of threats that could ruin the American vision of a peaceful future based on global dominance. One threat has to do with trying to eliminate those countries seen as potentially able to challenge the power structure, even though they seem like secondary and tertiary countries if their capabilities are traditionally assessed. Such countries were singled out by the Bush administration with great fanfare in 2002 as the "axis of evil" countries. It is this preoccupation that explained, at least partially, the obsession with Iraq as a sufficient threat to justify recourse to a major war, despite the disconnect between Iraq and the menace of megaterrorism, as well as the need to magnify actual Iraqi capabilities in order to make its alleged threat seem at all plausible. The second kind of adversary that cannot be located or destroyed is, of course, the new kind of networked, nonstate adversary exemplified by al Qaeda.

Because this second challenge cannot be successfully addressed, American society needs to be misled into believing that a war against "axis of evil" countries somehow facilitates the struggle against al Qaeda rather than aggravating it. In addition, to be sure that the patriotic mandate does not dissipate nor criticism mount of the Bush administration's regressive economic policies, a state of fear and anger is officially manipulated by issuing periodic warnings of imminent terrorist attack at home. Such alarms are helpful in maintaining a high level of domestic support for the expansive and expensive role of the United States as the guardian of global security. There exists an insidious underpinning for these policies that is not accidental but brings great anxiety and discomfort to the American people. The FBI director and the head of the CIA inform us in strong language calculated to cause widespread fear that it is a virtual certainty that suicide bombers will soon be stalking our cities and shopping malls, that a "dirty bomb" with radioactive effects will be released in densely populated urban areas, or that there is evidence of plans to attack crucial bridges, tunnels, nuclear power plants, and the like. Such warnings, especially if some incidents do occur, are likely to produce a mood of national panic, inviting the government to encroach further on the rights of American citizens and others resident in the country.

This condition of collective fear and uncertainty has been disabling our collective critical faculties. We as a society seem unable to critically think about existing policies or to envision and evaluate alternative courses of action. An individual or a people facing severe danger is unable to assess and understand the true nature of the situation, and will often be politically paralyzed. America has been frozen like this since the attacks on the World Trade Center and Pentagon, although the imminence of a war against Iraq has awakened many citizens, but without yet giving rise to a politically relevant strategy of resistance and renewal, or to a viable alternative image of security to that of the armored fist.

The Magnitude of the Crisis

It is first necessary to acknowledge the magnitude of the crisis confronting the American people. It appears we are facing, nationally and internationally, the first real challenge that is directed at our system of government, our way of life, and the manner in which the whole world is organized. With reluctance, I think we need to escalate the language used to identify properly the precise nature of this danger. I have come to the unhappy conclusion that the danger we and the world faces is the distinct possibility that American foreign policy, as now practiced, and to the extent it is successful, will eventuate in a form of world order best described as "global fascism." Why global fascism? The Bush administration's grand strategy seems intent on achieving a monopolistic concentration of military power to be used to destroy opponents who are perceived as embodiments of evil. Being evil means that it is both pointless and immoral to rely on diplomacy to resolve conflict. Further, given the depravity of such enemies, there is no need to admit the existence of legitimate grievances that might call for changes in American policy. The impulse is to destroy and to regard an adversary as "the other," an unconditional enemy, an evil that is defined by this evangelical Christian underpinning and nurtured by a new form of geopolitical ambition that seeks to build security on the basis of political purification. Such a worldview is so threatening to the rest of the world that it is generating waves of spontaneous opposition in many places, which, in turn, gives rise to governmental impulses here in America to rely on repressive techniques. (See Chapter 9.)

The assault on traditional American liberties, and more generally on human rights here and abroad, began immediately after the September 11 events. This assault was rhetorically justified as part of the antiterrorism campaign, but without any reasonable or convincing connection with actual security threats. Such sweeping claims were exaggerated responses by enforcement agencies that gave the impression, probably correctly, that our attorney general and those making national policies found this challenge of terrorism a wonderful excuse for doing a lot of things that they wanted to do anyway. Osama bin Laden opened an enormous window of opportunity for John Ashcroft. Many dubious moves were taken against this inflamed background. Among the first occurred when President Bush issued an executive decree in November 2001 that authorized the creation of military commissions able to operate in secret and allowed to inflict a death sentence — without giving any kind of assurance of a fair trial and without providing the accused with any kind of appeal, thus institutionalizing a very extreme form of quick kangaroo justice for the prosecution of any noncitizen alleged to be connected with terrorist activities. It was a dragnet capable of almost indefinite abuse as it proceeded behind institutional veils of secrecy, especially given a vague definition of terrorism that could be stretched to cover virtually anyone the government wanted to punish or repress.

Soon after the end of the Afghanistan War, the world was treated to the appalling spectacle of captured al Qaeda and Taliban soldiers and civilian suspects exhibited like caged animals in Camp X-Ray, located on the American base at Guantanamo in Cuba. This was a gratuitous, shocking display of official cruelty that could not be plausibly justified on the basis of security considerations. Such behavior encouraged, I think, a widespread sense of anxiety overseas about how the United States was dealing with megaterrorism. What sort of message did we want to send the world about the way in which we deal with those who oppose us? There was no acceptable reason to explain these departures from the standards of international humanitarian law as set forth by the Geneva Conventions. These standards were drafted and agreed on by governments, and are designed to be compatible with the pursuit of military victory in war, and as such, are minimally demanding.

And then, of course, there was the rush to enact the USA Patriot Act in 2002, a sweeping legislative enactment hardly debated in Congress despite the comprehensive enlargement of governmental enforcement powers that included a dangerously broad redefinition of terrorism that could be used to sweep up whoever the government wanted to apprehend, including many of those engaged in innocent activities. Such a definition of terrorism, if applied fairly, could indict our leaders for relying on violence to achieve political ends not consistent with law, or due to their harboring violent exile groups in this country that rely on terrorist tactics. The legislative powers given to the U.S. government enabled unwarranted intrusions on privacy, a capacity to detain individuals on frivolous charges, often denying the accused access to lawyers or the possibility of confronting the evidence. It subjected nonresidents, noncitizens, and even permanent resident noncitizens to deportation for all sorts of minor law infractions that could have been quite innocent, or at least were trivial, and certainly not justification for disrupting families and lives in an anguishing and likely permanent manner. Much of the repressive fury was directed toward young males from the Islamic world who were placed under special forms of surveillance and control, with the threat of arbitrary deportation hanging over their heads. We have learned recently that the Justice Department wants even more power and has prepared a very extensive proposed legislative enactment called the Domestic Security Enhancement Act that is proposing to give the state many additional powers, including authority to look at credit cards and Internet activity and enlist citizens in a campaign to report suspicious activity by neighbors. Such initiatives appear as deliberately Orwellian moves to create a controlled society in the United States while all the time singing the praises of freedom. It is revealing that a patriotic cover for such legislation was explicitly used, even extending to the name of the legislation.

We already have the sorry experience of two American citizens — Yasser Isam Hamdi and José Padilla, both members of an ethnic minority, who have been denied their constitutional rights as citizens by being declared "enemy combatants" by the Justice Department. These individuals are American citizens but because they are regarded as enemy combatants, they abruptly lose their "inalienable" rights. They are not entitled to consult with a lawyer. They are potentially subject to indefinite solitary confinement without charges and they are, in effect, stripped by unilateral fiat of their privileged status as citizens. This pattern is extremely troublesome for its own sake, but even more so because it is related to the kind of official American response that can be expected of this wider international movement of opposition and resistance to the U.S. project of global dominance. More and more grassroots militancy is present in this country and overseas.

The very untenability of the American global strategy and its penchant for aggressive war making is, as a byproduct, leading to the transformation of America into a militarist society reinforced by a submissive citizenry and media. This process gives rise to a vicious cycle, it engenders opposition and the very fact of opposition leads the government to seek more and more control over what people, including citizens, are allowed to do by way of political dissent within the society. We are unwittingly part of a vicious cycle, internationally and nationally, that is placing extraordinary pressure on our constitutional system, both in relation to our rights as citizens and with respect to the functioning of a governmental process that is legitimate only so long as it is based on checks and balances and the separation of powers.

Finding Hope

It is against this depressing background that I now want to offer something about what we can do to find hope for a better future.[5] It is worth recalling an often quoted observation made early in our history by Benjamin Franklin: "Those that can give up essential liberty to obtain a little temporary safety, deserve neither liberty nor safety." And I think we should all, as individuals, ponder what that sage remark means in the concrete reality of our own lives because we are being profoundly challenged as individuals to act now as citizens, not as subjects. This response to al Qaeda represents the most difficult test of whether American democracy is rooted deeply enough to withstand this shock treatment administered against it from outside and inside. Such circumstances make it plain that this is not a time when we as individuals can remain spectators on the sidelines, which reminds us of Lincoln's call to heed "our better angels" in times of national crisis. An analogous sentiment was also well expressed by a great conservative philosopher, Edmund Burke, who declared that "the hottest fires in hell are reserved for those who remain neutral in times of crisis." We are unquestionably faced with a forbidding crisis, but there is fortunately more on the global stage of history than these negative developments.

Some extraordinary things are happening in the world that should give us at least vectors for the struggle to create a better world and provide us a sense of what is possible from the perspective of global reform. To begin with, we have the unfolding of the first genuinely global peace movement that is mobilizing large segments of the population of free societies everywhere. It was unprecedented to have between 85 and 95 percent of the world's countries opposed to the American war directed at Iraq, even when these countries are led by governments supportive of Washington, as was the case for England, Italy, and Spain. These governments, ignoring the overwhelming sentiments of their own people, for various reasons supported the Iraq war policy pushed so hard by the White House. We are witnessing the unfolding of a great popular movement of global scope that subscribes to a vision of a better world that is not addicted to militarism and violence as the path to global security. It is perhaps an occasion of perverse encouragement that the United States government felt so isolated so as to somewhat pathetically boast that it acquired a new ally, Bulgaria, to demonstrate that it was winning over uncommitted governments throughout the world to support the Iraq War. In contrast, let us give thanks for the "old Europe" of France and Germany for their principled opposition to the war against Iraq, which at the very least stimulated a debate, especially in Europe, and lent credibility to grassroots opposition. Let us wish now for the return of "old America," along with the continued antiwar and anti-imperial vitality of "Old Europe"!

Other encouraging things are happening in reaction to this growing sense that it is a time to propose alternative ways to arrange the world, that it is not enough to oppose the American global design. The prime minister of Malaysia, Mahathir Mohamad, gave an extraordinary welcome speech in Kuala Lumpur on February 24, 2003, to the Non-Aligned Movement, which brought together the representatives of more than a hundred countries from the south.[6] Mahathir said that it was time for the countries of the world, led by the countries of the south, to mount a campaign to make war unconditionally illegal, and that it would be a welcome contribution to world order if the nonaligned states would take the lead by repudiating war as an instrument of their own national policy. Mahathir also proposed a concrete initiative: "Isn't it time that all the countries in the world were put under the same constraint as Japan and limited to spending one percent of their GNP on military budget?" When Mahathir put forth this simple yet startling suggestion, he reportedly received huge applause from the assembled leaders of the 116 member states of the Non-Aligned Movement.

I believe we live increasingly in a time of renewed receptivity to bold ideas that might have been dismissed scornfully as utopian just a few years ago. Jonathan Schell has published a deeply researched book, *The Unconquerable World*, on the futility of war as a way of solving the problems confronting humankind.[7] More and more people here and abroad are turning away from their fears of terrorists to their fears associated with the pursuit of global dominance by the sole remaining superpower. Such a dramatic turn of mind can help us build our own movement that will represent a commitment to a future based on liberty at home, peace with equity abroad, and a restored confidence in the continuing viability of our constitutional arrangements.

What it means to be an American, or for that matter "a patriot," should definitely not be understood as the USA Patriot Act would have us believe and act. (See Chapter 9.) It is both interesting and worrisome that these repressive initiatives should seek to preempt the language of patriotism as if what it means to be a patriot is to renounce our liberties! Even choosing the word "patriot" to describe this legislation reveals a manipulative mentality in our government and exhibits a profound disrespect for our great national traditions of citizen liberties.

We have an opportunity, at this challenging time, to turn toward the traditions of Mahatma Gandhi and Martin Luther King, adopting the tactics and values of nonviolent struggle, a type of faith and militancy that can truly claim Jesus and the Buddha as spiritual forebears. We need to infuse our educational experience from start to finish with the relevance of a nonviolent pedagogy, from the earliest moments of schooling to the last hours of our lives. We need to purge our own political culture of the violence that finds security in an arsenal of weapons, whether stockpiled at home or collectively expressed by the deployment of weapons of mass destruction around the world. I am convinced that if we are able to disseminate this nonviolent pedagogy, good things will begin to happen in ways we cannot now anticipate. Such an altered climate will also affirm a culture of human rights as integral to the quest for an alternative to the kind of future than what the Bush Administration is offering Americans and the peoples of the world.

It is also empowering to remind ourselves that a series of extremely positive global developments occurred in the 1990s. I stress the relevance of reviving a global justice revolution that was beginning to take hold during the final decade of the twentieth century. We need to recall the legal pursuit of dictators like Pinochet and Milosevic, seeking to impose criminal accountability on individuals responsible for the commission of terrible crimes of state. These initiatives, in turn, inspired social movements and many governments, rapidly leading to the establishment of an International Criminal Court in mid 2002, which may in time prove to be the most important international innovation at a global level since the United Nations was founded after World War II. We also experienced, during the 1990s, significant international efforts to protect vulnerable societies facing ethnic cleansing and genocide. The humanitarian interventions, although controversial for some weighty reasons, did, at least, express a rising sense of responsibility on the part of the international community to prevent atrocities from being committed behind the walls of sovereign states. The liberating idea of human solidarity was beginning to prevail over the excesses of sovereignty and tribal passions fueled by nationalism, making the supreme authority of the state no longer sacrosanct if those governing states grossly abused their power by committing crimes against humanity.

There was also born at the end of the 1990s a robust antiglobalization movement that was, in an exciting way, developing a grassroots global consensus dedicated to achieving more equitable, democratic, and sustainable ways of governing the world economy. A significant part of that vision expressed the conviction that we needed to build a global democracy in a world that was growing more interdependent, complex, and fragile by the day. Among the many proposals for making global democracy into a practical reality was the proposal to establish a Global Peoples' Assembly that could begin to represent directly the peoples of the world rather than have their voices muffled by the more parochial concerns of governments.[8] We can only begin to imagine how different the prewar debate within the United Nations on Iraq policy would have been if there was a peoples' assembly that spoke for the 90 percent of the world's population opposed to this war, rather than the kind of discourse on the nuances of coercive diplomacy that has dominated the Security Council debate. In this debate, the governments negotiate within a framework set by geopolitical power relations, calculating their own benefits, seeking their own piece of the economic pie that will result from the occupation of Iraq, and acting to avoid the wrath of Washington. However grateful we may be for the role of France and Germany and other governmental opponents of war against Iraq, the debate was officially framed by an unfortunate unanimous acceptance of the premise that if Baghdad resisted inspection or was found in serious violation of its obligations under the ceasefire restrictions imposed in 1991, then a war against Iraq should be authorized by the Security Council. This framing avoided the essential, indispensable question as to whether war against Iraq is legally, morally, and politically justified given the factual circumstances and taking into account Iraq's sovereign rights, as well as whether the burdens of "disarmament" had been fairly imposed on a defeated Iraq in the first place back in 1991.

We Need to Reinvent Our Democracy

It is essential that activists around the world revitalize these elements of a global campaign for a more democratic world. If we genuinely want to restore our security and our sense of democracy, we have to reinvent what it means to have a functioning representative democracy that isn't distorted by money or a sense of electoral impotence. We have a problem within this country that is far deeper than the dangers posed by the Bush administration. We have a Democratic party that is scared to act as an opposition party even when the country is deeply divided and confused — and on a matter as vital as the ultimate choice of war or peace. We have a Congress that is awkwardly impassive and largely silent when it should be impressively active and impassioned. We have a media that is orchestrating the society for war and conformity, rather than facilitating an invigorating debate about what policies are in the best interests of the country. We must address these issues in a spirit of civic urgency if we as a people and as a world are to reinvent the kind of democracy we all need for the twenty-first century to become a success, eventually overcoming this most disturbing of beginnings.

I continue to hope and pray that there will come into being richly imaginative forces of resistance and change that will halt this drift toward the sort of political catastrophe that I have identified with global fascism. (See Chapter 13.) More and more of us do understand that this is a moment where we have to accept a share of responsibility for the future. It will not be easy to change the course of world history or to rein in the exercise of American power. Formidable obstacles are arrayed against such a change of direction, but we should be engaged on the basis of what we believe is right and necessary, not by a sober calculation of the odds of success. Because the obstacles seem so great, yet the cause seems so just, we must learn as quickly as we can that a "politics as the art of the impossible" has become our best hope. Throughout human history the great strides forward all seemed "impossible" until they happened.

Endnotes

1. See Richard Hofstadler, *The Paranoid Style in American Politics, and Other Essays* (New York: Knopf, 1965).
2. "Rebuilding America's Defenses," Report of Project for a New American Century, Washington, D.C., Sept. 2000.

3. "National Security Strategy of the United States of America," document issued by White House, Washington, D.C., Sept. 2002.
4. For critique see Rahul Mahajan, *Full Spectrum Dominance: U.S. Power in Iraq and Beyond* (New York: Seven Stories Press, 2003).
5. See David Kreger, ed., *Hope in a Dark Time: Reflections on Humanity and Future* (Santa Barbara, CA: Capra Press, 2003).
6. Mahather Mohamed, Opening Speech, XII Summit Meeting, Non-Aligned Movement, Feb. 24, 2003. Citing Prime Minister Mahamine speech on war in no way endorses his anti-semetic views expressed on other occasions.
7. See Jonathan Schell, *The Unconquerable World: Power, Nonviolence, and the Will of the People* (New York: Metropolitan Books, 2003).
8. See Richard Falk and Andrew Strauss, "The Deeper Challenges of Global Terrorism: A Democratizing Response," in Daniele Archibagi, ed., *Debating Cosmopolitics* (London, UK: Verso, 2002) 203–231.

Chapter 12
Will the Empire Be Fascist?

The United States is by circumstance and design an emergent global empire, the first in the history of the world. Prior empires have had frontiers and boundaries, although they occupied large expanses of territory, and exerting control from a distant center that due to available technologies of communication and transportation were further away in time than is any part of the world from Washington. In purely temporal terms, the American Empire is thus smaller than earlier great empires associated with China, Rome, the Ottomans, the Persians, the Austro-Hungarian, and the overseas empires of the British, French, Dutch, Spanish, and Portuguese.

It is important to appreciate the consequences of an empire of global scope. Such an empire, to the extent that it is established and sustained without significant resistance, raises a special challenge to world order. Over the course of modern history, in particular, stability in international relations has been maintained primarily by reliance on countervailing power, often interpreted by reference to "the balance of power," and giving rise to various schools of "realist" thinking to explain the central ordering role of power. Such an international equilibrium was complemented in the Westphalia era by "war," which served as a crude and cruel legislative substitute, introducing periodic changes in maps portraying the boundaries of territorial states.

An imperial ordering instrument was by way of various forms of "hegemony" that established geographic zones of control, known as "spheres of influence," by which powerful states exerted control over the behavior of weaker states, as illustrated by such patterns as the Monroe Doctrine, the Soviet Bloc, and the Atlantic Alliance. An ethical approach to ordering world politics remains weak, yet for the future it is the most promising, prospect, relying on the strengthening of international law, especially as institutionalized within the United Nations. Such a framework of international law, the struggle to find an alternative to war in the setting of conflict and change, has taken on a sense of urgency since the development of weaponry of mass destruction, but lacks the independent capabilities to ensure respect for its constraints by powerful states and by newly formidable nonstate actors (the al Qaeda network).

Against this background the shape of the world order crisis becomes more evident. An American empire that repudiates international law and is unchecked by countervailing power is a political actor that possesses an abundant arsenal of nuclear weapons and is confronted by a nonstate enemy that has been pronounced as "evil," justifying an exterminist approach to resolving the conflict. Beyond this, the American approach to global security extends its response to antiterrorism to encompass states that are perceived as hostile, and possess or may possess weaponry of mass destruction. The Iraq War is an expression of this extension, made particularly disturbing because the alleged *casus belli* was not endorsed by the United Nations Security Council and cannot be reconciled with international law.

This chapter explores the implication of these trends as defining the American empire, and specifically argues that the prospects associated with such a reality no longer support, if indeed they ever did, the school of benign imperialists who, while acknowledging the imperial moment for the United States, insisted that it was a benevolent political configuration as compared to prior imperial projects, and provided the world with the global public good of security without oppression and exploitation.[1] Indeed, I believe that the American empire is turning toward a system of militarized control that includes a repudiation of the authority of international law and of the United Nations. To underscore my sense of concern about this style of imperial control, I treat these trends as posing a threat of "global fascism." It is a threat that has begun to be realized in the context of the American response to the September 11 attacks, but especially by the extension of this response by way of aggressive war making to the "axis of evil" countries.

Such a threat is also accentuated by the development of resistance to this American project by the peoples of the world, as evident in the antiwar movement that took shape during the Iraq crisis, including in the United States itself. The response of cynical disregard by the U.S. government occurred in an atmosphere in which sweeping claims to curtail liberties have been given legislative backing by the Congress and where discriminatory policies have been formally and informally pursued with respect to Muslim residents in the United States, especially young male Arab Americans and noncitizens. Given this rising tide of resistance that encounters an official mindset empowered by a dangerous blend of religious and geopolitical zeal, the moves toward fascist modes of control are plausibly feared and anticipated.

An Imperial Moment

Andrew Bacevich clearly expresses a view that is increasingly encountered in mainstream American commentary, acknowledging for better or for worse a new imperial role for the United States: "The question that Americans can no longer afford to dodge — is not whether the United States has become an imperial power. The question is what sort of empire they intend theirs to be."[2] Bacevich ends his book by stressing the importance of this acknowledgement of empire, insisting that concealing such an imperial reality will lead to "not just the demise of the American empire but great danger for what used to be known as the American republic."[3]

A similar theme was influentially intoned by Michael Ignatieff, who calls for an American understanding of its imperial role as "a burden" that is the consequence of its preeminence in the world. Ignatieff gives empire a potentially favorable gloss, arguing that "the case for empire is that it has become, in a place like Iraq, the last hope of democracy and stability alike."[4] Ignatieff couples his advocacy with the warning that empires decline and fall when they overreach, ignoring limits on their capabilities. As with Bacevich, Ignatieff believes that overcoming the American inhibition to mention the "E-word" is the first requirement for reinterpreting the appropriate U.S. global role given its preeminent power.

Clarifying this American role did not begin with the presidency of George W. Bush. Ever since the collapse of the Soviet Union in 1991, there have been strong official and unofficial statements based on a new American-dominated power structure, including celebrations of a so-called unipolar moment (Charles Krauthammer) and assertions that the United States is "the indispensable nation" (Madeleine Albright).[5] These sentiments as intoned during the Bush Sr. and Clinton years were mostly understood as leadership challenges to be met by the United States in the aftermath of the Cold War. In the wings of American policymaking were shrill, more radical neoconservative voices arguing that the end of the Cold War presented the U.S. government with an extraordinary opportunity to fill the vacuum created by the Soviet collapse with American power for the benefit of the world. Such a vision was hatched in the ideologically overheated incubators of such well-financed think tanks as the American Enterprise Institute and the Heritage Foundation. This historic possibility, it was argued, could only be realized if the U.S. government would consciously pursue a global dominance project by way of an *increased* investment in military capabilities, that is, going against the flow of the liberal consensus at the time that "a peace dividend" and nuclear disarmament were the best ways to take advantage of the end of the Cold War. It was further contended that if the United States failed to rise to the occasion, it would encourage forces of disorder throughout the world, producing a variety of dangers and setbacks. In a sense, there was no choice but to make use of American power, *as enhanced by an expanded global military capability.*[6]

In the same period, more centrist figures in the United States were articulating more modest versions of a parallel vision of a reconstituted world order.[7] Joseph Nye suggested that American superiority in the increasingly important domains of "soft power" would allow the U.S. government to establish a more stable and beneficial world order that was anchored in multilateralism and patterns of cooperative, international problem-solving.[8] These centrist leadership models relied on nonmilitary means to sustain American global dominance, and avoided illiberal designations such as "empire" or "imperial" to identify the process. Yet, by so framing the grand strategy debate in this period after the Cold War, it provided space for those more neoconservative perspectives that insisted that these goals could only be reached by "hard power," the ability and willingness to project superior military force to all four corners of the planet.[9]

This commentary on the global scene was basically overshadowed during the 1990s by the preoccupation with economic globalization as the defining reality of a new era of international relations in which market forces associated with trade and investment assume priority over traditional security concerns, given the absence of serious strategic or ideological conflict among leading states. From this perspective, a principal world order concern was the future of the sovereign state, as well as the struggle of non-Western peoples to sustain their distinctive identities in a consumerist world shaped by the materialist tastes of the American people and their hegemonic popular culture. This challenge mounted by the economic globalizers energized global civil society, giving rise to a global democracy movement designed to make the world economy more equitable in its distribution of benefits, and accountable to the peoples of the world as well as to their corporate boards. It also gave rise to a religious resurgence of global scope, which in certain manifestations, especially in the Islamic world, posed a direct challenge to globalization and American global leadership.[10]

The September 11 attacks occurred against such a background and almost immediately moved the global security agenda back onto the center stage of world politics, and once again removed global economic issues from active public concern. But what became clear almost from the first responses by the U.S. government was a decision by the White House to frame its response to megaterrorism in terms that incorporated the radical neoconservative conception of a future world order. President Bush immediately insisted that other countries have the choice of either being on the side of the United States or "with the terrorists." At the same time, the net was spread much wider than the defensive necessities of the situation, encompassing "terrorism" in general, and not just the "megaterrorism" of al Qaeda.[11] This enlarged conception of "the war" allowed the Bush administration to shift the focus of the American response from the al Qaeda presence in Afghanistan to "the axis of evil" countries that had essentially no connection with megaterrorism, but were definitely standing in the way of the American espousal of global dominance as a goal to be actively pursued. It is this shift that has brought the issue of "empire" into the open and raised the question of what type of empire, what repercussions it would have for America as a constitutional democracy, and how it would play out in world politics. The international turmoil generated by the White House resolve to wage war against Iraq has placed these issues in the sharpest possible relief, and gave rise to a massive popular mobilization of resistance throughout the world and a diplomatic revolt by some of America's closest allies and traditional friends. The Iraq crisis played out in part within the United Nations Security Council posed a dreadful choice for the membership, to go along with aggressive war making in violation of the UN Charter or to find the UN and Western governments bypassed by American military unilateralism.

Depicting the Radical Vision of the Bush Administration at Home and Abroad

President Bush has set forth the American commitment to an imperial world order with relative clarity. Elements of this vision were promoted by the Bush presidency well before September 2001. The priority accorded to the militarization of space, which included the unilateral scrapping of the Anti-Ballistic Missile Treaty, was certainly an expensive, destabilizing step taken in the direction of American global dominance. Beyond this, an imperial and unilateralist U.S. approach to the rest of the world was disclosed by its repudiation of the Kyoto Protocol on the emission of greenhouse gasses, by rejecting the treaty setting up the International Criminal Court, and by an overall diplomatic posture that was dismissive of humanitarian undertakings by the United Nations. Also, to fill the most influential governmental positions, the Bush administration appointed the most extreme cold war hawks who were the principal authors of the neocon worldview in the 1990s, including Paul Wolfowitz and Dick Cheney — the reputed architects of a Pentagon-leaked document in 1992 that advocated an American grand strategy that was centered on ensuring that in *no region* of the world should the United States allow a military power to emerge that might be capable of challenging American dominance within its own region.[12]

The American response to September 11 has greatly accelerated the drive for global dominance, although it has been masked beneath the banners of antiterrorism. The rapid military buildup of American forces, their adaptation to the challenges of hostile forces in the non-Western world, the extension of antiterrorism to "axis of evil" countries, and the general acceptance of this role by mainstream American public opinion have all had the effect of moving the project of American empire into the center of political consciousness. The Bush administration in its formal public presentations has been careful to discuss its goals as premised on antiterrorism, but the broader claims, although expressed in an indirect form, lent undeniable support to imperial allegations. President Bush has made his most authoritative statement in a June 2002 address at West Point, and more comprehensively in The National Security Strategy of the United States of America (NSS 2002) released by the White House in September 2002.

At West Point Bush repeated the familiar litany about American goals in the world as fully compatible with traditional ideas of world order based on the interaction of sovereign states. The president told the graduating cadets that "America has no empire to extend or utopia to establish." He then went on, after describing the threats posed by weaponry of mass destruction in hostile hands, to articulate precisely American plans for global dominance and a utopia of sorts. The utopian element was the promise to eliminate war among "civilized" states from the international scene, insisting that "civilized nations find themselves on the same side ... thereby making the destabilizing arms races of other eras pointless, and limiting rivalries to trade and other pursuits of peace." But such a promise was coupled with the dominance theme, indeed, present in the same sentence: "America has, and intends to keep, military strengths beyond challenge." And so the global security system is based on the combination of demilitarization for the rest of the world, while the United States relies on its military might to keep the peace.[13]

This double emphasis is repeated in a more oblique yet unmistakable form in the White House National Security Strategy document. In his signed cover letter introducing the document, Bush says "Today, the international community has the best chance since the rise of the nation-state in the seventeenth century to build a world where great powers compete in peace instead of continually prepare for war. Today, the world's great powers find ourselves on the same side — united by common dangers of terrorist violence and chaos. The United States will build on these common interests to promote global security." Such expectations are accompanied by embracing "the democratic peace theory" so popular among the benign imperialists during the 1990s. In Bush's words, "the United States will use this moment of opportunity to extend the benefits of freedom across the globe. We will actively work to bring the hope of democracy, development, free markets, and free trade to every corner of the world." Such a design combines ideas of American dominance associated with economic globalization, ideas that were prevalent before September 11, with more militarist ideas associated with the antiterrorist climate of the early twenty-first century.

There is the further disclosure of a deliberate bid to impose a hierarchical form of world order, in other words, an imperial structure on the rest of the world, by the official approach taken in NSS 2002 toward its one plausible geopolitical rival, China. In discussing American plans for the Asia–Pacific region, China is given some patronizing advice sure to cause consternation in the policy institutes at work in Beijing and Shanghai. The language is worth quoting: "In pursuing advanced military capabilities that can threaten its neighbors in the Asia-Pacific region, China is following an outdated path that, in the end, will hamper its own pursuit of national greatness. In time, China will find that social and political freedom is the only source of that greatness."[14] Apparently oblivious to the inconsistency, a few paragraphs later NSS 2002 suggests the essential reliance of the United States on its military superiority: "It is time to reaffirm the essential role of American military strength. We must build our defenses beyond challenge." And further, "The unparalleled strength of the United States armed forces, and their forward presence, have maintained the peace in some of the world's most strategically vital reigons."[15] To lecture China (and presumably others) about the outdatedness of military power while devoting more resources to its military budget than the next fifteen countries combined can only be understood as a message from the imperial capital to a subordinate part of the empire.

It seems safe to conclude the following about the drift of American power in the early twenty-first century. The basic move is to adopt policies that anchor the imperial project in a military approach to global security. While not abandoning the ideological precepts of neoliberal globalization, the Bush administration places its intense free market advocacy beneath a security blanket that includes suspect advice to other governments to devote their resources to nonmilitary activities. Such advice is coupled with an acknowledgement of the new and acute American vulnerability to megaterrorist attack by nonstate actors, and an accompanying call for unity at home and internationally to help in confronting such a threat. There was a considerable show of such unity in the aftermath of September 11, but it started to fray when the Bush administration extended its response to Iraq, raising suspicions that it was deliberately confusing the challenge of megaterrorism with the ambition to establish an American empire.

There is another quite different line of interpretation, suggested by Nelson Mandela, that September 11 had a disorienting effect on President Bush and his entourage of advisors. In Mandela's words, "What I am condemning is that one power, with a president who has no foresight, who cannot think properly, is now wanting to plunge the world into a holocaust."[16] In effect, Mandela is implying that the imperial option to the extent pursued by the Bush approach will produce a massive war, not an era of peace, prosperity, and security.

What is meant by "think properly" can be understood in different ways. If taken to mean in a clear and self-interested way, it is a prediction that aggressive American military moves will provoke forms of resistance that eventuate in a war that is a disaster for America and the rest of the world. But Mandela's phrase "think properly" can also be interpreted to mean in accordance with ethical and legal norms, in which case the disregard of this framework of restraint will itself lead to an all-encompassing tragedy.

Why Global Fascism?

The benevolent empire school that surfaced in the 1990s, and maintains a subdued voice on the sidelines at present, was based on an acceptance of American claims of "moral exceptionalism." It focused on America as the vehicle for the spread of democracy and the only political actor willing to and capable of managing humanitarian interventions. Its advocates also believed that to the extent that countries could be induced to enter the modern world of industrial development and technological innovation within the setting of a globalizing world economy, the problems of disorder and political extremism would be abated.[17] The Bush approach seemingly repudiated such a path, insisting that the alleged "nation-building" of the 1990s was not serving America's strategic interests, and that much more emphasis should be placed on military capabilities to project American power to the four corners of the earth. This course of action suddenly became national policy, reinforced by support from the entire political spectrum, in the patriotic climate of opinion that has prevailed since the momentous events of September 11.

But to some extent, the idealism of the benevolent school has been incorporated into the refashioning of the imperial project by the Bush leadership. While other countries have interests, the United States has sustained the pretension that it additionally embodies, unlike other great powers of the past, values of benefit to all, a claim repeated as if a mantra by President Bush and his main advisors. These values are designated as "the nonnegotiable demands of human dignity: the rule of law; limits on the absolute power of the state; free speech; freedom of worship; equal justice; respect for women; religious and ethnic tolerance; and respect for private property."[18] In the NSS 2002 document: "The U.S. National security strategy will be based on a distinctly American internationalism that reflects the union of our values and our national interests. The aim of this strategy is to help make the world not just safer but better."[19] In relation to both the Afghanistan and Iraq wars, the U.S. government has defended its war making by pointing to alleged humanitarian and emancipatory gains associated with its reliance on military power. The U.S. government also disavowed any self-aggrandizing goals, angrily dismissing widespread accusations of antiwar critics that recourse to war against Iraq was driven by its oil ambitions, and promising to hold oil in trust for the people of Iraq during any period of American occupation.

Given this kind of emphasis, isn't it misleading to suggest that there has been a shift from the benevolent empire model that was articulated in the 1990s? And further, hasn't the reliance on military power been justified by the changed global circumstances brought about by the September 11 attacks? Is not, in fact, the American advocacy of democracy and human rights both a continuation of the nation-building of the 1990s that the Bush Administration had initially? Is not this approach to world order an expression of an antifascist geopolitics? The weight of such questions does suggest that the debate about American empire is far from over, but it does not undermine the argument of an emergent global fascism.

The analysis offered here is largely structural, although bolstered by the way in which the authority of the UN Security Council (UNSC) was manipulated by the United States prior to the Iraq War, and then disregarded. The structural element arises from the facts of American military, economic, and diplomatic preeminence and its explicit resolve to keep that edge. The U.S. government is devoting huge resources to the monopolistic militarization of space, the development of more usable nuclear weapons, and the strengthening of its world-girdling ring of military bases and its global navy as the most tangible way to discourage any strategic challenges to its preeminence. True, the realities of dominance are unlikely to be translated into formal relations of governance and subordination, but noncompliant actors in the world will either be destroyed or replaced with compliant actors. Compliance will be measured by accepting the American approach to global security, including the espousal of a free market ideology and the practice of a nominal constitutionalism. This combination of factors adds up to "empire" according to my assessment.

But why fascist? I would stress three elements. First of all, there is the combination of unchallengeable military preeminence with a rejection by the U.S. government of the restraining impact of international law and the United Nations. The Iraq debate brought this global militarist posture into the open. The Bush administration has relied on a novel and extensive doctrine of "preemption" (redescribed as "preventive war" by some critics to emphasize the absence of any show of imminent threat) that claims a right by the United States (but presumably no others) to initiate war against a foreign state without sustaining the burden of demonstrating a defensive necessity. It has further strained credulity and weakened world order, by applying this doctrine to the circumstances of Iraq without even making a minimally credible showing of justifying evidence of an Iraqi threat. Taking advantage of the antiterrorist mood in the United States to mount the war in Iraq was widely understood as the practice of vengeful geopolitics against an essentially helpless country.

The fact that this policy was filtered through the United Nations revealed both the imperial structure and the prospect of resistance. The imperial structure was evident in the manner with which the issue of Iraqi inspections was unanimously framed by UNSC Res. 1441, which accepted implicitly the central unsubstantiated claim that Iraq's possession of weaponry of mass destruction posed a war threat, which if not immediately removed by inspection and Iraqi disarmament, would lead to an American-led war outside the United Nations. If the Charter had been the true guideline for global action it would be Iraq that would have received protection against such American provocations as constant military intrusions on its airspace over the course of years, ill-concealed programs of support for armed uprising by the enemies of the Baghdad regime, covert operations designed to destabilize governmental control in Iraq, and a military buildup that was shamelessly threatening a "shock and awe" attack unless the regime of Saddam Hussein capitulated to the demands being made that encroached centrally on Iraqi sovereign rights. Instead, the UN membership tried to reach the proclaimed American goals by relying on inspection leading to disarmament. But the proclaimed American goals were rather evidently not fully expressive of American objectives, and so even effective inspection was not acceptable to Washington as an alternative to war and "regime change."

It is here that the membership of the Security Council has drawn the line and rejected an abandonment of inspection despite the increasing evidence that it was accomplishing what the United States contended was the basis of the Iraqi threat and the grounds for the hypocritical claim that it was important to the credibility of the UN that its resolutions be implemented. It did not take observers long to note the U.S. unwillingness to take steps over the years to implement the numerous Security Council resolutions directed at Israel with respect to withdrawing from the Palestinian territories occupied during the 1967 War and applying the Geneva Conventions specifying the obligations of Israel as the occupying power in the West Bank and Gaza.

The UN was placed in a tenable position from the moment the United States agreed to seek support for war at the UN, a seemingly multilateralist step that was vigorously opposed by the administration's ultrahawks who sought to fashion American foreign policy without the bother of collective procedures. President Bush's speech on September 12, 2002, to the General Assembly gave the UN the choice of supporting the U.S. position, which seemed from the outset irreconcilable with international law and the UN Charter, or finding its authority bypassed by action undertaken by the United States and whatever coalition partners it could muster. The UNSC struggled hard to avoid an outcome that appeared to make its authority "irrelevant," bending 80 percent of the way in Washington's direction — but in the end it was not enough.

The first and major point here is that the United States put its strategic approach above the claims of international law and the procedures of the UN on the most vital matter of the decision to embark on a nondefensive war. Its shaping of the issue at the UN confirms the imperial structure of world politics, but the outcome reveals anti-imperial tensions that threaten to shrink the American Empire from its pretensions of *global reach*. The Iraq debate can thus be seen as both confirming the existence of an American empire, but also as expressive of an emerging geopolitical resistance. The American defiance of this resistance and its abandonment of diplomacy and accommodation is expressive of *global fascism*. It represents a consolidation of unaccountable military power on a global scale that overrides the constraints of international law and disregards the procedural role of the UNSC in authorizing uses of international force that cannot be encompassed within the right of self-defense enjoyed by all sovereign states.

Second, in attempting to counteract terrorism, the U.S. government has claimed sweeping powers to deal with the concealed al Qaeda network. Some of these claims are necessary and justifiable to deal with the magnitude and nature of the threats posed by megaterrorism. The character of the powers claimed include secret detentions, the authority to designate American citizens as "enemy combatants" without any rights, the public consideration of torture as a permissible police practice in anti-terrorist work, the scrutiny applied to those of Muslim faith, the reliance on assassination directed at terrorist suspects wherever they are found, and numerous invasions of privacy directed at ordinary people. These mechanisms of state power are given legal backing in the USA Patriot Act and are awaiting expected strengthening in proposed legislation now called the Domestic Security Enhancement Act prepared by the Justice Department. The slide toward fascism at home is given tangible expression by these practices, but it is also furthered by an uncritical and chauvinistic patriotism, by the release of periodic alarmist warnings of megaterrorist imminent attacks that fail to materialize, and by an Attorney General, John Ashcroft, who seems to exult in an authoritarian approach to law enforcement.

The third main concern about the onset of fascism arises from an impending collision between Washington's imperial geopolitics and the rising tendencies of grassroots resistance to the American Empire, along with the planetary spread of anti-American resentment. If such a movement from below becomes more aggressive, as is likely, and to the extent the other elements of the American approach continue, an intense pressure to control and repress this populist resistance will arise. Such an interaction will inflame feelings on both sides, making relying on a fascist conception of control likely to prevail, despite continuing American professions of belief in the ways of democracy and freedom.

For all these reasons, the dangers of global fascism cannot be discounted as imaginary or alarmist. Hopefully, countertendencies within the United States and the world will be sufficiently awakened by these dangers and fashion an effective response. America has proved to be resilient in the past, as when antidemocratic forces were unleashed by the rabid witch-hunting anticommunism of McCarthyism during the 1950s. But this resilience is now being tested as never before because the proponents of this extremist American global strategy currently occupy the heights of political influence in and around the White House and Pentagon, and seem to have no intention of giving ground despite the growing challenge mounted by American grassroots opposition as reinforced by international public opinion.

Along the lines of the overall argument presented here, removing the threat of global fascism would not entirely dispose of the existence of an American empire. There would still be the advocates of benevolent empire and the structural possibilities of reviving an economistic approach to globalization as it existed in the 1990s.[20]

Endnotes

1. Prime explicit imperialists of this stripe are Robert Kagen, "The Benevolent Empire," *Foreign Affairs* 77: 24–35 (1998); Michael Ignatieff, "The Burden," *New York Times Magazine*, Jan. 5, 2003, 22–27, 50–54.
2. Andrew J. Bacevich, *American Empire: The Realities and Consequences of U.S. Diplomacy* (Cambridge, Mass.: Harvard University Press, 2002), 244.
3. Bacevich, *American Empire*, 244.
4. Michael Ignatieff, note 1, at 54.
5. Krauthammer, "The Unipolar Moment," *Foreign Affairs* 70, 1 (1990–91).
6. These neocon views were influentially laid out by the contributors to Robert Kagan and William Kristol, eds., *Present Dangers: Crisis and Opportunity in American Foreign and Defense Policy* (San Francisco, Calif.: Encounter Books, 2002); and again in the report of the project of The New American Century Project entitled "Rebuilding America's Defenses, Strategy Forces and Resources for a New Century," published in September 2000.
7. For example, under the auspices of the Council of Foreign Relations, see Jan Lodel, *The Price of Dominance* (New York: Council of Foreign Relations Press, 2001; also G. John Ikenberry, ed., *America Unrivaled: The Future of the Balance of Power* (Ithaca, N.Y.: Cornell University Press, 2002).
8. Joseph S. Nye, Jr., *Bound to Lead: The Changing Nature of American Power* (New York: Basic Books, 1991); also, Nye, *The Paradox of American Power: Why the World's Only Superpower Can't Go It Alone* (New York: Oxford, 2002).
9. See Frank Carlucci, Robert Hunter, and Zalmay Khalilzad, eds., *Taking Charge: A Bipartisan Report to the President-Elect on Foreign Policy and National Security* (Santa Monica, Calif.: RAND, 2001).
10. For an assessment of this dynamic, see Richard Falk, *Religion and Humane Global Governance* (New York: Palgrave, 2001).
11. This distinction is a central theme of my book, Falk, *The Great Terror War* (Northhampton, Mass.: Olive Branch Press, 2003.
12. David Armstrong, "Dick Cheney's Song of America: Drafting a Plan for Global Dominance," *Harper's Magazine*, Oct. 2002, 76–83; Nicholas Lemann, "The Next World Order," *The New Yorker*, April 1, 2002, 42–48; and see Robert Kagen, note 1.
13. Quoted passages all from the text of the West Point speech as available from the White House website www.whitehouse.gov/news/releases/2002/06/print.html (accessed Month, day year).
14. National Security Strategy of the United States of America, White House Document, September 2002 (NSS 2002), 27.
15. NSS 2002, 29.
16. This is quoted from a speech at the International Women's Forum in Sandton, South Africa, Feb. 2003.
17. For example, see Thomas Friedman, *The Lexus and the Olive Tree: Understanding Globalization* (New York: Farrar, Straus, Giroux, 1999).
18. NSS 2002, 3.
19. NSS 2002, 1.
20. See Falk, *Predatory Globalization: A Critique* (Cambridge: Polity, 2000); also Michael Hardt and Antonio Negri, *Empire* (Cambridge, Mass.: Harvard University Press, 2000).

Index